Praise for *In the Event the Flower Girl Explodes*:

"*My Best Friend's Wedding* with a rainbow twist! From the first page, readers will be sucked into Nicole Winger's world. Smart, funny, new-grad Nicole wrestles with territory all too familiar to twenty-somethings--trying to launch her career, navigate a relationship, and carve out her identity an adult. Throw into the mix family drama in the form of a beloved brother announcing his new enthrallment with a fur-coat-flaunting, stiletto-stomping southern belle who seems intent on stealing Nicole's brother away, and you find all the ingredients for your next summer novel. An entertaining read for anyone who likes their beach material with a bit of bite, enjoys their black humor with a side of substance (and a little frill), or has had to navigate the ever-treacherous waters of a loved one pairing off with someone utterly loathsome."

- Sara DiVello, bestselling author, *Where in the OM Am I? One Woman's Journey from the Corporate World to the Yoga Mat*

"*In the Event the Flower Girl Explodes* is an amazing coming of age story that truly captures the feelings that build when we don't know how to communicate about them. It culminates in lessons learned and renewed faith in oneself."

- Sarah Woodard, author of *Adri's Big Dream*

"Abby is a fresh, relatable voice. Once you start reading *Flower Girl*, this February you won't want to stop until the ice thaws. Well, okay, you'll probably read it too fast to make it last you through spring, but you get what I mean."

- Carina Sitkus, author of *Grandma's How-To List for Getting Through Life*

"I'm sure it's nice, dear."

- my mom

In the Event the Flower Girl Explodes

Other Books by Abby Rosmarin:

I'm Just Here for the Free Scrutiny
Chick Lit & Other Formulas for Life
No One Reads Poetry: A Collection of Poems

In the Event the Flower Girl Explodes

Abby Rosmarin

ISBN: 978-0-9966313-2-7 (print)
ASIN: B078RQ54N4 (ebook)

For my rock, my partner in crime, my most trusted editor-in-chief.

For my husband, Isaac.

Chapter One

26 STEPS TO THE BOSS'S OFFICE

There were 26 steps from Nicole's cube to Cassandra Evans's office.

This was a general estimate. The final number didn't include long strides, foot shuffles, or the moments when Nicole took a tentative step back, believing it would be easier to just retreat back to her cube and make up an excuse to her family.

Yup, couldn't get the time off. I tried, but it looks like I'm stuck up here instead. Enjoy the wedding without me, and send my regards.

Nicole focused only on moving each foot forward. She had no clue what she'd say to Cassandra – which, to be honest, was probably for the best. Having a plan meant she could back out of the plan. Instead, she was freefalling, and there's no real way to stop a freefall, save for reaching the point of impact.

After those 26 steps, Nicole found herself at Cassandra's door. Before Nicole could knock on the frame, Cassandra looked up and gave a polite smile.

"How can I help you, Nicole?"

The printer is jammed. The toner is out of ink. The kitchen faucet is leaky. The office is on fire. Oh God, please let the office catch fire.

"Um, I – uh." Nicole swallowed and pressed her

tongue to the roof of her mouth. "I was hoping to get some time off."

"That can be arranged," said Cassandra. "What day would you need off?"

Nicole bit at the inside of her cheeks.

"Um, I actually need more than a day."

"More than a day?" said Cassandra. "How many days are we talking about, then?"

Nicole cleared her throat.

"Like, three?"

"Three." Cassandra folded her arms. "Is there a medical emergency?"

"No," said Nicole, her eyes back at her feet. "I'm actually going to Florida."

Cassandra leaned forward and placed both hands on her desk.

"You do understand that we typically don't give vacation days to temp employees, right?" Cassandra said slowly.

"Yes, yes, I completely understand." Nicole faltered. "It's not a vacation so much as... a wedding?"

"A wedding," Cassandra repeated. "Well, congratulations to them. Who's the happy couple?"

"My brother, actually," Nicole replied, gritting her teeth.

A smile broke across Cassandra's face.

"Well, why didn't you tell me that in the first place?" said Cassandra. "I'm sure we can arrange something. You do understand that this will be unpaid though, correct?"

"Of course," Nicole answered.

"I wouldn't dream of having you miss your brother's wedding. You're the sister of the groom." Cassandra sat back in her seat. "I remember when my own brother got married. Those last few days were chaos. I think I was more worked up than the bride herself. It was hectic, but what a memorable time. I bet it'll be the same for you."

The corner of Nicole's mouth twitched.

"Of course."

"So what dates are we looking at?" Cassandra pushed her chair closer to the desk.

Nicole sighed and licked her lips.

"The fourteenth through the sixteenth."

Cassandra's brow furrowed.

"Of September?"

"Of August." Nicole gave a tight smile.

"So, this month," Cassandra stated slowly. "Next Wednesday, to be precise." Cassandra paused and sighed. "Couldn't you have told me this earlier?"

"I'm sorry about that. I..." Nicole trailed off and swallowed. "I guess I've had a lot on my mind."

Cassandra sighed again, this time more audibly.

"It's not favorable, but I guess it can still be done."

Nicole dragged her fingers through her hair.

"Thank you. Thank you so much."

"No worries. Have fun next week."

Nicole nodded absently, started to turn toward the door, and immediately turned back to Cassandra.

"I can work while I'm there," Nicole offered. "I can even put more hours in today and next week, so I don't fall behind in anything."

"That won't be necessary." Cassandra smiled. "Your tasks are easily transferable. We'll be just fine while you're gone."

"Great," said Nicole, forcing her expression to stay blank. "Good to hear."

"Is there anything else you need from me?" Cassandra asked.

"No, no, that's it." Nicole gave a wavering grin. "Thank you again. I know this was short notice..."

Cassandra waved away Nicole's words.

"Not worth groveling over," said Cassandra. "Besides, if I were in your shoes, I'd choose gaining a sister over some temp gig anyway."

The blood drained from Nicole's face as her mouth went dry.

"And, if I don't see you beforehand, I hope you have a nice weekend," said Cassandra.

"Yeah, you too," Nicole croaked. Cassandra turned back to her computer and resumed typing at a pace that gave no hint that she had ever paused in the first place. Nicole pressed her lips together as she exited Cassandra's office, taking a longer, more circuitous route back to her cube.

Nicole stared at her desk, desperately trying to continue what she was working on. She moved a few papers around. She opened an email and looked at the words without actually reading them. Within minutes, Nicole gently placed her head in her hands. She pressed her fingers into her brows and sighed. She moved only when her elbows started slipping out from under her.

***

Nicole called her girlfriend the second she stepped out of the office building that evening.

"I shot myself in the foot at work," said Nicole.

"Oh no – what happened?"

"I just..." Nicole paused long enough to check for traffic as she crossed the street. "I messed up and my boss let me know I was expendable. They'll never hire me as a full-time employee now."

"What happened?" asked Laura. "How did you mess up?"

"I... I asked for time off."

"Wait, I'm confused – why would time off do that? If they were okay with you taking time off for Andrew's wedding..."

"No, no... that's the thing." Nicole pressed a hand to her forehead. "It *was* for Andrew's wedding."

"Wait... you asked for that... *today*?" said Laura. "Nicole..."

"I know, I know, I just..." Nicole sighed. "I kept putting it off. I was scared that my boss would be pissed. And then I... kinda got the opposite."

Laura paused.

"So... did your boss really say you were expendable?"

Nicole faltered.

"Not in so many words. But she made it pretty clear that I wasn't an asset."

Laura sighed again.

"If she gave you that much time off on such short notice, I would just be thankful that she wasn't upset by it," she said. "Better to have a happy former boss who will gladly give you a recommendation than a boss who is mad at you and probably wasn't planning on hiring you permanently in the first place."

Nicole clenched her jaw. Her hand holding the phone tightened.

"Was that really necessary?" she said.

"I'm just trying to give perspective," said Laura. "Temp jobs are temp jobs. Sometimes people get hired from them. Sometimes people don't. Given the circumstances, the only thing we can do is be thankful it went as well as it did."

Nicole kept silent, her teeth locked, until the anger started to dissipate.

"I'm just..." Nicole sighed, her face hot. "I'm frustrated and mad and..."

Nicole paused and sighed again.

"And you resent the fact that you had to take time off for a wedding that you don't even want to go to in the first place," Laura finished.

"I hate that you know me so well," said Nicole, her shoulders drooping with a sudden fatigue.

"And, in a way, you blame your brother for putting you in this position in the first place," Laura continued.

"I don't blame my brother..." said Nicole.

"You blame his fiancée, then."

"That sounds more like it."

Nicole rounded the corner and made her way up the steps to the elevated train platform.

"And, in a way, you blame your brother for making her his fiancée in the first place," Laura added.

Nicole let out a small grunt. She pressed her toes into her shoes, tensing up her legs in the process. She waited for Laura to say something else. When she didn't, Nicole cleared her throat into the phone.

"Am I coming over tonight?" Nicole asked.

"Of course," said Laura. "I figured you would."

"I'm getting on the train now," said Nicole. "I'll probably get there in like a half hour or so."

"You're coming over straight from work?" Laura asked.

"Figured as much," said Nicole. "Don't really feel like

going to my apartment anyway."

"Works for me," said Laura. "I'm at the grocery store now. I'll just make sure to be back before you get there."

"Sounds good to me," said Nicole.

"I'll see you soon, okay?"

"Okay."

"You know I love you."

Nicole smiled faintly.

"And I love you too."

"See you soon."

"I'll see you soon."

Nicole leaned back against the wall and breathed slowly until her train pulled up to the platform. She boarded the last train car, found a seat in the back corner, and called her mom. The phone rang two or three times before someone picked up.

"Hey there, kiddo," her mother's voice sung out. "How are you doing?"

"Fine, fine," said Nicole with a half-hearted singsong. "I just wanted to let you know that I was able to get the time off."

"Oh wow. They took this long to get back to you?"

Nicole pressed her lips together and stared at the train car's floor.

"Something like that."

"Still though, so good to hear," said her mom. "I was worried, you know..."

"Mom..." Nicole began.

"I know it hasn't been easy," she continued. "But this is important to him. He's still your brother. He needs you there."

"I really don't want to get into this now." Nicole turned in her seat and faced the wall. "I had a long day."

"Okay, okay." There was a pause. In the silence, the train came to a stop. It opened its doors, let its passengers exit and board, and closed its doors again. "Have you talked to Andrew recently?"

"No, Mom." Nicole answered flatly. "No I haven't."

"I'm sure he misses talking to you," said her mother. "You two were so close."

"Mom." Nicole tried to keep her voice steady and

firm, but found it wavering, like she was a young child pleading to her mother.

Nicole could hear her mom sigh on the other end of the line.

"The flight is at 7:30," said her mother. "Do you think you guys will get here in time?"

"Yes, Mom, we will," Nicole answered with a weary smile to no one.

"And Laura was able to get the time off too, right?"

"Of course, Mom," said Nicole.

"A mother always worries," she said. "And that worry extends to significant others. You'll learn someday, if you ever have kids."

"I bet, Mom," Nicole replied. "I appreciate the concern, either way."

"Well, if I don't hear from you beforehand, I'll see you next Tuesday."

"Heh. 'See you next Tuesday'," Nicole replied.

"What?"

"Nothing, nothing," Nicole responded. "Just a bad joke."

"Well, all right then," said her mother, her voice saturated with concern. "You take care, okay?"

"I will, Mom," Nicole replied. "And I'll see you at O'Hare. I'll call if we get held up."

Nicole ended the conversation, placed her phone in her purse, and stared out the window. Her eyes darted from the ground, to the buildings, to the sky. The train slowed to a stop and the doors opened again. She let the train rock her as she closed her eyes, the dings of the train doors ringing in her ears. She hugged her purse closer to her stomach and leaned her head back, counting down the stops until she'd be in Laura's neighborhood.

Abby Rosmarin

Chapter Two

RED LEATHER LEGGINGS AND A MINK COAT

"I just don't get it."
Nicole and Andrew's mom brushed off a piece of lint from Andrew's shoulder.
"It's really no big deal, Mom."
"But it's your senior year," their mom pressed, stepping back from her son. "Homecoming is so important for the seniors..."
"I'm saving money on corsages," said Andrew. "Just being financially conscious."
"I just don't understand why you'd rather go alone," their mom continued.
"Because I don't have a girlfriend?" Andrew responded.
"She doesn't have to be your girlfriend," their mom offered. "At least not yet."
"And who is this mysterious 'she'?" Andrew asked, checking his hair in the living room mirror.
"Any of the nice girls who seem to like you so much," their mom answered.
"I know a few of my friends who would gladly volunteer," Nicole spoke up from the couch.
"You know, I was talking with Mrs. McGregor," their mom

continued. *"You know her daughter, Patricia? She won't stop talking about you, but she wouldn't ask you to Homecoming. She was worried sick that you'd say no."*

"That's because I would," Andrew answered.

"And why would you do that?"

"Because she follows me around enough as it is," Andrew said, straightening his suit jacket as he did so. Outside, a car stopped in front of the driveway and honked its horn.

"Besides..." Andrew pulled her mom in for a hug. *"I've already got two great girls in my life."*

"You flatterer," their mom said and gave her son a kiss on the forehead. She had to rise up on her toes to do so, and even then Andrew had to duck slightly.

"And don't think you're getting out of a hug, either." Andrew turned to the couch. Nicole looked up just in time to get scooped up and slung over Andrew's shoulder.

"This is not a hug!" Nicole shouted out between laughs.

"Close enough!" Andrew shouted, spinning her around before putting her down. Nicole held onto him as she tried to gain her equilibrium. Andrew wrapped his arms around her shoulders, giving her a long bear hug. The car outside honked again.

"Why don't you invite your friends in first?" their mom asked. *"Maybe they'd like a soda?"*

Andrew smirked.

"I'm sure they'll be fine, Mom."

"Okay, well, you have a good time, then," she said, brushing another invisible piece of lint off Andrew's shoulders. *"Be home at a good time. And no drinking."*

"Yes, Mom. I promise." Andrew gave his mom a kiss on the forehead before walking to the front door. *"What was that again? Stay out late and drinks lots of booze?"*

"Not funny, Andrew."

"Fine, fine. I'll be back before midnight." Andrew opened the door and took a step out.

"You're in charge while I'm gone, Nicky. Take good care of Mom."

Nicole gave a salute.

"Aye aye, Captain."

The car gave one more honk.

"I'm coming, I'm coming!" Andrew shouted at the car,

letting the screen door close behind him as he jogged across the lawn.

***

Her name was Cora, and Nicole had met her that previous November.

She didn't know much about her, minus the fact that her name was Cora and Andrew had met her sometime during the summer. And that it took Andrew until the fall to even tell Nicole about Cora in the first place.

"We've been together, ah… three or four months?" Andrew had said off-handedly in October. "We met in July, so… I guess so. Yeah. Four months."

"Four whole months?" Nicole had responded with dramatic gusto. "That's like a decade in Andrew-time. So, when's the wedding?"

Andrew had waited a beat before calmly replying with, "Ha. Ha ha. Very funny."

"So, where did you meet her?"

"Y'know," said Andrew. "Around."

"At a beach, at a party…" Nicole pressed. "In jail, at a strip club…"

"Y'know, through friends," Andrew responded.

"So long as she's not a mail-order bride, I'm set." Nicole paused before adding, "She isn't a mail-order bride, right?"

Andrew gave a small, tired laugh, before saying, "No, no. She's legit."

It took an additional month before Andrew would even agree to letting Nicole meet her – and then an additional two weeks before Andrew would finalize a date and time.

"And I'll bring Laura, too," Nicole had offered. "We'll make it, like, a double date, so she doesn't feel pressured to pass the Sister Test."

"Doesn't she have to pass the Sister Test anyway?" Andrew chuckled nervously.

"Well, obviously. But this way she'll feel better about the testing process."

A date was finally set. That following weekend,

Nicole and Laura waited for Andrew and Cora at a café in the downtown area. It was an unpleasant afternoon, the kind that foretold an exceptionally dreary and cold winter. The sky had been overcast since the previous day. The air was cold enough for snow, but not a single snowflake had dropped. The winds whipped around the buildings, turning even the busiest streets into wind tunnels.

Nicole was on her second cup of coffee while they waited for Andrew and Cora.

"What do you think she looks like?" Laura asked after a few minutes.

Nicole shrugged.

"I don't know. Maybe tall, maybe not. Maybe brunette. Maybe not."

Nicole sighed and tapped at her cup.

"You're terrible at this game," Laura said with a smirk.

"And it's because I don't know. I genuinely don't know," Nicole countered, shrugging again. "I guess I never gave any thought to who would be a proper girlfriend for him." Nicole slouched forward over her cup.

"Well, what were his other girlfriends like?"

"If he ever had a girlfriend before, I could tell you."

Laura tilted her head to the side and cocked an eyebrow.

"Are you honestly telling me that he has never been in a relationship, ever," said Laura. "Not even in high school?"

"That's the God's-honest truth," Nicole replied. "And it wasn't even for lack of opportunity. Girls were always throwing themselves at him in school."

"Most guys would've lost their minds to get that type of attention," Laura noted.

"Yeah, most guys would," Nicole agreed. "I don't know why, but it was just annoying more than anything else for him."

"I'm finding that hard to believe."

"It's the truth, though," said Nicole. "I don't know. Maybe it was a case of too much opportunity. Or maybe he was too focused on everything else to care."

"Like...?" Laura asked with a knowing smile.

"Well, like, school." Nicole shrugged again. "And sports, and getting into college, and..."

"You?" Laura chided.

"Well, sure." Nicole moved her purse from the table to the floor. "And my mom..."

"No, I get it. I really do," said Laura. "He was the man of the house. He probably felt an obligation to look after you."

"Well, yeah." Nicole shrugged again and picked up her cup. "And I owe a lot to him as well."

"That makes sense. From the sound of it, he really looked after you."

"He really did." Nicole took a small sip and smirked. "He's why I never got made fun of in school – at least not more than once."

"Let me guess," Laura stirred her drink before blowing on it. "Because all the girls loved him and all the boys were afraid of him."

"When an 18-year-old varsity football player tells you to stop messing with his kid sister, and you're a puny 12-year-old boy, you listen," said Nicole. "Or, if you're a 12-year-old mean girl with a crush the size of Illinois on said football player, you listen."

"Sheesh, I could've used a brother like that," said Laura. "Middle school would've been a completely different playground, then."

"You would've also had to have lived in Hampshire, most likely," said Nicole. "The good thing about smaller towns is that everyone knows everyone else. Not the case in, say, Chicago."

"Touché," Laura replied.

Both girls let the silence fall easily between the two of them. They focused on their cups, on the outside windows, on the clock by the registers.

"They're running late," Laura said matter-of-factly.

"My brother has never been on time for anything in his whole life," Nicole stated.

Laura nodded, her gaze going back toward the windows.

"Holy crap," Laura breathed out. "You need to see this."

Nicole turned to where Laura was looking and immediately bit at the inside of her cheek. Outside, by the front door, stood a girl with her back to the café. She appeared to be about average height, but that was the only thing that anyone around Chicago would have labeled as "average". She wore 5", glittered stilettos that turned her medium stature into something downright Amazonian. Skintight, bright red leather pants wrapped their way around her legs, matching the fire-engine-red hair that had been teased to be three sizes bigger than its natural state. But all of that paled in comparison to the full-length fur coat that skirted the ground, even with the stilettos on.

"Jesus!" Nicole yelped, her voice loud enough to attract the attention of the rest of the café, who in turn looked out the window as well.

Laura pressed her lips together and shook her head, her eyes still locked on the girl outside.

"Is that *mink*?" Nicole went on, her voice still loud enough to attract attention.

"I wouldn't even know," Laura answered in a casual, low tone.

"Someone needs to tell her that Halloween was three weeks ago," Nicole continued, this time in a whisper.

"Where would you even *get* something like that?" Laura asked.

"Do you think she's getting paid to look like that?" Nicole quipped. "Because I can't imagine actually paying *money* to wear that."

The girl started pacing the sidewalk by the entrance, her eyes darting from her phone to somewhere off in the distance. Nicole watched her as she played with her hair, checked her phone, and tapped one of her stilettos against the pavement.

A tall, broad-shouldered figure walked down the sidewalk from the opposite end of the café. An unsteady smile crept across Nicole's face.

"This can't be good," Nicole murmured. "Andrew is alone."

Nicole watched as her brother bypassed the entrance and walked over to the girl in the stilettos. The fur aficionado had her back turned to Andrew as she stared blankly down the opposite end of the road. He tiptoed behind her before poking her torso from either side. The girl jumped up with a squeal – a squeal that could be heard inside the café as well – and jumped into Andrew's arms. After a quick spin from Andrew, the girl slid back onto the sidewalk, wrapped her arm around Andrew's waist, and followed him into the café. Nicole turned and faced her coffee, her hands now gripping around the cup.

"Nicky!" Andrew called out from the entrance. Nicole turned toward her brother, feigned a bemused surprise paired with a forced smile, and slid out from her seat.

"Hey there, big brother!" she said far too loudly. She got up and, with arms outstretched, went in to give Andrew a hug. But the girl had not removed her arm from Andrew's waist, and Andrew had not removed his hand from her shoulder. Nicole gave an awkward side hug before immediately stepping back.

Nicole scanned the café. She caught the eye of a few patrons, who averted their gaze and went back to whatever it was they were doing before.

Laura pushed her seat back and stood up.

"Good to see you again," she said, shaking Andrew's free hand.

"And likewise!" he replied. "This is Cora, everybody."

"Hi there, y'all," she replied in a thick southern accent.

Nicole stood there with a dumbfounded grin on her face.

Andrew picked up the conversation after a moment of silence.

"Cora, this is Nicole," he said. "Nicole, Cora."

"So nice to meet you," said Cora, her arm still around Andrew's waist.

"And likewise," Nicole said in monotone.

"Cora, this is Laura." Andrew gestured over. "Nicole's girlfriend. Laura, Cora. Cora, Laura."

"Hmm," Cora replied, looking at Laura briefly before turning her gaze back to Andrew.

"Hey, my name rhymes with yours," Laura offered. "Cora, Laura."

"It does, doesn't it," Cora replied, offering nothing else to the conversation.

Laura shuffled her feet and looked towards the cash registers.

"Yeah," Laura answered to no one. "And it's, uh, great meeting you."

"And great to meet you, too," said Cora, a warm smile on her lips but nothing more to say. Laura smiled back in response while Nicole looked on with her arms crossed.

"Do you want anything?" Andrew turned to Cora.

"Do you think they have sweet tea here?" Cora asked.

"I don't know," Andrew replied slowly, scanning the chalkboards above the registers. "But I can ask. And if they don't?"

Cora sighed.

"I guess a water with lemon will do."

Andrew gave Cora a quick kiss on the temple before getting in line.

"I swear, there is no place around here that serves a proper sweet tea." Cora crossed her arms.

"I have to admit: I don't think I've ever drank sweet tea before," said Nicole.

Cora laughed.

"Oh, bless your heart! Y'all're missing out! I don't know how you yanks handle it. Unsweetened tea's so bitter!" Cora flipped her hair back and looked over at Andrew. "Well, things are always sweeter in the South, as they say."

"I actually have family who live in the South. What area of the South are you from?" Laura asked.

Cora turned back.

"Florida."

"Florida," Nicole found herself echoing.

"Yeah, Florida," Cora repeated, her accent now stronger, if not slightly different. "The Great State of Florida. Born and raised."

"Oh, nice," Laura continued. "My aunt actually lives in Florida, right by the Georgia border. What part of Florida are you from?"

Cora shrugged.

"South."

Laura glanced at Nicole before directing her attention to Andrew's return.

Andrew cradled his ceramic coffee cup while he handed a plastic cup to Cora.

"They didn't have sweet tea, so they mixed sugar with their morning blend," said Andrew.

Cora looked at the cup for a second before taking it and playing with the straw.

"Well, I appreciate the effort," Cora said with a sigh.

The group stood there for a second. Nicole found herself nodding absently to the scenery around the room.

"Shall we sit?" Laura offered. "We saved one of the best spots in the place."

"Of course, that sounds great," said Andrew.

Laura led the way as the group surrounded the small wooden table. Nicole moved her cup and her jacket over a seat and pulled out the chair in the corner next to Laura. Andrew placed his cup in front of his seat, shrugged off his coat, and draped it over the back of the chair.

"It's so great to finally meet you," Cora said as she took the spot where Nicole had been seated, her fur coat still fully buttoned up. "Andrew's told me so much about you."

"Really?" Nicole replied, her voice sounding every bit as incredulous as she felt.

"Of course!" Cora downright squeaked. "Andrew told me you just got your degree in design."

"Yeah." Nicole slowly and deliberately drew out her words. "Um... in May. I graduated with my degree in May."

"Oooh, how exciting," Cora said with a broad smile. Nicole couldn't be certain, but she swore Cora's accent had shifted again, like she had gone from one type of southern accent to another. "So what do you do now?"

"Uh..." Nicole tapped the edge of her cup. "I've been looking. Just signed up with a temp agency, so we'll see."

"Oh, bless your heart, that's a tough situation to be in." Cora's right hand twirled the straw of her sweetened unsweetened ice tea. The straw danced in slow, methodical circles. "Which college did you go to again?"

Nicole took a long sip from her coffee and carefully set the mug down.

"UIC."

"Oh, nice," Cora replied. "That's near Northwestern, isn't it?"

Nicole looked to Andrew, then Laura, then back to Cora.

"Kind of." Nicole looked away and out the window. "Like a thirty-minute drive by car, in good traffic."

"Aah, never mind, then." Cora giggled. "This city is *way* too big. How everyone is not wandering around completely lost is totally beyond me." Cora sighed and followed Nicole's gaze to the window. "Almost done, though. Seven more months and I'm out of this place."

Nicole stared at Cora as Cora contently stared out the window. Nicole looked over at Andrew, who had not looked her way since they had sat down.

"What brings you to Chicago, then?" Laura asked, straightening herself in her seat.

"Northwestern University, of course." Cora gave Laura another one of her huge smiles.

"Are you in the same graduate program as Andrew or..." Nicole asked in monotone, her eyes still on Andrew. Andrew played with his cup before looking over at Cora.

"*Graduate* program?" Cora laughed out. "Goodness! I'm not even done with my *bachelor's*." Cora giggled and shook her head. "Did Andrew never tell you how we met?"

Nicole let out a steady breath while she stared at her brother.

"No."

"He was my TA last semester," said Cora. "Chemistry 101. It was *such* a brutal class. Wouldn't've survived if it weren't for his tutoring. In fact, a good portion of the class would've failed if it weren't for his help. He's *incredible* at chemistry, isn't he?"

Nicole opened her mouth to reply, before clenching her teeth shut. She took a deep breath and picked up her coffee cup.

"Yes, yes he is," she eventually said.

"So, as a way of saying thanks, we all went to a celebration dinner after the final exam." Cora looked over at Andrew and touched his arm. "One thing lead to another and, by the end of the night, we were an item."

Nicole played around with the dates in her head, her eyebrows slowly furrowing in the process.

"So was this a... summer semester?" Nicole asked.

Cora grinned and shook her head.

"Oh my, you yanks are funny. Summers are for havin' fun!" Cora's grin broke into a smile. "This was my spring semester."

"Ah, so you guys started dating in... May... then?" Nicole said coolly.

Cora looked at her tea quizzically.

"Well, I guess so!"

"Ah." Nicole contorted her lips. "And you're... a senior, I'm guessing?"

"Yes ma'am," said Cora. "I'll graduate this coming May, God willin'."

"So, that's make you... 21, then," Nicole said slowly.

"Turned 21 just this past July!" Cora answered.

Nicole stared at Andrew, who was now busy reading the chalkboard menu to the side of him.

"Ah."

Laura cleared her throat.

"So, what brought you to Northwestern?" Laura asked.

"It's, like, one of the best pre-law places around, ain't it?" Cora lifted her shoulders slightly. "And they gave me a full ride, so I wasn't gonna complain."

"That's impressive," said Laura. "Full scholarship at Northwestern. Are you planning to become a lawyer?"

Cora shook her head.

"Goodness, no."

"Why are you getting your bachelor's in pre-law, then?" Nicole inquired. Nicole turned to see Laura staring at her.

Cora shrugged.

"I like rules. I like arguing. Why not?"

Nicole tilted her head to one side.

"Ah."

Laura gave Nicole another look before saying, "So, what are your plans for after college?"

Cora twirled a lock of hair between two fingers.

"Well, gosh, I just don't know yet," Cora responded.

That time, Nicole was certain her accent shifted. It sounded downright Texan.

"You could always be a paralegal," Nicole offered.

"Nicole and Andrew's mom is a paralegal, actually," Laura added.

Cora waved away the idea.

"To be perfectly honest, I hope to never spend a day in a law office, or any office, if I can help it." Cora paused and looked over at Andrew. "But... we'll see."

Nicole's eyebrows furrowed.

"Hmph."

"So, Andrew," Laura piped in again. "How's the PhD coming along?"

"It's uh, it's coming," Andrew sighed out. "Feels like I'm going in circles with my research, but what can you do."

"You'll be done before you know it," Laura reassured. "And then we'll have to call you Doctor."

Andrew shrugged.

"I still have at least a year, if not more, before that happens."

"All in due time," Laura replied.

Nicole removed her gaze from Andrew and stared at her cup.

"Well, shucks," Cora pushed the sleeve of her fur coat up. "I'm gonna miss my nail appointment if I'm not careful." Cora got up and pushed her seat in. "It was lovely meeting y'all. Hopefully I'll see y'all later."

"Have fun at your appointment," said Laura. "It was nice meeting you."

Nicole looked up at Cora with a tight smile.

"And likewise," Cora responded. "I enjoyed meeting you two." Cora leaned over and planted a small kiss on Andrew's forehead. "Babe, I'll see you tonight, okay?"

"Of course," Andrew replied. "See you soon."

"Alrighty, toodles!" Cora turned and exited the café, attracting every patron's attention again as her high heels clicked across the tiled floor, her mink coat brushing behind her like a cape. Nicole, Laura, and Andrew watched Cora leave before turning back towards each other. Andrew looked at the full cup of tea that Cora had left behind.

"She's nice," Laura said after a moment of silence.

"She's young," Nicole added.

Andrew shrugged his shoulders.

"She's not *that* young."

"She's 21, Andrew," Nicole stated. "And you're almost 30. You were in college when she was graduating elementary school."

"So?" Andrew defended. "It's not like I started dating her when she was *in* elementary school. She's an adult."

Nicole made a low, grunting laugh and rolled her eyes.

"Barely."

"Hey, I didn't ask for your opinion," Andrew snapped.

Nicole shot her brother a look, her fingers tightening around her coffee cup. She sat up stiffly in her seat. She took in a long breath, ready to let Andrew have it.

Before she could get it out, Nicole felt Laura's hand on her leg. It pressed lightly but firmly onto her thigh. Nicole met Laura's gaze before Nicole released her grip on her cup and relaxed a bit in her seat. Laura brought her hands back up to the tabletop and took a sip from her own cup.

"I'm impressed that she got into Northwestern on a full scholarship," Laura added in. "I mean, part of the reason why I didn't go to Northwestern was because it was so expensive. They refused to grant me any type of scholarship."

"It all worked out for the best, though," Andrew replied, his voice noticeably softer. "If you had gone to Northwestern instead of UIC, you would've never met Nicole."

He glanced quickly at Nicole, if only for emphasis, before looking back at Laura.

"Point." Laura looked over and grabbed Nicole's hand, which had been resting in defeat by the coffee cup. She looked back at Andrew and said, "I would've met you instead, which would've been way awkward."

"Tell me about it," Andrew said with a laugh.

The laugh filled the space between them for a second, before dissipating into the air. Silence crept its way to the table again, making everyone painfully aware of the words they weren't saying.

Andrew took in a deep breath.

"Well, I think I've spent as much time out of the lab as you're legally allowed to do as a grad student," Andrew finally said. He stood up, pulled his jacket off the back of the chair, and draped it over his arm. "I'll see you guys later."

"Yeah, we'll see you later," Nicole said weakly. Andrew grabbed Cora's cup of tea, turned from the table, and immediately exited the café, pausing to put on his coat only after he was outside and on the sidewalk.

Nicole and Laura sat there, their backs to the wall, the rest of the café spread out before them. They were surrounded by idle chatter, the muffled sound of music through headphones, the intermittent rustle as someone turned a page in their newspaper.

"You should've just let me yell at him," Nicole said, her hand still entwined with Laura's.

"What good would've come of that?" Laura asked.

"He had no right snapping at me like that," Nicole continued.

"He's obviously feeling defensive," Laura offered.

"Well he's got a lot to feel defensive about," said Nicole. She leaned back in her seat before adding: "I'm just happy we weren't near an open flame. Her hair would've gone up like a mushroom cloud."

Laura laughed and shook her head.

"I like the *sihmple* things in life!" Nicole mocked in her thickest southern accent, "like my sweet *tay* and my coat of dead an-nee-mals! And I just don't know what to do with all y'all big city folk!"

"Oh, come on," Laura said with a tilt of her head. "She wasn't that bad."

"She wasn't that good, either," Nicole countered. "I mean, of all the people Andrew could be dating, he goes with *that*? An underaged flamingo with a hatred for plain iced tea?"

"You mean *unsweetened*," Laura replied, her voice mimicking Nicole's fake southern accent.

"Things are just sweeter in the South!" Nicole

singsonged back.

"Your accent is terrible, by the way," Laura noted, dropping the accent entirely.

"Almost as terrible as hers."

"Now, that's just mean," said Laura.

"I'm pretty sure she was switching regional accents mid-conversation," Nicole added. "I think she went country-western at one point."

Laura smiled and shook her head.

"I thought that's what was happening," Laura replied. "It sounded... really off."

Nicole let go of Laura's hand and finished the last bits of her coffee.

"Honestly, I don't know what has gotten into Andrew," she said with a sigh.

"Whatever it is, yelling at him about it won't fix things," Laura advised.

Nicole placed her cup down and played with the rim.

"What do you think I should do then?" Nicole asked.

Laura got up and pushed in her chair.

"Nothing," she said. "Absolutely nothing. If she really is as ridiculous as she makes herself out to be, this relationship won't last. Andrew is too smart to stay with a girl like that. All you can do is wait it out and be there for him when things inevitably go south."

"No pun intended, I imagine?" Nicole pushed her chair back and grabbed her coat.

"Am I ever one for puns?" Laura asked, picking up her and Nicole's cups. She briefly checked under the table before walking over to the basin above the trash bin. Nicole followed, shrugging on her coat and fixing its collar.

"Not even when they're funny?" Nicole asked. "I mean – *punny*?"

Laura smiled.

"Not even then."

"Hey, you never know," Nicole offered. "You might wake up and realize you need to pun-tificate more."

Laura turned back with a cocked eyebrow before carefully placing the cups into the basin.

"Really, now."

"What, do you want pun-ch me in the face?"

"Thinking about it."

Nicole followed Laura out of the café, sucking in her breath as the cold air hit her straight on. She found Laura's hand again as they walked down the street together, their strides matching in pace as they rounded the corner.

"You know, in this weather, a mink coat kind of makes sense," Laura said, her face contorted against the bitter wind.

"Okay, my puns might've been bad, but *that* was unforgivable," said Nicole with a smile. Together, they crossed over a small footbridge, the Chicago River semi-frozen underneath them. A train passed by on a parallel bridge, the sound of wheels rolling on the steel echoing off the building walls. Nicole squeezed Laura's hand as they continued walking.

Chapter Three

TERMINAL

Nicole spent the last few hours of work on Tuesday staring at her computer screen before sneaking out early.

Since Monday morning, Nicole had watched her work dwindle down to nearly nothing, effortlessly passed on and reassigned, never making its way back to Nicole's desk. By 1 p.m. on Tuesday, Nicole had absolutely nothing to do. She spent an hour looking busy, spent another hour looking the opposite of busy, and – by 3:15 – snuck out of the office undetected.

There was nothing really waiting for her on the outside. Laura wouldn't be getting out of work for another hour. She didn't feel like going back to her apartment. She had nowhere to go, but she knew she had to get out.

She pushed open the main door of the office building and scanned the street. The world around her was consumed with the beginnings of rush hour. Nicole stepped onto the sidewalk and followed the crowd of people until she got to a train platform. She rode across town, eventually making her way to the Ohio Street Beach.

At the edge of Lake Michigan, Nicole slipped off her shoes and walked along the beach's tiny shoreline, the skyscrapers of Chicago behind her. The warm water slid effortlessly over her bare feet with every gentle wave.

People laid about on towels, some silently sprawled out, others propped up on their elbows and chatting. In the water, a few children splashed each other with unbridled delight. A handful of adults stood off to the side, the water up to their knees.

Nicole stopped, lifted one of her feet out of the water, and watched as the incoming wave danced just below it. She settled her foot down and turned to face the water. She stared out at the horizon, her gaze lingering, following the water as it snaked away from the rocks and into the horizon. She closed her eyes and took in the sounds of the waves, the squeals, the idle chatter, the muffled music.

For a brief moment, she felt like herself again. She loved the Ohio Street Beach, and returning to it always brought a warmth to her heart. She felt like kicking at the water as the waves rolled in. She felt like running her hands through the lake and grabbing fistfuls of sand. She felt like calling up Andrew and scheduling an impromptu hangout at the beach, just like old times.

Nicole opened her eyes and sighed. Andrew was nowhere near Chicago, and hadn't been for the last two weeks. Nicole took in another heavy breath and walked away from the shoreline, letting the sand dry off her feet a little before she placed back on her shoes.

***

"Did you pack sunscreen?"

"Yes, Mom."

"Did you *both* pack sunscreen?"

"Yes, Mrs. Winger," Laura answered.

"And it's a proper SPF?" Nicole's mom went on. "The sun is a lot stronger in Florida. Have you ever been to Florida before, Laura?"

"A few times," Laura answered, looking back as her luggage teetered over a chipped sidewalk stone. "Mostly around the Tallahassee area."

"Nicole, how strong is your SPF?" Mrs. Winger turned to her daughter, who had been trailing three or four steps behind both her mom and Laura.

Nicole shrugged.

"I don't know. 50?"

"Hun, I hope it's more than that," said her mom.

"Okay, you're right. It's 150," Nicole teased, tilting her head at her mother.

Her mother sighed and shook her head.

"You have your father's complexion," she warned. "And he always got sunburns. You out of everyone should be worried about sunscreen."

"I'll put on a lot of it, then," said Nicole.

"Well, I packed some aloe vera lotion, just in case," her mom offered.

Nicole took in a breath, ready to quip something back at her mother. Her mom looked back with an earnest, worried face, and Nicole sighed it out instead. The trio of ladies hung a right through a set of double glass doors and into the airport. Nicole tugged at her suitcase and tried to catch up.

"Thanks, Mom, for bringing aloe vera." Nicole gave her best grateful smile as they cross the main entrance. "I appreciate it."

Nicole let her attention scatter as they checked in and checked their luggage. She focused briefly on a screaming toddler, who had tried to run away from his mom only to reach the end of his child leash. In another corner, a couple was having what Nicole could only deduce was a whisper-screaming match. Across the way, a father sat on his carry-on luggage as he spread out a map over his lap. There were families moving about, carting more pieces of luggage than Nicole would probably ever own in her lifetime.

"We're meeting your Aunt Barbara and Uncle Pete in Miami," her mom tried to explain as they got in line for security. "We'll be renting a van and driving out to East Braedonton together."

"Deep in the dirty south," Nicole mumbled. Nicole stepped up to the gate agent and handed him her ticket and driver's license. She unconsciously gave him an awkward semi-smile, ironically matching the smile on her license. He gave her a polite grin as he handed everything back and motioned for the next person in line.

Nicole walked over to the next line, removed

everything into the appropriate x-ray bins, and walked through the metal detector. She gathered her stuff on the other side, plopping her bins onto a nearby bench. She flopped her flats against the tile floor and shimmied her feet into them while she reassembled her bag and returned pieces of jewelry to their rightful places. She turned and watched as her mother and her girlfriend started going through the exact same process, waiting barefoot in line like everyone else.

Nicole scanned the airport terminal, at the people who were about to leave Chicago. She watched as people walked past her, their carry-on luggage trailing behind. She wondered how many of them would be on the Miami flight with her. She wondered if any of them would be visiting Miami on vacation. These hypothetical people, who'd land at the Miami airport with high hopes, where they'd hail a cab to the hotel and get a chance relax and recharge. She could imagine them strolling out onto the balcony first thing in the morning, taking in the Atlantic air and getting ready to go down to the beach. She could imagine how peaceful that would feel.

She wondered how many of them regarded Chicago as their tourist destination and were now returning home, ready to return to the real world after a stint of sightseeing. She could imagine them going up to the Skydeck, going down to Millennium Park, making all the necessary vacation stops before returning back to Florida and going on with their everyday lives.

Nicole followed her mom and Laura down the hallway until they reached their gate. After searching in vain to find three empty seats in a row, Nicole grabbed an empty spot by the window and dropped her bag by her feet. She sat down with a *plop*, disturbing the person next to her who had been reading a mass-market paperback with a scowl on his face.

"Mhm!" The man next to her dramatically cleared his throat, his head slightly turned in Nicole's direction, his scowling eyes still on his book. Nicole gave a sheepish grin that he didn't see, took in a deep breath, and looked out one of the windows.

Parts of the Chicago skyline were still visible, albeit

covered in a slight haze. A moderately sized airplane was already taxiing the outer runway. She followed the plane as it sped down the runway, lifting up just as it went out of Nicole's view. She let her gaze linger where the airplane had disappeared from sight before returning back to the skyline.

The sky was beginning to turn, with lavender and pink hues gathering at the base of the city. The sun was starting to set earlier now. The first sign that summer was coming to a close.

Another plane slowly moved into view and pulled up to the gate. It came to a gentle stop in what Nicole felt was mere inches away from the window. The boarding bridge stretched out, connecting with the side of the plane and shifting into its final position. Within minutes, people began streaming out of the gate entrance to Nicole's right. A cheerful flight attendant reminded everyone that the boarding process for Flight 421 to Miami would begin momentarily. The people around Nicole began to shift in their seats, gathering their belongings before standing up. Some were already congregating by the front desk. Nicole looked back to where Laura and her mother had been sitting. She caught the gaze of her mom, who waved her over, all three airplane tickets in her hand. Nicole looked down at her bag for a heartbeat longer than necessary, picked the bag up, and made her way over.

Abby Rosmarin

Chapter Four

A SENSE OF POISE AND RATIONALITY

"You stand there," Nicky *instructed, pushing her brother into place. "And I'll stand here. I'll be the bride and you'll be the Daddy."*

Andrew chuckled and moved himself into position. "And who are you marrying?"

Nicky scanned the room before picking up one of her dolls.

"I'll marry this one," Nicky proclaimed, holding it out as if inspecting it. She paused again, picking up a second doll. "And this doll can be the Mommy." Nicky went over and placed the second doll by Andrew's feet before going back to her original position.

"And which doll is going to be the priest?"

"Why do I need a priest?"

"Because every wedding has a priest," Andrew explained.

"Do you want to be the priest?" Nicky asked.

"Am I the priest and the daddy?" Andrew gave a knowing smile.

"Can you be both?" Nicky asked.

Andrew shrugged.

"Sure. I'm sure some weddings have that."

Nicky held up the first doll above her head.

"I now announce you married!" Nicky proclaimed. "You

may kiss the bride!" Nicky brought the doll to her face and gave it a quick peck before hugging it to her body.

Andrew laughed.

"You have no idea how weddings work, do you?"

"Yes I do," Nicky said with an indignant pout. "And now I'm married."

"Where's your maid of honor?" Andrew jibed. "Or the best man?"

Nicky pursed her lips.

"Do you want to be best man?"

Andrew picked up the doll by his feet and dusted off the dress.

"I don't think I can be all three things. I'm sure there's a law or something."

"Well, then I'll be the best man," Nicky decided.

"But you're a girl," Andrew responded. "Don't you want to be the maid of honor?"

"I don't want to be made of honor." Nicky crossed her arms. "Whatever honor is, I don't want to be made of it."

"Not that type of made, silly." Andrew laughed. "Like maid-maid. Like cleaning maid."

"That's even worse!" Nicky shot her hands out to the ceiling. "I don't want to be a maid during my wedding!"

Andrew shook his head with a smile.

"Maybe we should just play something else."

"But I need to get married," Nicky whined.

"I thought you were already married." Andrew pointed to Nicky's doll, who was now lying on the couch. "To Princess Jessica."

"It didn't count," Nicky pouted. "I didn't have a best man or a maid of honor."

"Okay then, I can be the best man," Andrew offered. "And the priest, and the Daddy, and the maid of honor, too."

"You don't have to be the maid of honor," Nicky replied with a sigh. "I can clean up after the wedding."

"Andrew!" Their mom called down from the second floor. "Football practice is in 15 minutes! Are you ready?"

"Not yet, Mom!" Andrew called back from the living room.

"I need you to get ready, then, honey!" she called out again.

"Yes, Mom!" Andrew shouted out. Andrew turned to Nicky. "We'll have to finish this wedding later."

Nicky nodded absently, her mind lost deep in thought. Andrew exited the living room, crossed the kitchen, and disappeared into the laundry room. Within minutes, Andrew reappeared, lugging his pads behind him.

"Hey, Andrew?" Nicky asked with all the sincerity a 5-year-old can muster.

"Yeah, kiddo?"

"If you ever get married, can I be your best man?"

Andrew gave an understanding sigh.

"Sure thing."

"And not the maid of honor. We can hire the maid of honor."

Andrew laughed and looked down at his pads.

"Alright. We'll hire the maid of honor."

***

The first of two engagement parties happened that January, eight months before the wedding and almost two months to the day from when Nicole had first met Cora.

The invitation to the engagement party was how Nicole found out that Andrew and Cora were engaged in the first place. She received a delicate, ornate letter in the mail just a few days after New Year's, inviting her to come to her brother's engagement party at one of Chicago's nicest restaurants. Nicole nearly dropped her phone as she scrambled to call Andrew.

"You're engaged?" Nicole began the call with, her voice more accusatory than she meant it to be.

"You got our invite, I see," Andrew replied calmly.

"When did you plan on telling me this?" Nicole asked.

"Well, you found out now, right?" Andrew said off-handedly.

Nicole drew in a sharp breath and bit her tongue. She could feel the venom swell up to the point that she could taste it. Every thought, word, and emotion bottlenecked in Nicole's throat. She stopped biting her tongue just long enough to move it back and clench down on her teeth instead.

"So, are you coming?" Andrew asked.

Nicole remained silent, her hand gripping her phone

with a force that would've snapped a lesser phone in half.

"I really hope you can make it," Andrew continued. "Laura's invited too, of course."

Nicole let out a sigh and pressed a palm against one of her eyes.

"I'm coming," Nicole said, suddenly feeling very exhausted. "Of course I'm coming. I'll be there."

"That's awesome to hear," Andrew replied. "It really is."

Nicole closed her eyes.

"Yeah."

"But, anyways," Andrew said, without missing a beat. "How's the temp gig going? Have they finally moved you onto a better project or are they still putting you through busy work?"

***

The engagement party was held at a swanky restaurant at the very top of one of Chicago's finest hotels. The restaurant had a U-shaped floor plan, with glass windows along three of the walls, providing breathtaking views of the city. To the right of the elevators was the Prudential Tower, standing alongside the other skyscrapers, all so close to the windows that Nicole probably could've reached out and touched them. That is, if the windows actually opened. To the left was Lake Michigan, stretching out into the horizon, the Ohio Street Beach blocked from view by the buildings. Something pinged at her heart. She'd give anything to be there instead of where she was now.

Nicole had to be led out of the elevator by Laura. She would've gladly stayed where she was, allowing the elevator doors to close on her before bringing her back to the ground floor. But Nicole had a death grip on Laura's hand; all it took was one gentle tug by Laura and Nicole hop-stepped out of the elevator.

From what Nicole could see from the elevator lobby, the restaurant looked like any other upscale restaurant. Smooth white linens covered the tables, with small glass candleholders adorning the centers. By the maître-d's podium stood a two-foot-tall chalkboard, held up by an ornate iron stand and accented with a delicate, antique frame. In colorful chalk, the sign read, "Cora & Andrew's Engagement Party! They met, they fell in love, and now they are getting married!" Before Nicole could roll her eyes, the maître-d stepped forward and clasped his hands.

"Table for two?" he asked in a gentle voice. "Or are you guests of Cora and Andrew?"

Nicole pressed her lips together, tempted to ask for a table in the farthest corner of the restaurant.

"We're here for Cora and Andrew," Laura answered with a polite smile.

"But of course," the maître-d answered, in a way that made Nicole wish he had a French accent to go along with it. "Right this way."

The maître-d led Nicole and Laura around the corner to the opposite end of the restaurant. As if turning a corner transported them into another world, the polished restaurant quickly melded into a large, crowded party. The crisp, white linens were replaced with pink, ruffled tablecloths. White Christmas lights had been strung from the ceiling, looping around and under the ceiling tiles before gathering at the end of the room. The simple candleholders had been replaced with pink, rhinestoned letter Ws, surround by thick, round candles.

The wall opposite the windows hosted three or four long, rectangular tables, draped in the same ruffled tablecloths and adorned with more flowers than Nicole had ever seen together at one time. Flower arrangements hung from the corners and edges and sides of the tables, with rose petals scattered across the surface. The petals danced around the trays upon trays of food and congregated at the base of a 5-tier cake. At the top of the cake stood a delicate porcelain figurine of a bride in mid-twirl, her gown frozen in time as it fluttered around her legs.

"I hope you enjoy your evening," said the maître-d. "I'll be here if you need anything."

"Thank you," Laura replied. The maître-d turned and disappeared around the corner as Nicole and Laura continued to stand at the base of the party.

"So *this* is what happens when a bridal magazine explodes," Nicole mumbled.

Laura pressed her lips together and stifled a laugh.

"Come on now," Laura began, hiding her smile as best as she could. "Let's see if we can find Andrew."

Nicole took a tentative step forward before letting Laura lead them through the masses. Laura wove her way around people who were standing with plates of food in hand, chatting idly with whoever was around them, apparently unaffected by the two women attempting to walk by. Nicole scanned the area for Andrew, or her mom, or anyone she knew, and found herself at a complete loss. Her eyes darted around until it landed on a tall, skinny man with a mop of blonde hair.

"There's Jacob, at least!" Nicole said over the drum of the crowd.

"Jacob?" Laura asked, her voice straddling the line between talking and shouting.

"His best friend in high school," Nicole explained. "At least I know *someone* here."

Nicole fished her way to the other end of the room, with Laura following behind.

Nicole stopped just short of Jacob and smiled.

"Glad to see a familiar face."

"Geez, Nicky, look at you!" Jacob put his drink down on the table next to him and gave Nicole a bear hug. "I swear you were in diapers the last time I saw you."

"I doubt it's been that long." Nicole rolled her eyes and smirked. "But I've missed you. How's things been?"

"Eh, same old, same old. Living in Des Plaines right now." Jacob shrugged his shoulders. "And how about you?"

"Good! Good," Nicole answered. "Graduated from UIC in May. Been working at a design company."

"That's awesome," Jacob replied. "What do you do there?"

Nicole bobbed her head from side to side.

"Eh, I'm a temp there right now. Originally, I had been doing mostly clerical stuff to help them get through the Christmas rush. But I've been able to get my hand in a few specific projects, so hopefully that's enough to keep me on for longer."

"Not bad. I like it," said Jacob. "How long are you scheduled to be there?"

"I was actually supposed to be done after New Year's. But they've yet to send me packing and I'm not going complain," Nicole went on. "With any luck, I'll be on their payroll by the summer." Nicole reflexively looked over at Laura. "And this is my girlfriend, Laura."

"Pleasure to meet you." Laura stepped forward and stuck out her hand.

Jacob stepped in and shook her hand.

"And likewise," he said. "How long have you two been together?"

Laura looked at Nicole before turning back.

"Almost two years," Laura answered. "A mutual friend introduced us."

"I certainly need a friend like that," said Jacob. "I'm still holding out for Mrs. Right. We'll see if she actually exists."

"She's out there," Laura reassured. "Just a matter of time."

"Hey, if Andrew can find someone that he'd actually want to settle down with, then there's hope for the rest of us," Jacob laughed.

Nicole held her breath, pressed her lips together, and scanned the crowd.

"Have you seen Andrew, by any chance?" she said, changing the topic.

"Um, no, not yet," Jacob answered. "But they're also not expected to make their entrance for another ten minutes."

"Their entrance?" Nicole repeated.

"Yeah, it said so on the invitation," Jacob went on. "It had a rundown of when guests should arrive and when Andrew and his fiancée would arrive."

Nicole felt one corner of her mouth pull up with a twitch.

"I guess I missed that."

Jacob shrugged.

"Happens to the best of us. At least you got here on time."

"At least there's that," Nicole mumbled. "Is there anyone else from Hampshire here?"

"Um, I'm not sure." Jacob scanned the room. "I'm sure there are some old teammates here as well, or something. I just haven't run into them."

Nicole sighed and looked around the room. There were easily a hundred people in their section of the restaurant. Maybe even two hundred. A small portion of the guests were around Nicole's age, but the majority of the people were considerably older. Some were sitting at the tables, but most were standing around, some standing directly behind a chair or leaning against a table.

After a moment, Nicole noticed a set of small disturbances in the crowd. Two women zipped around the room. One looked about Cora's age with jet-black hair. The other was in the heart of middle-age with frosted blonde hair, teased a mile high just like Cora's. The young woman with the black hair darted from table to table, clipboard under one arm, talking to people in short, sharp segments, before quickly moving on to the next set of people. The middle-aged woman, who was so skinny that the jagged angles of her shoulder bones accented her arms, walked at a calmer pace, meandering from group to group, chatting up each and every person for a minute or two at a time. Her teeth were long and white and her smile seemed to take up her entire face.

"Well, hello, you guys. I'm Sarah," Nicole heard a nasal voice with a strong, synthetic southern accent coming from her right. Nicole turned away from the pair of women to see a short female, bordering on obese, who had already draped her hand out to Jacob. Jacob held Sarah's hand by her fingers and gave it a tentative shake.

"Jacob. Pleased to meet you."

Sarah turned and presented her hand to Laura.

"I'm Sarah."

Laura repeated Jacob's semi-handshake with an awkward smile.

"Laura. It's, um, nice to meet you."

Sarah turned one last time and draped her hand at Nicole.

"Sarah."

"Nicole," she answered flatly, touching Sarah's fingers and giving one limp shake.

"So are you friends of Andrew's or…" Sarah took a step back and clasped her hands together.

"I'm his sister, actually," Nicole answered, trying to smile but finding her lips curling into a subtle snarl instead.

"Ah, well, that's nice." Sarah sighed and tossed a lock of hair behind her shoulder in a dramatic sweep. "I'm one of her bridesmaids. The third bridesmaid in line, but not like that matters."

Nicole and Laura exchanged glances before looking back at Sarah.

Sarah looked around the room, shook her head, and let out a dramatic sigh.

"Now, I'm not one to speak ill of such a festive engagement, but Cora's doing her engagement party all wrong," Sarah said. "Just look at this. A party like this shouldn't be inside. It's far too stuffy."

Sarah paused for emphasis, her left arm extended out as if demonstrating how incorrect the party was.

"No, when I have *my* engagement party, I'm going to have it on a terrace," Sarah went on. "In a place that's much nicer than Chicago. Like Bermuda. Or the Bahamas." Sarah paused again and bought her left hand up to her face, pausing just long enough so that the diamond ring on her finger was directly under her jaw, before tossing another lock of hair back.

"Ah, you're engaged, too?" Laura asked.

Sarah covered her left hand with her right.

"No, not yet, but… details!" Sarah rolled her eyes and uncovered her left hand, jutting it out at Laura. "But isn't this ring *amazing*? This is exactly what I want my engagement ring to look like."

"It's quite…" Laura looked down, her brow furrowed, before looking back up. "Sparkly."

"I know, isn't it?" Sarah's face lit up. "According to the jeweler, this size is the equivalent of a 5 karat diamond. So whoever I end up marrying better be rich, because this was expensive enough in CZ."

Nicole looked over to see that Jacob had somehow

slipped away sometime during the cubic zirconia showcase.

"But, yes, when I get married, I'm so not doing any of this," Sarah continued. "First off, terrace in Bermuda. Or the Bahamas. And white *roses* would be strung from the ceiling. Not white *lights*. And I would have a 6-tier cake, because I would have, like, way many more guests."

Sarah looked down at her ring one more time.

"Well, that's life for you. Cora can't have it all, I guess," she said, her face tightening as she finished her sentence. "Even though she already has the looks, the good figure, and a fiancé." As if snapping out of a trance, Sarah shook her head and smiled. "But, anyway, so nice to meet y'all!" Sarah shook her fingers at Nicole and Laura before snapping them back against her palm. "Toodles!"

Sarah cut across the space between Nicole and Laura before approaching another group, greeting the people there by stick out her left hand.

"Well, now…" Nicole trailed off, awestruck.

"My thoughts exactly," Laura replied.

"I thought everything is sweeter in the South," Nicole mumbled.

Laura shrugged and shook her head.

"Maybe she just ate all the sweets," Nicole added.

Laura looked up at Nicole, her eyes wide with astonishment. She pressed her lips together and snorted.

"That was mean," she said.

"And yet you laughed," Nicole countered.

The girl with black hair and the clipboard weaved her way over to Nicole and Laura.

"And you are?" she demanded as she walked over, her lanky figure towering over Nicole, her accent similar to Sarah's.

"Uh… Nicole?" Nicole tilted her head to one side. "And Laura?"

The girl fished through the pages on her clipboard before pressing a finger onto one page.

"Nicole Winger and Laura Reynolds?" she said, her eyes never leaving her page.

"Uh, yes," Nicole replied, one eyebrow cocked.

"I'm only telling you guys this once." The girl shifted

her clipboard under her arm again. "Entering and/or exiting is now a complete no-go until Andrew and Cora arrive. Is that clear? Even for the bathroom. Even if there's a fire. We need everyone on this side of the restaurant until they arrive. We need to keep the area completely clear for their grand entrance and *no one* is going to trespass until they have firmly established their presence. Is that clear?"

"Clear as crystal," Nicole answered, the corners of her mouth tugging up into a bitter grin.

"Good. Stay." The girl turned and wove around people before asking the same question to the group that Sarah was currently a part of. Nicole watched as the girl gave the same speech about Andrew and Cora's entrance. Sarah looked on with a scowl on her face, twisting her fake diamond ring back and forth on her finger.

"Sit. Stay. Rollover. Good boy," Nicole muttered mostly to herself.

"Who do you think that was?" Laura asked.

"Someone with severe control issues." Nicole looked around the room. She couldn't find her mom, or Jacob, or anyone that she knew. She felt anchored to her spot, surrounded by faces of people who were a little too cheerful for her liking. Nicole pursed her lips and shifted her weight from one foot to the other.

All at once, the music stopped and the lights went out. Everyone's conversations came to an abrupt halt as everyone looked up and around the area.

"Ladies and gentleman, please find your seats," said a voice on a loudspeaker.

"In the dark?" Nicole asked.

As the crowds slowly dispersed around the tables, Nicole and Laura started walking around, looking for two empty seats and finding some in the farthest corner of the room.

The lights stayed off as people sat down, stunted chatter now taking over their once lively conversations.

"Ladies and gentleman!" the announcer called out again. "Please rise for the future Mr. and Mrs. Andrew and Cora Winger!"

"Did they honestly tell us to sit down just so they

could tell us to stand back up?" Nicole muttered over to Laura.

A spotlight turned on as an intricate orchestral song started. Everyone stood up and clapped. The spotlight moved and focused on the inside corner by the entrance of the party. A red carpet appeared from around the corner, rolling out until it reached the center of the room. Andrew and Cora soon walked out, arms linked, feet in perfect synchronization. Everyone started cheering as they walked their way to the end of the carpet. Cora used her free hand to wave at her guests. She was decked out in a tight, white, sequined tube dress and stilettos so tall that they made her the same height as Andrew.

After a few moments of hand waving, Cora and Andrew departed from the red carpet and made their way to a small section of floor that separated the rectangular food tables from the circular guest tables. Cora turned to Andrew, wrapped her arms around his neck, and began swaying back and forth. Without any transition whatsoever, the music cut from orchestral to a slow country number.

Nicole looked around, wondering when she could sit back down again. When she saw that everyone around here was standing tall with their eyes fixed on the couple, Nicole sighed and crossed her arms. Andrew and Cora continued to dance until the song finished, at which point they stood side by side and bowed to the guests.

The announcer repeated, "Ladies and gentleman, the future Mr. and Mrs. Andrew and Cora Winger!" and the crowd erupted into applause.

The lights slowly turned back on as the applause died down. Groups of people came up to talk with Andrew and Cora. Nicole looked around one last time, a feeling of isolation sweeping over her.

Nicole sat back down at the now deserted table. Laura followed suit and sat next to her.

"That was... quite the entrance," Laura said after a moment.

"You can say that again," Nicole muttered.

"Okay. That was... quite the entrance," Laura repeated.

"Hey, I'm supposed to be the smartass in this relationship," Nicole warned.

"What can I say?" Laura shrugged. "You rub off on me."

Nicole turned to Laura with a wicked grin, ready to say something in response, until she spotted a familiar face coming in with the maître-d. The lady, with her gray hair neatly clipped back, walked out into the area, careful not to step on the red carpet. She gave a smiling nod to the maître-d and continued into the party.

Nicole started waving her hands in the air.

"Mom!" Nicole shouted. "Over here!"

Mrs. Winger scanned the room with a puzzled look before finding Nicole. With a broad smile on her face, she made her way over to Nicole and Laura's table.

"How are you girls?" said Nicole's mom. She gently touched Nicole's shoulder before sitting down at the table.

"Oh, just great," Nicole replied.

"We're good. Thank you," Laura added. "And you?"

"Oh, I'm good," Mrs. Winger sighed out, placing her purse onto her lap. "Looks like I missed the grand entrance, though."

"Trust me, it wasn't that grand," Nicole mumbled.

"Oh, be nice," her mom said reproachfully. "I'm sure it was lovely."

Laura cleared her throat.

"So, did you just get here?" Laura asked.

"About five or so minutes ago, I did," Mrs. Winger answered. "But I was told that I couldn't come over here until the lights for the party were turned back on." She looked over to the dance floor and sighed. "But that's all right. At least I didn't miss their first dance at their wedding. And it gave me a chance to chat with this lovely couple from Ohio. They were waiting for their table and wanted to know why the lights were out in one half of the restaurant."

"Still curious about that myself," Nicole said in monotone.

"Again, be good," her mom repeated. "It's not every day one has an engagement party."

Nicole sighed and looked down at the place setting by

her seat. Everything, she noticed, was pink. From the dishes to the silverware to the cups to the pink candles on silver trays sprinkled with pink rhinestones. It gave her a headache if she looked at it for too long.

"Did you see where Andrew and Cora might've gone off to?" Mrs. Winger looked around the room.

Nicole gestured to where a large group had gotten up from their tables and stood in a large circle.

"Over there is probably a good guess," she said.

"Well, then, let's say hi." Mrs. Winger gave her daughter's forearm a gentle shake.

Nicole tilted her head to one side, grimacing.

"Um, I don't know, I…" Nicole swallowed and stared at the rhinestones until her temples throbbed.

"Come on now, don't let the large groups scare you," said her mom.

"I'm not scared of large groups…" Nicole began. She searched for what to say next while staring at the tulle that peaked out from under the tray. She eventually shook her head and said, "Fine. Fine. Let's go say hi."

Nicole followed her mother through the crowds, originally side by side with her mom and Laura but, as they swerved around the tables, Nicole fell more and more behind until she was trailing both women. Mrs. Winger stood on her tiptoes at the base of the group before tapping an elderly gentleman on the shoulder.

"Excuse me, sir, I hope you don't mind." Mrs. Winger gave a nervous laugh as she stepped around the man. "I just wanted to say hello to my son and his fiancée."

"Oh, you're the mother of the groom, then!" A high-pitched voice with a southern accent rang in Nicole's ear. She turned to find the frosted-haired woman who had been moving about from group to group at the beginning of the party. She stepped past Nicole and wrapped her impossibly-thin arms around Mrs. Winger. "It's so good to finally meet you!"

"And… and you," Mrs. Winger replied, returning the hug after a pause. "It's good to meet you as well."

"Oh, bless your heart, you have no idea who I am." The lady stepped back, threw her arms out, and smiled broadly. "I'm Sue-Anne, Cora's one and only mother!"

"Well, it is great to finally meet you," Mrs. Winger replied, hugging herself at the waist. "This is a lovely party."

"I know, isn't it?" Sue-Anne replied. "Although that Cora, what a little firecracker. She should've *told* me she was getting *engaged*. A proper daughter calls her mama up the day she can get her boyfriend to agree to propose."

"Agree to propose – like, she should've known and told you before he did it?" Nicole asked.

"Oh, bless your heart, that's exactly what I meant!" said Sue-Anne. "But, no matter: the beauty of my party-making abilities is that I can design a gorgeous get-together like this, in a town I've never been to, in one month's time, with no problems! Which is good, since I only *had* a month to plan this!"

"So Andrew and Cora got engaged before Christmas, then?" Nicole asked, doing the math quickly in her head.

"Why, bless your heart again, of course they did! Got engaged right after Thanksgiving!" Sue-Anne's smile broadened. "Poor boy felt so guilty about abandoning Cora for Thanksgiving. He flew out to see us that weekend and proposed just as soon as he got there! What a romantic, that boy. Truly a gentleman, for a yank."

Sue-Anne gave a contented sigh and stroked her pearls.

"So, was your husband unable to make it?" Sue-Anne asked.

Mrs. Winger gently touched her wedding band.

"Um, I'm not sure if Andrew told you about his father, but..." Mrs. Winger began slowly.

"Oh, yes, yes, yes." Sue-Anne raised one hand up and closed her eyes. "And may that good man rest in peace."

"He was quite the good man," Mrs. Winger replied softly.

"Oh, just pardon my rudeness, I didn't mean to conjure up some sad thoughts on such a happy day," said Sue-Anne. "I simply meant your *new* husband. Was he able to make it tonight?"

"Oh, I, uh..." Mrs. Winger looked down at her hands and smiled awkwardly. "I haven't remarried."

Sue-Anne cocked her head one side, her face contorted

in confusion.

"Huh. How strange is that?" she replied, as if working out an equation in her brain. "You're a pretty lady. How is it that you haven't snagged another husband yet?"

Mrs. Winger shifted her weight from foot to foot.

"Well, I guess I never saw the need to," Mrs. Winger said with a gentle shrug of the shoulders. "My focus was on my kids and my job."

"Well, if that isn't just the saddest thing I've heard today," said Sue-Anne. "And you had to get a job on top of all that mourning. Goodness, gracious."

"I already had the job," Mrs. Winger gently corrected. "I've been working as a paralegal since Nicole was 3."

"Well, isn't that nice," said Sue-Anne. "You know, my husband has a secretary as well. She can type up a letter or make photocopies like no one I know."

"Well, actually, paralegals aren't like secretaries," Mrs. Winger explained, in a tone used for a tourist who needed directions. "You really help out in the legal process. You conduct interviews, obtain affidavits..."

"Oh my, I believe you," Sue-Anne chuckled out. "Maybe we'll have to start telling Dan's secretary to start conducting interviews, too."

Nicole took a protective step forward, filling the space between Sue-Anne and her mother.

"Hi, we haven't met yet." Nicole gave a sight wave from a tightly-tucked arm. "I'm Nicole. Andrew's brother."

"Oh, how lovely to meet you, then, Nicole," Sue-Anne cooed. She turned and faced Laura. "And who might you be, darlin'?"

"This is my girlfriend, Laura," Nicole said, searching Sue-Anne's face for a reaction.

"Oh, how lovely!" Sue-Anne clasped her hands. "It's always important to have girlfriends! I just don't know what I'd do if I didn't have my girlfriends to chat with."

"No... she's... my *girlfriend*..."

"Oh, I know!" Sue-Anne exclaimed. "Men will come and go, but girlfriends are forever."

Laura gave a slight nod, hiding the amused grin that

was spreading rapidly across her face.

"Well, I certainly shouldn't keep you from your very own son." Sue-Anne turned back to Nicole's mom. "Let's go and say hi to the happy couple."

Sue-Anne led the way through the group of people, pausing to say hello to every person she walked past. Eventually they came to the heart of the group, where Andrew was talking to an elderly woman, with an arm around Cora's waist.

"Oh, my handsome future son-in-law!" Sue-Anne sang out. She emphatically wrapped her arms around Andrew before Andrew could even acknowledge Sue-Anne. Andrew let go of Cora's waist and returned the hug warmly.

"Mrs. Bachman, how are you?" Andrew asked as he removed himself from the hug.

"Oh, just peachy!" Sue-Anne replied. "How can I not be? Look at how this party turned out! You could just cry, it's so beautiful!"

"Oh, Ma," Cora replied with gentle admonishment.

"And look who I found tailing around the back!" Sue-Anne stepped aside, revealing Nicole and the rest.

"Hey," said Nicole. Her shoulders rose up and her lips tensely pressed together.

"Hey there, kiddo." Andrew smiled. "I'm so glad you guys could make it." Andrew looked over at his mom and his smile grew bigger. "You look wonderful this evening, Mom."

"You always know how to flatter, sweetheart." Mrs. Winger walked over and gave her son a gentle kiss on the cheek. "But look at you. The man of the hour. I can't remember the last time I saw you in a suit."

Andrew tugged at the cuffs with a sheepish grin.

"That's actually a gift," Sue-Anne piped in. "From his future in-law family. I asked for his measurements and had the finest tailor in our little town make him a suit fit for a king."

"You do look very regal in it," Laura noted.

"Well, of course he does," Sue-Anne replied. "You have to, if you're gonna marry a princess like my little Cora."

Cora looked to the floor, cheeks red, suppressing a smirk.

"Oh, but how rude of me!" Sue-Anne stepped back. "I was interrupting a lovely conversation! How are you today, Mrs. Cromer?"

"Barely surviving this dreadfully cold weather," Mrs. Cromer replied, her southern drawl accented with an elderly vibrato. "But I'm having a wonderful time at your party."

"Oh, that is lovely to hear," Sue-Anne replied. Sue-Anne turned to Mrs. Winger and said: "Mrs. Cromer flew all the way from East Braedonton to be here today." Sue-Anne paused and gestured to the crowd around her. "In fact, almost everyone here flew all the way from our little hometown, just to be here today."

Nicole let out a sigh as she followed Sue-Anne's gaze around the room.

"That's really kind of them," Laura noted.

"But don't think for a second that this means they won't bother to come to the *Florida* engagement party!" Sue-Anne continued.

"There's an engagement party in Florida?" Nicole asked flatly.

"Of course!" Sue-Anne retorted, as if Nicole had asked if plants need water.

"When will that be, Sue-Anne?" Mrs. Winger asked. "I want to make sure I can make it."

Sue-Anne raised a hand and tossed her fingers out to the side.

"Oh, whenever," Sue-Anne responded. "I was too busy planning this one." Sue-Anne stepped in closer to Mrs. Winger. "Between you and me, I would've preferred the party in Florida in the first place. But our little girl was in Chicago, and I didn't want her to have to skip class to come celebrate catchin' a husband. So I made do with what I had."

"Well," Mrs. Winger replied. "You really outdid yourself. I could never dream of planning something like this."

Sue-Anne smiled and pressed a hand to her chest, as if holding onto Mrs. Winger's compliment.

"I must say, I am certainly happy that my fellow townspeople were able to come all the way up to Chicago," Sue-Anne went on. "First off, the guest list for people from Chicago alone was pitifully small. And secondly, half the guests had the nerve to not RSVP! Even one of Andrew's own groomsmen!" Sue-Anne huffed. "At least the groomsmen from *our* side of the family are here, so it won't look totally lopsided when we take our photos tonight."

Cora touched her teased hair and puckered her lips into a small dot.

"I mean, imagine the nerve! Acceptin' an invitation into one's weddin' party, but not acceptin' an invitation into that couple's *engagement* party?"

"Is Jacob in your wedding party?" Nicole asked Andrew, her voice steadily getting faster. "Because I saw him. He definitely RSVPed. Is he a groomsman?"

"Yeah, yeah, of course," Andrew replied, his eyes searching the crowds. "I guess the guys from Northwestern couldn't make it."

"Which includes a groomsman!" Sue-Anne butt in. "Really, I have half a mind to tell him his groomsman title has been revoked."

"Oh, Ma, no need to be harsh," Cora spoke up, her eyes still on the ground. "He wasn't being rude. He simply didn't know."

Andrew looked at Cora.

"Come again?"

"I somehow missed a whole page of the guest list. They never got their invites... and I didn't realize it until just days before the party," Cora said with a jovial shrug to her shoulders, as if laughing off someone else's mistake. "It happens to the best of us."

"Oh, darlin', this is why I should've been in charge of sendin' out the invitations," Sue-Anne reprimanded.

"You could've just called them," said Nicole.

Cora turned to Nicole, confusion sweeping over face. "Pardon?"

"You could've just called them," Nicole repeated. "I'm sure they wouldn't have minded."

"Call them?" Cora repeated with an incredulous

laugh. "How ghastly."

"Might as well tell them to bring their own beverages, or give us cash in lieu of gifts!" Sue-Anne picked up.

Sue-Anne and Cora broke into laughter. Andrew cast his eyes to the ground and gave another sheepish grin. Nicole gritted her teeth. She attempted to smile, but found herself grimacing instead.

"Oh, we don't mean to be mean," Sue-Anne explained. "But there is a proper way of doing things, and an improper way of doing things. I don't expect you yanks to understand."

Nicole's ears began to ring. It took her a moment to realize that she had been holding her breath. When she finally inhaled, her mother was in the middle of complimenting Cora's dress. Laura was responding to something Mrs. Cromer had said.

"I'll be back," Nicole stated to the gap between her mom and Laura, hoping no one heard her, and started to walk away.

"Where are you going?" Laura said, turning around suddenly.

Nicole stopped and turned.

"Oh, um, I'm going to get something to drink," Nicole lied. "I'll be back in a bit."

Before Laura could respond, Nicole lost herself in the crowd of people. She wove her way around, doing her best to avoid eye contact as she excused herself across the dance floor and back to the circular tables. With a heaving sigh, Nicole sat at the first table by dance floor and buried her head in her hands.

"Well, hi there, stranger," said a twangy female voice next to her.

Nicole looked up and turned to her left. In the table next to Nicole's sat two girls. The one closest to Nicole broke into a wide, welcoming smile.

"I said, 'hi there!'"

"Hi," Nicole said in a tired voice.

The girl turned her seat away from the table until she was fully facing Nicole.

"The name's Ashley," she said, in a drawl that was definitively country-western. "That one over there's

Karen."

Karen, a petite girl with mousey brown hair, sat across from Ashley, her head buried in her phone.

"Hey, Karen!" Ashley called out. "Stop chatting with the beau and say hi."

Karen gripped her phone until her knuckles went white and looked up.

"Hi," she chirped out in an accent Nicole couldn't put her finger on, before going right back to her phone.

Ashley sighed and rolled her eyes.

"Puppy love. What can you do?" Ashley flipped a lock of hair over her shoulder, as if that were the answer to the question. "Anyway, how do you know Cora?"

"Cora?" Nicole repeated. "Um... uh, she's my brother's fiancée..."

"Oh, so you know Andrew!" Ashley piped up. "I guess that was silly of me for assuming."

"That's all right," Nicole replied, resting her elbows against the edge of the table. "I guess you know Cora, then?"

"Of course!" Ashley replied with a smug certainty. "We're sisters!"

"Oh, you're Cora's sister?" Nicole asked. "I haven't met much of Cora's family yet."

Ashley laughed and slapped her hand against the table.

"No, silly! My *sister*. Like, sororities?" Ashley jutted her chin out, which felt like the sign language way of saying, "duh!"

"Oh, okay," Nicole replied, her eyes back on the dance floor. From where she sat, all she could see was a sea of people from the hip up. She had absolutely no clue where her mother or Laura was.

"Cora, Karen, and myself, we're all part of Northwestern's sorority devoted to girls from the South," Ashley went on. "Kappa Kappa Kappa is a bit of a sanctuary for those who are exhausted by the north."

Nicole cocked her head to one side.

Did she just say Kappa Kappa Kappa – KKK?

"Oh, I know what you're thinking," Ashley went on. "But it's not what it seems. The Kappa Kappa Kappa sorority – Kappa-cubed – is not just about southern pride. We help out in the community. We have fundraisers. We volunteer and stuff. We do a lot of good."

"Ah." Nicole scanned the room again. No Mom. No Laura, or even Jacob. She began to regret leaving any of them in the first place.

"Kappa-cubed is such a Godsend," Ashley continued. "It's easy to feel out of place when you're used to cities like Memphis. I don't know where I'd be without my sisters. Little wonder Cora asked a few of us to be her bridesmaids. Are you Greek, too?"

"Greek?"

"Well, you'd obviously not be in the Kappa Kappa Kappa sorority, but there's a sorority out there for every type of girl."

"No, I was never really into that, in college," Nicole admitted, straightening up a bit in her seat.

Ashley laughed.

"A yank *and* a GDI. Chicago really is a diverse place."

"GDI?"

"Gosh-Darn Independent," Ashley answered, her lips puckering into a smirk.

Nicole sucked in the air between her teeth and widened her eyes for a moment.

"Well, this has been quite... informative," Nicole said at last. "If you'd excuse me, I'm going to get myself a drink."

"Oh, of course, of course," said Ashley pushing her chair in more to give Nicole space to move her seat. "It was a pleasure meeting you."

"And, uh, likewise," Nicole said with tight lips. Nicole looked over to the other girl – Karen, was it? – and saw that her eyes were locked back onto her phone.

"Well, I'll see you around, then!" said Ashley.

Nicole pushed in her chair.

"I'll see you, too."

Nicole skirted around the edge of the party until she made it to the food table. She looked at the vast arrays spread out from end to end. The bits of fruit shaped like fish and seahorses and starfish. The platter tiers of sandwiches, with each tier showcasing a different sandwich shape and variety. The rose pedals on the table were starting to creep onto the serving platters. The bar was located on the opposite end of the dance floor, by the cake with the dancing bride on it. Even if she wanted a drink, Nicole was not ready to go through all those people just to get there.

She stood where she was, feeling equal parts stranded and isolated. She couldn't find Laura, or her Mom, or Jacob – or anyone from her hometown, anyone that looked even vaguely familiar. She wanted to go and find at least one of them, but feared she'd run into Sue-Anne again, or the Clipboard Master, or Bridesmaid Sarah with her cubic zirconia pre-engagement ring. Or, worse, Andrew and Cora.

The songs from the DJ bled together, as did the conversations and movement of the partygoers. Nicole wasn't sure how much time had passed before Laura came out of the crowd with Mrs. Winger.

"There you are," Nicole's mom said. "We were wondering where you went off to."

"Oh just... around," Nicole replied.

"They're going to do the cake cutting in a minute," said Mrs. Winger. "Lovely young girl named Rachel came by and told us that the DJ would be announcing the cake cutting in five minutes."

"So... she announced the announcement?"

"I think it's very nice that Cora has a friend who wants to make sure everything goes according to plan," Mrs. Winger went on. "There are worse things to have in this world."

"You can say that again," Nicole mumbled.

"Why don't we find a seat," said Laura. "Y'know, before the good ones are taken."

"That sounds like a great idea," Mrs. Winger agreed. "Are you ready, Nicole?"

"As ready as I'll ever be," Nicole sighed out and followed her mother to a nearby table.

Abby Rosmarin

Chapter Five

TOUCHING DOWN

The sound of the landing gear lowering into place was enough to stir Nicole awake. She fluttered her eyes open as she felt the ground vibrate underneath her, as if the landing gear was moving directly below her feet. Nicole peeled her cheek off the window, straightened in her seat, and attempted to move her neck back into a normal position. She looked over at Laura, who had narrowed her eyes and crinkled her nose while reading her book. After a moment, Laura paused and looked up, glancing over in Nicole's direction as if to confirm Nicole had been staring at her.

"Good morning, sleepyhead," said Laura. "Enjoyed your nap?"

"Sure," Nicole answered, placing a hand on the stiff part of her neck. "Slept like a baby."

"You woke up just in time," Laura went on. "We're almost in Miami."

Nicole looked out her window and at the world. The sun had long set, leaving nothing but illuminated dots below her. As the plane descended, the dots became more defined, until they eventually made buildings and streetlights and passing cars. She sighed and let her forehead rest against the window. Slowly but surely, the buildings and streets grew bigger and bigger, until the plane was on the same level as the tops of the trees. Nicole lifted her head just in time for the plane to land, jolting everyone as it touched down and slowed down and taxied down the runway.

"Ladies and gentlemen, we have arrived in Miami, Florida. Local time is 10:45 pm. If this is your final destination, we want to thank you for flying with us today. If you are returning from a trip, we want to welcome you home. To everyone else, welcome to Miami."

Nicole clicked her tongue against the roof her mouth, staring out at the runway tarmac and the walls of the airport. She remained seated as the rest of the airplane's inhabitants stood up, opening the storage compartments and pulling out their luggage. It wasn't until both her mom and Laura were making their way into the aisle that Nicole got up and grabbed her bag.

***

"Howdy, stranger!" a familiar voice called from the baggage claim area.

"Pete!" Nicole's mom called out, leaving the luggage belt and approaching a middle-aged man with a polo shirt and an Army haircut.

"How's my favorite sister-in-law?" Uncle Pete asked, wrapping his arms around Mrs. Winger's shoulders and giving her an emphatic hug.

"I've been good!" she replied. "How about you?"

"Not too bad, not too bad," Uncle Pete responded. "As far as flights go, I definitely can't complain. Just happy to get out of Jersey."

"Well, Florida is a wonderful place to be, regardless of where you're coming from," Mrs. Winger responded.

Nicole watched them out of the corner of her eye as she waited for the luggage belt to start moving. She sighed and readjusted the shoulder strap of her bag for the third time.

"Well, I definitely needed a break. Let me tell you!" Uncle Pete went on. "It's been crazy this last year. Did I tell you about the time a grizzly bear was found in an elementary school playground?"

"Yes, Pete, you mentioned that last November," Mrs. Winger responded. "A very peculiar story indeed."

"In the town next to my own!" Uncle Pete continued. "Trying out the swings like he was a kid! And then there was the man who ran his SUV into a convenience store just miles down the road from me! Just this past April! Absolute chaos. To think I moved to New Jersey to get away from the madness!"

"It certainly sounds like you've had an interesting year," Nicole's mom replied. "You never know when something out of the ordinary is going to happen."

The baggage claim alarm snapped everyone around Nicole to attention. She lost what her mom was saying to her uncle. Within moments, the luggage belt began to move. Identical pieces of luggage started coming into view, picked up and away sporadically by the passengers along the edge. Nicole and Laura scanned each piece as it passed by until they found Nicole's and Laura's and Mrs. Winger's. They took turns pulling each piece off the belt. Then, with Nicole managing her suitcase and Laura dragging both hers and Mrs. Winger's, they made their way over to Uncle Pete.

"And how's my little Nicky?" Uncle Pete asked when seeing Nicole.

"I'm good," Nicole replied.

"And Laura!" Uncle Pete turned to Laura. "It's been ages!"

"Not since Christmas," Laura agreed.

"Did I tell you about the daycare center that burned down two towns over from me?" Uncle Pete asked. "No one was in there when it happened, thankfully. They say it was two employees who did it!"

"You don't say," Laura replied.

"Where's Aunt Barbara?" Nicole asked.

"Barbs is with the kids getting the car. Well, the van. We needed a van in order for all of us to fit."

"It certainly makes sense for us to carpool," Mrs. Winger replied.

Uncle Pete patted his pockets before pulling a folded set of papers out of his breast pocket.

"So it turns out that the closest hotel is just outside of

Miami," said Uncle Pete, unfolding the papers. "I hope that's all right."

"Of course it's all right," Mrs. Winger replied. "Thank you again for setting all this up."

"No problem. No problem at all." Uncle Pete glanced briefly at the papers before folding them up again. "Do you guys have everything?"

Mrs. Winger looked back at Nicole and Laura.

"Looks like we have everything," said Mrs. Winger. "Thank you, girls, for getting the luggage."

"No problem, Mrs. Winger," Laura replied.

"Here, let me get mine." Mrs. Winger gingerly reached over. Laura let go of her own bag and used both hands to maneuver Mrs. Winger's luggage over. "Should we meet Barbara outside?"

"Well, best place to meet a car is outside." Uncle Pete tapped his breast pocket one more time and turned towards the exit doors. "Unless you're the type of person who drives their SUVs into convenience stores. Did I tell you about that, girls? Not even a few blocks away from my house!"

Uncle Pete led the way out of the airport. Nicole lagged behind, the backs of her feet bumping against her luggage. She passed through the double glass doors and felt a blast of hot air. She took a step back against the wall of heat and humidity before forcing herself forward. Everyone gathered around the edge of the sidewalk, glancing down the roadway.

The heat made the outside feel like it was high noon instead of the middle of the night. The bustle around Nicole mirrored that same discrepancy in time. Even at 11 p.m., the Miami airport was alive. Buses and shuttles of all shapes and sizes pulled up to their designated locations, with hordes of people getting on or off. Countless cars pulled over to the side, its passengers spilling out only to loop around to the trunk and grab their luggage. Off in the distance, a cop leaned against his car, watching everything with crossed arms.

"So, how is Barbara?" Mrs. Winger asked.

"Oh, just doing great," Uncle Pete answered.

"And Kevin, and Ella? How have your kids been?"

Mrs. Winger asked.

"Both are doing great as well," Uncle Pete answered. "Ella's starting her third year of law school."

"Well, that's exciting," said Nicole's mom.

"Still can't believe my babies are old enough to be doing things like go to college, let alone become a lawyer," Uncle Pete said wistfully.

A light blue van soon pulled up to where Nicole and the rest stood. A middle-aged lady exited the driver's side and walked around the front of the van.

"Annette!" the lady sang out, her arms outstretched at Nicole's mom.

"Hi there, Barbara!" Mrs. Winger gave Aunt Barbara a huge smile as she walked over to meet her. Aunt Barbara wrapped her arms around Nicole's mom and rocked her back and forth, to the point that Mrs. Winger almost lost her footing.

The side door slid open. Out first was a young woman in a knee-length skirt and tank top, her flip-flops slapping against the sidewalk as she touched ground. Behind her was a man roughly the same age as Andrew, a pair of square glasses adorning his face.

"It has been forever," Ella stated as she hugged Nicole.

"It definitely has been way too long," Nicole replied, returning the hug.

Ella turned to Laura.

"You know I hug everyone," Ella warned.

"And you know I don't have a problem with that," Laura chuckled softly, stepping in for the hug.

"Ah, kid Nicky," said Kevin, his arms open as he approached Nicole. He embraced her tightly and then took a step back. "You're looking more like an actual adult which each passing day."

"I'll let you know if I ever start feeling like one," Nicole replied.

"You really need to come out to New York sometime." Ella turned back to Nicole.

"I know, I know. Soon. I promise." Nicole shifted her weight to the backs of her heels. "Did Roger not come?"

"Oh, you know..." Ella looked down as she twisted

her wedding ring, stopping only when it started catching her skin. "He's got the bar exam coming up. He basically doesn't exist until he takes the test."

"Yikes," Nicole responded. "I'm sorry."

Ella shrugged.

"Such are the lives of lawyers. Gives me a preview of what I'll be doing next year. We got a chance to celebrate our anniversary in between studying, so there's at least that."

"Congratulations, by the way," said Laura, "on your anniversary."

Ella shrugged again.

"Thanks," she replied half-heartedly. "Here, let me help you guys with your luggage. We can just throw yours on top of ours." Without the slightest hesitation, Ella went and grabbed the handle of Nicole's luggage.

"Oh, it's all right. I can do it," Nicole began.

"Just consider it a bit of cousin-ly help." Ella tugged at the handle until the luggage tipped onto its wheels before she rolled it around to the back of the van. Kevin walked over and grabbed Mrs. Winger's bag. Empty-handed, Nicole followed Kevin and Ella, stopping at the end of the sidewalk and watching them as they loaded the van.

"How's Chicago?" Ella asked, lowering the cargo door.

"Oh, the usual," Nicole replied. "A whole lot of crime and homicides that never seem to affect me. How's New York?"

"Oh, the usual," Ella answered with a smirk. "A whole lot of crime and homicides that never seem to affect me."

"Touché," said Nicole.

"Is everybody ready to roll?" Uncle Pete asked, unfolding the paper in his breast pocket and checking it one more time.

"I don't know about rolling, but I'm definitely ready to drive a car," Aunt Barbara deadpanned.

"So *you're* the one driving us to the hotel?" Uncle Pete asked.

"The car's in my name." Aunt Barbara tilted her head. "And I *did* drive it up to the terminal after you refused to meet me at the rental lot."

"Well, can't argue with that." Uncle Pete gave Kevin a wink. "I'll just make sure my seatbelt is working."

"Save the office humor for the office, honey," Aunt Barbara chided before opening the driver door.

Uncle Pete folded up his paper and slipped it back into his pocket.

"Well then – all aboard!"

Uncle Pete opened the passenger door while the rest of the family filed into the back of the van. Ella, Nicole, and Laura took the bench in the back, while Mrs. Winger and Kevin sat in the bucket seats in the middle. Kevin slid the door closed and took a long, surveying look back before buckling himself in.

"So, we need to go to the Spade Poolside Hotel and Suites." Uncle Pete pulled out his paper again, unfolded it, and pointed to the upper left-hand corner. "We need to pull onto Route 836..."

"Honey? I got it."

"Are you sure? The directions say we then need to pull onto Route 94..."

"I got GPS on my phone," Aunt Barbara reminded. "As does anyone who lives in the twenty-first century."

"When I need my phone to do more than make phone calls, I'll let you know," Uncle Pete declared. "Much like when I need my microwave to start transcribing documents or my fridge to order pizza."

"I wouldn't mind a fridge that ordered pizza," Kevin chirped in.

"Ha, ha, Kevin. Very funny." Uncle Pete looked back at his son. "I don't get all the hoopla over making everything you own do five things at once. The microwave doesn't make phone calls and the TV doesn't surf the internet."

"Some TVs surf the internet, Dad," said Kevin.

"Well, my TV doesn't, and that's the important part!"

Kevin looked back at the girls and rolled his eyes before turning back around.

From the middle seat, Nicole stared out the front of the window. The world around her was so bright for so late at night. Street lamps casted orange glows against the palm trees lining the roads. Downtown Miami briefly came into view before the highway slanted right and the miniature gathering of buildings drifted out of sight. She looked around, hoping to see a bit of the ocean, but was met with buildings and pavement and trees.

"What do you think the wedding will be like?" Ella asked.

"Andrew's wedding?" Nicole mumbled out.

"Who *else's* wedding?" Ella retorted.

Nicole shrugged and readjusted herself in her seat.

"I don't know," Nicole answered. "Probably big."

Ella snorted.

"If the invitations are any indication, this is going to be on par with a royal wedding."

"Do you think the BBC is going to broadcast it, then?" Kevin asked from his seat.

"I'm sure it was considered," Ella added.

"Have you guys met Cora yet?" Laura asked, her voice oddly displaced, as if it were coming from outside the van.

Ella sighed.

"Not yet. Honestly, I didn't even know Andrew was engaged until Aunt Annette told Mom."

"I'm sure they've been quite busy," Nicole's mom defended. "I remember how busy I was when I got engaged."

"Hey, I was busy, too," Ella replied. "I was in my first year, for crying out loud. Barely had time to sleep and I still found the time to tell my family."

"Ella, we don't need to get defensive," Aunt Barbara chided, her head barely turning from the steering wheel.

"I'm not getting defensive. I'm just saying..." Ella rolled her eyes.

"Nothing says, 'I'm not defensive,' like immediately defending why you're not defensive."

"Kevin." Aunt Barbara's voice was low and monotone.

"Oh, it's not that important, anyway," Mrs. Winger brushed off. "Anyway, Ella, how have you been? How's Roger?"

"I'm good, he's good," said Ella. "He's taking the New

York bar exam in September."

"How exciting," Mrs. Winger replied. "He is going to make an excellent lawyer."

"That's assuming he passes the bar," Ella warned.

"Oh, I'm sure he will," Mrs. Winger reassured.

Ella laughed.

"Don't tell him that. He says he hates it when people say he'll pass. In his words, how do we know how the future will play out, and won't we look like idiots if we're proven wrong?"

"Well, I'm sure that's just the nerves talking," said Mrs. Winger, her shoulder pressed against the seat so she could better face Ella. "I can only imagine how stressful it is for him."

"Either way, I think we'll all be happy after he's taken it," Ella stated.

"True, true..." Mrs. Winger let her words drift off a bit before turning her head to the man sitting across from her. "Kevin, I haven't even asked you how you've been! How rude of me. How are you?"

Kevin shrugged, his shoulders changing the shadows on the carpet as he moved.

"Oh, you know. Same old," said Kevin. "Wish I could give you a more exciting update."

"Do you still live in New York, like Ella?" Mrs. Winger asked.

"I commute in from Long Island now. It's cheaper that way."

"Well, I can only imagine how expensive it can be to live in New York City," Nicole's mom remarked. "Andrew and Nicole will tell me what they pay in rent in Chicago and I'm just beside myself. I bet New York is even more expensive."

"You hemorrhage money for the right to have no AC," said Kevin. "And I don't mind the LIRR. Gives me time to read."

"Oh, I'm sorry – the leer?"

"Long Island Rail Road."

"Ah, I see." Mrs. Winger readjusted herself so her back was touching the backrest again. "Well, I'm glad to hear it. And your job is going well?"

"It pays the bills and I don't hate it," Kevin responded. "That's really all you can hope for."

"Well, still, I'm glad things are going well," said Mrs. Winger.

Outside, the world was glowing orange from the highway lights. The van made a right and exited the highway. Nicole closed her eyes and imagined that they were pulling onto a hotel by the beach, with nothing but sand and waves and water disappearing into the horizon. For a brief moment, Nicole imagined hiding in the hotel room until everyone left and spending her day on that imaginary beach.

"We should be coming up on the hotel soon," Aunt Barbara said after a few minutes. Nicole opened her eyes as her aunt turned left at a gas station and pulled up to a two-story hotel.

The hotel was a yellow-walled, U-shaped building with a white-trim ceiling and white iron railings along the second floor walkway. In the center portion of the U stood a modest pool surrounded by white lounge chairs and patio furniture. The pool area was gated off with the same type of railing used for the balconies. Palm trees and grass and small bushes stood between the first floor walkways and the pool, giving the area in the center an eerie oasis feel to it.

"It's not much," Aunt Barbara remarked as she pulled her van into an empty spot, "but it's what we could find that was both close to the wedding and had at least four rooms available."

"Cora didn't reserve a block of rooms for her guests?" Ella cocked her head.

"Ella, don't start..."

"I'm just saying. It's kind of rude to the people who are coming in from out of state," Ella continued. "What if someone couldn't get a room in time?"

"Well, we did, and that's what we should focus on," Aunt Barbara said sternly. "Now, I'm going to go check in, and I'd appreciate it if you helped unload the van instead of complaining about every little thing you think is going wrong with the wedding."

Aunt Barbara turned off the engine and yanked the

keys out from the ignition. She pushed opened the driver's side door, stopping it inches before it hit the car next to hers. Uncle Pete got out next, making his way to the back before opening the rear cargo door. Kevin pulled open the sliding door and hopped out, pausing at the opening to help Mrs. Winger down. Laura got up and followed out, graciously taking Kevin's hand as she hopped down.

"And they say chivalry is dead," Nicole remarked when it was her turn.

"Just in a mild diabetic coma," Kevin replied.

Kevin, Mrs. Winger, and Uncle Pete took turns pulling out the luggage, setting each piece upright in the parking lot before going in for another. Within a few minutes, Barbara came out of the main office, four sets of keys in her hands.

"Alright, Kevin and Ella? You have 204. We have 205. Annette, you have 206. Nicole and Laura? You guys have 207. No breakfast, but free WiFi. Front desk said to ring if you guys needed anything."

"Like an elevator?" Kevin asked, looking over at the stairs leading up to the second floor.

"Ever the smartass, Kevin," Aunt Barbara said with a smirk. "I'm sure we're all exhausted from traveling. Let's get some sleep and we'll meet up in the morning."

Nicole shifted her bag onto her shoulders and tugged at her rolling luggage. She pulled her baggage up the stairs, the edge of the suitcase banging against each step. She played with the hotel key in her free hand, her thumb tracing the edges of the plastic oval keychain. The numbers on it were indented and blackened, as if the keychain had been branded. She smirked at the idea of a miniature set of pokers resting in the fire before being pressed into the plastic.

"Try to be up and ready by 9, alright?" Aunt Barbara said as she unlocked her room's door. "I'll be around to knock on everyone's door by 8:30. Hopefully everyone is already awake by then."

"I'll set make sure to set the alarm," said Mrs. Winger. "Although I can't remember the last time I slept in past 8."

"Welcome to being old, I guess!" Uncle Pete

remarked, chuckling to himself.

"Well, have a good night, everyone." Mrs. Winger pulled up to her door. "And pleasant dreams!"

"You too, Aunt Annette," Ella replied, one foot already in her room.

"And you too, Nicole." Mrs. Winger moved her head to face Nicole.

"Yes, Mom. And pleasant dreams to you, too."

Nicole pushed open the door to their room and stepped inside.

The room was almost exactly what Nicole was expecting. The walls were off-white, but the carpet hosted an ornate pattern of orange swirls and dark red flowers that irritated Nicole's eyes. The curtains were dark green and clashed with everything else in the room, including the bedspreads, which continued the floral pattern, only in lively purple and green and white hues.

Two double beds laid out before them, with a chest of drawers and a desk along the opposite wall. The wooden furniture was simple and elegant, like they had been created for a different hotel, but ended up here instead.

"Two beds," Laura remarked. "It's like an episode of 'Leave it to Beaver'."

"Like you ever watched 'Leave it to Beaver'," Nicole said with a smile.

"I took Intro to Media Studies," said Laura. "Besides, everyone knows that's how they did it in the early shows. They acted like no one ever shared a bed together, even the married couples."

"Of course." Nicole pulled her luggage to the wall by the bathroom and pushed it onto its side. "And children were brought in from the stork. Simpler times, obviously."

"They just don't mention the part where the husband ends up in the same twin bed as his wife," Laura remarked, lifting her suitcase onto the luggage rack and unzipping it.

"Or his secretary's," Nicole added.

"Oooh, touché."

Nicole rummaged through her things, pushing all of her folded clothing out of the way until she found her pajamas. She changed facing the wall and kicked the clothes she was wearing over to the side of the luggage.

Laura shimmied off her shirt and placed it on the chest of drawers, poking around gently until she found a white tank top. Nicole walked into the bathroom and pressed her palms into the counter. She stared into the mirror, the reflection of Laura changing appearing just above her shoulder. She took in a slow, sluggish breath, let go of the sink, and brushed both hands through her hair.

"Ugly comforters aside, they're really no worse than my own bed," Laura remarked.

Nicole turned from the mirror and exited the bathroom.

"Come again?"

"I mean, my bed's about this size, anyway. Mine probably has fewer bed bugs than this one, but it's not like we were actually given two twin beds." Laura opened her backpack and pulled out her book. She walked over to the bed by the window, pulled back its covers, and climbed in. Nicole shut off the lights to the bathroom, crawled across the second bed, and slid herself under the covers.

"You know, just because the room *has* two beds, it doesn't mean we have to use them both." Laura sat up and repositioned the pillow next to her. "Sharing is caring."

Nicole shifted her weight until she was resting on her side and let out a weary sigh.

"Eh, I think I need a bed to myself tonight." Nicole grabbed the pillow under her and pulled it closer to her face. She looked up and saw Laura staring at her. Laura pulled her knees up to her chest, creating two wobbly sides of a tent under the floral comforter. Her book rested against her hip, pinned there with one hand as the other hooked around her legs. The blankets indented inwards where her fingers had clasped.

"'Cause, y'know, we've been on a plane for the last, like, ever," Nicole tried to go on. "I think I need to spread out a bit to compensate."

"Hey, I get a bed to myself, then." Laura propped her book against her knees, opened it up, and smoothed out the page in front of her. "I totally get it."

"You're not mad, are you?" Nicole propped herself on

an elbow.

"Of course not," Laura replied. "Why would I be mad?"

Nicole shrugged and looked back down at her pillow.

"Maybe tomorrow night?" Nicole offered.

Laura gave a slow, tired blink and smiled.

"Why don't you get some sleep," said Laura. "We've got a long day ahead of us."

Nicole laid down and rolled onto her belly, her head turned so it was facing the bathroom.

"You're telling me," she mumbled into the pillow.

Chapter Six

ENGRAVED INVITATION

"If you're going, I'm going," Nicky said with her arms crossed.

"You're not going, and that's final," said Andrew, half-disappeared in the closet before coming out with his jacket.

"Why can't I go?" Nicky asked, following Andrew to the front door.

"Because you're ten and it's no place for a ten-year-old."

"Well, what are you doing that I can't do?" Nicky tapped her foot against the floor.

Andrew sighed and looked around the living room.

"Stuff. Hanging out with the guys from the team. Making a bonfire. Hanging out..." Andrew shifted his head from side to side. *"Stuff."*

"So why can't I do stuff?" Nicky pressed.

"Nicky, sometimes I'm going to go places that you can't go to. At least not yet. Not for a while," Andrew tried to explain. *"I'm older than you. A lot older. There's gonna be stuff that's okay for me to do, but not okay for you to do."*

"Like what?"

Andrew scratched his neck and brought his hand out.

"I don't know. Driving."

Nicky huffed in defeat and dropped her arms by her sides.

"Fine. But when I'm 16, can I hang out and build bonfires and do stuff?" Nicky asked.

Andrew shook his head and pushed his right arm through the coat of his sleeve.

"We'll talk then, okay?" Andrew offered.

"Why can't I do stuff and bonfires?" Nicky re-crossed her arms.

Andrew shifted his coat over his shoulders and zippered it up.

"You can, you can." Andrew pressed a palm into one of his eyes. "We'll just talk then, okay?"

"Talk about what?"

Andrew sighed and hunched over.

"Stuff."

***

Sue-Anne proved to be a woman of her word: Andrew and Cora were having a second engagement party, this time in Florida. Only Nicole didn't find out this time by invitation. In fact, she might not have known at all, had she not asked about Andrew's plans for spring break.

"So are you stuck in the lab for spring break, or am I actually going to see my brother next week?" Nicole asked during one of their phone calls.

"Actually, I... uh..." Andrew paused to the point that Nicole wondered if call had been dropped. "I'm going to Florida that week."

"Whoa, wait: you're actually using your spring break for spring break purposes?" Nicole laughed into the phone. "Who are you and what have you done with my brother?"

Andrew gave a meek laugh into the phone and the line went quiet again.

"Well, where to? Miami, Key West..."

"East Braedonton."

"What?"

"East Braedonton," Andrew repeated.

"What in the world is an East Briding-ton?" asked Nicole.

"It's a town," Andrew replied in monotone. "Cora's hometown, in fact."

"Oh." Nicole's hold on her phone loosened a bit as her

shoulders dropped. "Meeting the family, then, I guess?"

"I kind of already did that," said Andrew. "A while ago."

"Oh," Nicole repeated with the same flat response. "I forgot." Nicole paused. When Andrew didn't say anything else, she added, "Okay then, what's the occasion for going to Florida?"

The phone went silent and it made Nicole stop in her tracks.

"You there?" she asked.

"There's going to be a Florida engagement party," Andrew stated, his voice suddenly and completely unfamiliar. "That's why I'm going."

"So all those people flew out to Chicago from Florida for nothing?" Nicole responded with an incredulous laugh.

"It was really nice that they made the effort," said Andrew, his tone even more defensive than before. "But not everyone could make it, so they're having a second one in Florida."

"And when is this going to be?" Nicole tried to ask calmly, but found herself sounding accusatory instead.

"Next Saturday," Andrew mumbled.

"Next Saturday?" Nicole repeated. "And when are the invites supposed to go out?"

Andrew stopped talking again. This time Nicole bit her tongue and waited for Andrew to speak.

"They already did."

"So...am I not invited, or something?" Nicole asked.

"Like you'd even be able to come if you were."

Every word she wanted to say bottlenecked in her throat. Every emotion crowded her brain, only to be clouded by the understanding that, at the end of the day, Andrew was right: she didn't have the time or the money to just fly off to Florida for a party.

"Well, is *anyone* from Chicago invited?" Nicole asked. "Were Aunt Barbara and Uncle Pete invited? Kevin or Ella?" Nicole gritted her teeth. "You know, all the people who were *accidentally* not invited to the Chicago engagement party?"

"Hey, that wasn't Cora's fault," Andrew snapped.

"Mistakes happen. And I don't appreciate you harping on her like that."

Nicole nearly shouted out, *How is this harping?* She nearly shouted out that she didn't even bring up Cora – but, yes, now that you mention it, it was, indeed, Cora's fault. She nearly shouted out a thousand things at him, none of which she could fully form in her head. So instead she clenched her fists into tight, painful knots. Her head swirled as she started stomping around her studio, consciously and deliberately not caring what her neighbors below her would think.

"Do you want me to send you an invite or something?" Andrew asked, his voice suddenly softer. "Would that make you happy?"

Nicole let out a breath and closed her eyes.

"Because we can do that," Andrew went on.

"No, no. That's fine," Nicole replied, her eyes still closed. "I don't need an invite."

But an invite came anyway. Three days later, Nicole received a glittery envelope with her name and address written in quick, slanted penmanship on the front. She received a phone call that evening, this time from her mom, while Nicole was wandering through an arts supplies store.

"Hey sweetie," her mom cooed, the same way she always did when she wanted to ask something serious from Nicole. "Did you get Andrew and Cora's invitation?"

"To the Florida Engagement Party?" Nicole rolled her eyes to no one, her hands lightly touching the outside edges of a tube of acrylic paint.

"Well, yes, to their engagement party in Florida," said her mom. "It's going to be this Saturday. Did you know that?"

Nicole pressed a finger into the tube and watched as it caved inwards under the pressure, the paint moving towards the top and side edges.

"Yes, Mom. I did."

"Well, I didn't know if you want to try to see if we can get a deal on airline tickets," her mom went on. "I'm sure we can find a good group rate. Maybe on one of those traveling sites I always hear about on TV..."

"I'm not going, Mom," Nicole stated.

"You're not?" her mom said after a pause.

Nicole continued down the aisle at the store, her fingers dragging across a row of pastel markers. She watched as they shifted around on her, clinking back into place after her hand brushed by.

"No, Mom," Nicole replied. "It's last minute and I have enough to get done at work."

"Well, we can just fly in for the weekend, then," her mom offered. "We can go in on Friday…"

"I'm trying to get hired as a permanent employee," Nicole interrupted. "The last thing I want to do is take time off last minute and blow my chances."

"Then we'll go Friday night. We can find a late flight."

"I said I'm not going," Nicole repeated, her voice rising up more than she wanted to. She glanced around, making sure no one was in her aisle.

"But, why, honey?" her mom asked.

With her lips pressed tightly together, Nicole looked around one last time and exited the store.

"I already told you why, Mom," she mumbled into the phone as she ducked out.

"But he's your brother," her mom tried to reason. "Getting married is a very big thing in anyone's life."

"And I already went to an engagement party in Chicago," Nicole defended, her heart starting to thud in between her ears. She paced down the sidewalk, large cement buildings guarding both sides of the street. She passed by a restaurant with an area gated off for outside eating. The chairs and tables were stacked in a corner by the building, secured to the gate with chains.

"This is very important to Andrew, and I think that it's—"

"If it was that important to him, he wouldn't be inviting us last minute!" Nicole shouted. A cop by the outside gate of a parking garage glanced up at her, then immediately away.

"I'm sure things just got lost in the mix…" her mom began, but faded to silence before finishing her statement.

Nicole pressed the fingertips of her free hand into her

temple. She darted across the street, unaware if traffic was even moving in her favor, and under an overpass for the L. She continued walking, cold wind biting at her face. There was so much she wanted to say. That nothing got lost in the mix. That everyone, initially and intentionally, had not been invited. That the only reason why anyone was getting an invitation now was because Nicole had said something in the first place. And that, even if they did get invited originally, it was to an engagement party for a wedding to someone they didn't even know, someone that Andrew was keeping incredibly silent on and defensive about, someone that didn't even seem like someone worth getting to know in the first place.

"I'm not going," Nicole repeated instead.

Her mother sighed on the other end of the line. Nicole slowed her pace, to the point that she almost stopped walking.

"And you shouldn't, either," Nicole added.

"Why shouldn't I go?" her mom asked, the usual sweetness in her tone now missing.

"Because..." Nicole trailed off. She looked around her, as if she'd find the words to say next to a street lamp or on top of a car. Instead, all she found was concrete and glass and metal.

"He is my son, Nicole," her mom said firmly. "And I am happy he found a girl he wants to marry."

Nicole swallowed and took in an unsteady breath. She kept walking, periodically looking behind her, making sure no one was around her for too long. She didn't want anyone able to pick up on her conversation, piecing together what they could gather until they could create their own version of what was going on.

"I was so worried, for so long," her mom said slowly and quietly, as if the words were being drawn up from a hidden compartment. "He was never interested in dating. Not even in college. Just didn't care to be with a girl." Her mom broke her train of thought before stammering out: "Or-or boy, if that's what he wanted."

"I understand, Mom," said Nicole, her voice soft and careful.

"A boy shouldn't lose his dad when he's 10," she went

on. "It just shouldn't happen. And I spent so many years wondering if he refused to have a girlfriend because of it. A boy needs his dad to talk to him about things like that..."

"I don't think Dad had anything to do with it."

Nicole found an opening to another parking garage and hung a sharp right. She walked down the ramp meant for cars, found a snug spot by the stairwell, and pressed her back against the wall.

"I guess we'll never know," her mom replied with a level of defeated finality.

The phone call went silent again, save for both women's breathing. The cold from the cement wall started creeping through Nicole's jacket, making her shiver as her back turned to ice.

"Your brother is getting married and we need to be supportive."

"I can be supportive without wasting hundreds of dollars on last minute plane tickets," Nicole replied, pushing herself away from the wall.

"I really wish you'd come with me," said her mom.

"I can't," said Nicole, her voice echoing in the garage.

"I'll pay for your ticket. For Laura's, too, if she wants to come." The pleading in her mother's voice nearly broke her heart. She wavered for a moment before sighing into the phone.

"I can't. I really, really can't," Nicole said again. "And I don't want you to have to spend more money than you have to."

"I don't have to, sweetie. I want to." Her mom paused for a beat before adding: "It might be nice to take a break from Illinois winter."

Nicole made a circle on the floor of the garage with her foot. She watched as a car drove down the ramp and past Nicole, hooking a broad left at the end of the garage and disappearing into the underworld of parking spaces.

"I don't want to go," Nicole finally said. She couldn't help but notice that she sounded like a little kid who refused to go to school.

"It might give you another chance to get to know Cora better," her mom offered. "I'm sure she's a wonderful,

wonderful girl once you get to know her."

"I'm not changing my mind, Mom," said Nicole. "I'm sorry."

The area around Nicole felt impossibly stagnant. Like all life and movement within ear- and eyeshot of her had stopped. The air felt stale and the silence made her ears ring.

"It's your life, honey. At the end of the day, you decide what you do or do not do," her mom said. "I'll try to take lots of picture. Maybe I can come by your apartment after my return flight and show them to you."

"Sure, Mom," Nicole relented. "That sounds great."

***

Nicole never saw any of the pictures that her mother took of the engagement party. Her mother's flight back from Florida didn't get in until late that Sunday night. And, as she explained to Nicole on the phone, she needed to go straight home from the airport if she was going to get even a few hours of sleep before work the next day.

They continued to chat on the phone as her mom drove out of Chicago and back to Hampshire. Mostly, Nicole just listened. Her mom talked about East Braedonton and the engagement party – an involved and complicated event hosted at Cora's parents' home, taking over the entire first floor, plus the sprawling acres of manicured land in the front and backyards.

"Did you know anyone there?" Nicole asked, already knowing the answer.

"Well, I knew Andrew," her mom answered. "And I got to talk with Cora's mother a bit more. They have such a lovely house. I know you'll love it when you see it. And I took lots of photos, just like I promised. I can show you them the next time I'm in Chicago."

But that was another empty promise. The next time her mom was in Chicago was a month later, towards the end of March. She had come in for a client interview and stayed to have lunch with Nicole. The topic of the photos never came up; instead, they talked about the weather and Aunt Barbara's new business and how delicious the food was.

"Have you been able to see your brother as of late?" her mom eventually asked, a forkful of salad just inches from her mouth.

"Oh, you know, from time to time." Nicole grabbed a chunk a bread and stuffed it into her mouth. "He's been super busy with school, I think."

"And the wedding, too," said her mom. "It's a busy time for him. But I'm glad he still finds time to see you."

"Yeah." Nicole swallowed the bread with one large, painful gulp. "So, how has work been?"

Nicole spent the rest of the lunch with an uneasy pit in her stomach. She hated lying to her mom, but she couldn't bring herself to admit that she hadn't seen Andrew face-to-face in months – that, aside from a few quick and shallow phone conversations, she hadn't talked with him since the disastrous call before his spring break.

Abby Rosmarin

Chapter Seven

EAST BRAEDONTON

Nicole was awake long before anyone else. The sun was still low on the horizon when Nicole finally gave up on getting any more sleep. She tiptoed to her luggage, slipped on her shoes, and snuck outside.

The Miami morning air had a funny way of feeling just as new and fresh as it did stuffy and stale. It was going to be a muggy day and sweat was already gathering underneath Nicole's pajama top. Nicole stepped up to the railing directly outside of her room and leaned over it until her upper body was directly above the shrubbery on the ground level.

She closed her eyes and imagined for a brief second that she was stepping out onto the balcony at some resort. A place where she could open her eyes and see an open patio, a poolside bar, and a picturesque view of the Atlantic Ocean. She'd open her eyes and be met with the comfort of knowing that the only itinerary for the day would be things like lounging and drinking and maybe a ride on a jet ski if she felt up to it.

But instead, she opened her eyes and saw scuffed yellow walls and white metal with rust in the corners. The pool was perfectly still, the water reflecting back sections of the patio furniture around it.

Nicole walked down the stairs and around the

shrubbery, making her way to the pool. She removed her shoes and dipped a foot halfway into the water. The smell of chlorine filled her nose as the water danced around her foot. She lifted her leg, shook the water off her foot, and found a lounge chair to lie down on.

The sky took on a vibrant shade of red as the sun came up. It reminded Nicole of the old saying: "Red sky at night, sailor's delight. Red sky at morning, sailors take warning."

It was something her dad had taught her. It was one of the few memories she actually had of him. He would point out a particularly gorgeous sunset, where the clouds looked like they were on fire as the sun slowly disappeared into the plains. He would explain that a red sky at night meant that a storm had passed, but that a red sky in the morning meant that a storm was on its way. Sailors take warning, because they were in for some rough waters.

Nicole watched the sunrise, wishing she had packed something to draw with. Pencils or markers…she'd even take children's crayons if they were available. She couldn't remember the last time she drew anything, and part of her wished she could spend the morning drawing the sky, encapsulating it in a sketchbook, immortalizing its simplistic beauty.

Something moved in Nicole's peripheral vision. She looked over and up, only to find Aunt Barbara pushing open the shades of her room. Aunt Barbara paused at the window for a moment, before looking down and spotting Nicole. She tapped at the window and waved. Nicole gave a small smile and a wave back. She waited until Aunt Barbara left the window before sitting up and removing herself from the lounge chair. She padded over to the pool to dip a foot in one last time. With a sigh, she put her shoes back on and went back upstairs to get ready for the day.

***

"We'll find a nice place in East Braedonton to get breakfast, what do you say?" Uncle Pete asked from the passenger side of the van.

"If the GPS is correct, we're barely 20 minutes out from Cora's house," said Aunt Barbara, buckling herself in. "We can have breakfast and still have plenty of time to see Andrew and the rest."

"Am I the only one here who thinks it's a bit weird that this whole thing is playing out like some southern belle wedding when Cora lives in a suburb of Miami?" Ella spoke out from the back seat.

"Florida is technically as south as you can get," Kevin noted with a sly grin.

"You know what I mean." Ella lowered her eyes. "You don't think The South when you're in Miami."

"That's because you'd be too busy drinking at the Miami nightclubs to think."

"Do you two need to be broken up?" Aunt Barbara sighed out.

"No, Mom," the two said in unison.

"Then let's go," she said, and backed the van out of the parking space.

Nicole watched the world from the side door window. She stared at the blur of trees and orange rooftops as the minivan cruised along the highway, moving farther and farther away from the city.

For a while, the highway ran parallel with the neighborhoods, with nothing but a guardrail separating the two. Nicole felt like she could jump the railing and find herself in a brand new part of town. It felt weird, having the highways so barely separated from the towns. She had grown used to elevated platforms, or walls of concrete isolating the cars from the rest of the world.

"It's ridiculous, isn't it?" Ella mumbled quietly to Nicole.

Nicole looked over.

"What?"

"This isn't the South. This is Miami," said Ella.

Nicole smirked and leaned in closer.

"You should've seen her the day I met her," said Nicole. "Everything was 'southern' this and 'the South' that. But she refused to say exactly where she lived." Nicole glanced around, checking to make sure no one was listening in on her conversation. "Now I can see why."

"I gotta ask: does she do the southern accent?"

"The thickest you've ever heard," said Nicole. "It's so fake, too. It'll change midsentence sometimes."

Ella shook her head and laughed.

"This is gonna be good."

Aunt Barbara veered right onto an exit ramp. After a few turns, the scenery changed from small, yellow homes and busy streets to sprawling acres of grass and orange groves. The roads just as quickly descended into rough, uneven asphalt. Every once in a while, Nicole could spot an old Victorian-style house behind an acre or two of land. Off in the distance was a water tower, the words "East Braedonton" painted in blocky letters around its center.

"Holy crap," Ella muttered. "This is some Twilight Zone weirdness."

"Let's see if I can find the downtown area," Uncle Pete said, his brow furrowed, his hand now holding Aunt Barbara's phone, tapping at the screen the same way a hen pecks as its feed. "This would be a lot easier if I had a road atlas instead."

"Maybe if you look for Braedonton on the map, you'll find a downtown area? Or at least a town center?" said Nicole's mom.

"Yeah, yeah..." Uncle Pete tapped around again before throwing his hands up and jutting the phone towards Kevin. "Here, you take it. I can't figure this thing out one damn bit."

Kevin reached forward and slid the phone out of his dad's hands. He glanced at the screen for a few seconds before stating: "There is no Braedonton."

"What do you mean, 'there's no Braedonton'?" Aunt Barbara asked, her face turned towards Kevin but her eyes on the road.

"I mean: there's no Braedonton," Kevin repeated. "There's East Braedonton, then... the Everglades."

"Is there a South Braedonton? Or North?" Laura asked from the back.

"Certainly is no West Braedonton," Kevin replied, his eyes locked on the phone. After a moment he added: "And no North or South. Just East Braedonton."

"Well, that's peculiar," said Uncle Pete.

"Why even call yourself that?" asked Ella. "Do they think it gives them more charm?"

"I'm sure there's a perfectly reasonable explanation," said Mrs. Winger.

"I bet the rest of the town realized that they're actually part of the greater Miami area and changed their name accordingly," said Ella.

"Honestly, Ella. I do not know what has gotten into you," said Aunt Barbara. "You have been nothing but negative since we've touched down."

Ella shrugged her shoulders and gently clasped her palms, her fingers intertwining together before resting on her lap.

"I'm just calling it like I see it," she said. "From the ridiculous invitations to all the engagement parties – none of which we were invited to, mind you – to all this southern talk, there's a lot to call out."

"We can't all be super sensible and on top of everything as a bride," said Aunt Barbara. "I'm very happy that you were able to, but I think you were the exception, not the rule."

"I think someone is a bit jealous that Andrew is getting the big, fancy wedding *she* always wanted," Kevin stated without the slightest hint of mocking.

Ella scoffed.

"Like I would want to make my family fly down to Not The South and get married in an area that would make *Gone with the Wind* blush," she said. "Besides, I'm just honing my abilities to pick things apart. I *am* going to be a lawyer someday, after all."

"God help the state of New York when that happens," said Kevin.

"Kevin, stop antagonizing your sister," said Uncle Pete.

"The good news is, I think we found the downtown area," Mrs. Winger intervened.

The area around them morphed from fields to small, ornate houses with perfectly manicured lawns and flat, pristine sidewalks. After a few blocks, the homes were replaced with small one- and two-story buildings, which were then replaced with two rows of flat-roofed buildings pressed together, one on either side of the road.

The sidewalks grew wider. An American flag hung on every telephone pole. People strolled in and out of shops, walking in a way that Nicole could swear bordered on skipping. Even the older men seemed to walk with a bit of a hop. At the end of the main street, just as the road turned, stood a tall, white church, its bell tower and steeple longer and larger than anything Nicole had ever seen.

"I'm sure we can find a nice diner here," Aunt Barbara said, pulling into one of the empty parking spaces. "And we can enjoy the downtown area as well. Kill two birds with one stone."

"And also resolve two situations with the same action," Kevin added.

Aunt Barbara turned around and looked at her son.

"Y'know, after we're done killing the birds," said Kevin.

Aunt Barbara rolled her eyes before looking back. Uncle Pete smiled proudly.

"That's my boy."

Everyone slowly exited the van, each person stretching their arms out slightly before walking into the heart of the downtown area. Nicole held her breath as the heat hit her. She hung out in the back as they walked down the street, staring more at the shuffling feet in front of her than anything else.

"This certainly is quaint," Aunt Barbara said, leading the pack.

"It's like we went through a wormhole and ended up in 1953," said Ella.

Aunt Barbara sighed and swung her head back towards Ella.

"Don't you have anything positive to say?"

"You never know: that could've been positive," said Kevin. "Depends on what your views of 1950s are."

Aunt Barbara shook her head and continued walking.

"Well, that looks like a nice place to eat." Mrs. Winger pointed across the street to a small restaurant with tan siding and the words, "Jasonson Family Diner" painted on a long, white rectangle over the door.

"Jasonson," Kevin read aloud.

"I don't think we're going to find any other option," said Uncle Pete, his chin jutting forward as he scanned the rest of the street.

"Well, I'm starving, so this works for me," said Ella.

The group crossed the street, each person looking to the right and left of them, even though only a few cars had passed down the main street in the entire time they had been there. Uncle Pete opened the door and let everyone in before easing the door closed behind him. The rush of air conditioning chilled Nicole's skin and made her hold her breath a second time.

"Well hi there, y'all!" A young girl with a chipper voice and blonde hair pulled back with a ribbon walked up. "How are y'all doing today?"

"Oh, just fine," said Aunt Barbara. When her words hung in the air, she added: "We're here for breakfast."

"Of course, of course!" The girl picked up a stack of menus, her accent so thick it sounded like a parody. "There's seven of y'all, right, if I'm counting correctly? I'm Tiffany, by the way. Pleasure to meet y'all!"

"And... likewise," said Aunt Barbara.

Tiffany lead everyone to a large table in the back corner in the restaurant, placing a menu at each spot as Nicole's family found their respective seats.

"Can I get y'all anything to drink before y'all order?" Tiffany asked. "Water, orange juice, sweet tea, coffee?"

"Is everyone okay with waters at first?" Aunt Barbara asked, sitting down at her spot after everyone else was seated.

"I'm okay with that," said Laura, her menu already open.

"Can't see why not," said Uncle Pete.

"Let's do waters for now," said Aunt Barbara with a polite smile. The young girl disappeared into the kitchen. Nicole opened her menu and scanned the page without taking any of the words in.

"Do they really speak like that?" Ella whispered to Nicole.

"Like what?" Nicole asked absently.

"With that terrible, hyper-Nashville accent?" Ella

responded, her voice even quieter than before.

Nicole grinned.

"Oh, they do," she said, keeping her voice as low as Ella's. "All of them do."

"Sheesh. It doesn't even *sound* like Tennessee. Sounds like someone who has never even been to Tennessee attempting a Tennessee accent," said Ella, her head dipped towards her menu. "Would it be terrible I fake-southern-accented it right back at them?"

Nicole bit her lower lip and snorted.

"Everything all right over there?" Uncle Pete asked.

"Perfectly fine," Ella replied.

"Yeah." Nicole cleared her throat. "I'm fine. Held in a sneeze funny."

Tiffany came back with a large pitcher of water. She started leaning over the table, picking up the empty cups by the paper placemats and filling them three quarters of the way with water.

"I take it y'all're here for Cora's weddin'?" she asked in between pouring.

"Why, yes, we are," said Mrs. Winger. "How did you know?"

"It's the talk of the town!" Tiffany responded. "It's the event of the summer, aside from the kite festival. Plus, we don't get a lot of yanks in these here parts, usually."

Nicole took a long sip of her water and swallowed hard.

"So, what part of the North are y'all from?" Tiffany asked.

"Well, we're from New Jersey." Aunt Barbara gestured to herself and her husband. "My sister-in-law and her family are from the Chicago area."

"Which is technically in the Midwest," Nicole found herself saying.

"Oh, bless your heart," said Tiffany with a broad smile. "Midwest, North... it's all the same when you're a southerner!"

Nicole attempted to smile back, but found herself grimacing instead.

The waitress just beamed back, oblivious.

"Now, what can I get y'all?"

***

"Bless y'all's hearts but y'all are yanks!" Ella mimicked when they stepped out of the restaurant

"Honestly, Ella. Enough."

"Mom, I'm sorry, but... c'mon."

Ella hopped back into the van and plopped into her spot. Nicole and Laura followed behind her.

"I don't think she meant anything by it," said Mrs. Winger.

"Everyone knows that 'bless your heart' is a southern way of telling someone to go pound sand." Ella reached for her seatbelt and buckled herself in. "Either she was getting in a dig at our expense or she was just repeating something that sounds southern...because, y'know, she's not a real southerner."

"I mean it, Ella. Enough," Aunt Barbara said sternly, her voice louder than it had been the entire trip. "I don't want to hear another mean comment. No snarky remarks, no mocking, nothing. Is that clear?"

Ella sighed and leaned against the backrest.

"Fine."

A tense silence followed as Aunt Barbara started the van and pulled out of their parking spot.

"The food was really nice," said Laura, breaking the silence.

"Mmhmm." Uncle Pete rubbed his stomach. "That really hit the spot."

"Y'know, we never went for a downtown stroll," said Kevin.

"We can do that later," Aunt Barbara said flatly.

"There's no place like Florida for fresh orange juice," Mrs. Winger piped in with. "I'll have to make sure to buy some oranges before we go home."

"That's a good idea," said Laura. She looked at Nicole and added: "We can finally use that orange juice maker of yours."

Nicole smiled weakly.

"Yeah. Sounds good."

Aunt Barbara looped around the downtown area

Abby Rosmarin

before getting back on course for Cora's house. Nicole watched the neighborhoods shift from tiny, one-floored homes spaced just a few feet away from each other to vast, intricate houses with large porches or massive columns adorning the fronts.

Eventually Aunt Barbara pulled into a neighborhood that could've rivaled the nicest neighborhoods in Beverly Hills. Every home was walled off, with a large iron gate at the beginning of each driveway, with acres and acres of manicured lawns standing between the houses and the road. The houses that Nicole could see through the gates were colossal, commanding the attention of anyone who might pass by.

"Nicole, do you see these houses?" her mom asked. "Look at the architecture. Aren't they amazing?"

"Yeah, they're nice."

"You love architecture," said her mom. "They're all so gorgeous, in their own unique way."

"Yeah, they're nice."

Aunt Barbara slowed down and turned left onto a driveway, pulling up until the van's nose was inches from the gate and the driver's side window was next to the intercom system. She rolled down the window, pressed the "call" button, and tucked her arm back in.

"Bachman residence," an unfamiliar voice with a thick accent said through the speaker. "Can I ask who is visiting?"

"Barbara and Pete Winger. And Annette Winger, too." Aunt Barbara stopped and shook her head. "Andrew's family is here to visit. Is that all right, or are we here too early?"

"Hold on one minute. Let me check." The intercom went silent for a moment before the voice came back on and said: "You can come in."

With that, the gate opened, slowly swinging inwards and coming to a perfect stop by the edges of the driveway. Aunt Barbara drove through the entranceway and continued down the long and winding road. The van hugged a broad curve, driving around a line of trees and bushes and revealing a house that made even Nicole gasp.

Before her stood a three-story redbrick home. Several

- 88 -

chimneys jutted out of the tall gray roof. At the center of the roof was a rectangle of white fencing, holding in what Nicole could only assume was a rooftop patio. Bay windows curved out across all floors. Large white columns held up a balcony on the second floor. The house looked as if several different mansions from several different time periods had banded together to make one beautiful, intricate, awe-inspiring house. Even Nicole had to admit that it was impressive.

"Annette, you'd said the house was beautiful, but this..." Aunt Barbara pulled around the miniature cul-de-sac in front of the house and slowed to a stop. "This is beyond beautiful. They write articles about houses like this."

"They are certainly blessed to have such a beautiful home," said Mrs. Winger.

Uncle Pete unbuckled himself and looked around.

"Are we supposed to park anywhere?" Uncle Pete asked.

"I'm sure they have valet," said Ella.

"What did I say?" Aunt Barbara's low, stern voice made Nicole sit up a little straighter.

"It's an honest observation." Ella unbuckled as well and positioned herself, ready to leave the van at a moment's notice. "A house like this, I'm sure they have people to park your car."

Ella looked at Kevin until she could catch his eye and started lifting herself from her seat. Kevin shrugged his shoulders and pushed open the sliding door. He jumped out, but held the sliding door by the edge, as if it would close on someone at any moment. The three girls in the back got out before Mrs. Winger did. After a moment, Uncle Pete exited the passenger side and Aunt Barbara exited the driver's. A young lady with mousey brown hair tied back into a low ponytail came out.

"Good morning, Winger family," she said in an eerily formal tone, her accent clashing with the formality. "Sue-Anne and Dan are so happy you could make it."

"Well, we're happy to be here," said Mrs. Winger.

The young girl held out her hand to Aunt Barbara. "May I?"

"Um, excuse me?" Aunt Barbara asked, her right hand awkwardly by her ribs as if she had just stopped herself from shaking the girl's hand.

"Your vehicle," said the girl. "May I park it for you?"

"Oh, um..." Aunt Barbara gave a slight chuckle, fished the keys out from her purse, and gently placed the keys into the girl's hand. "Of course. Thank you so much."

"Sue-Anne and Dan are waiting for you all in the foyer. Would you all like me to show you inside?"

"No, no, I'm sure we can figure it out," said Aunt Barbara. "But thank you, though."

"It was wonderful meeting you all. I hope you all have a great time." The girl gave everyone a broad smile before hopping into the van and starting the engine.

"Well, then." Aunt Barbara turned to the group. "Shall we?"

"I *told* you they had valet," Ella whispered to Nicole with a cunning grin on her face.

"I'm surprised we didn't have to tip her," Nicole whispered back, her grin mimicking Ella's.

Aunt Barbara led the way as they walked up the granite steps to the set of double doors. Before Aunt Barbara could reach the top step, the front door swung open to the woman with frosted blonde hair, wearing bright pink jogging suit.

"Welcome, welcome!" Sue-Anne sung out. "Come inside!"

Nicole scraped her toes against the bottom of the doorframe as she walked in, causing her to lurch forward and almost into Uncle Pete. After steadying herself, Nicole surveyed the room in front of her. In a way, Nicole wasn't surprised by what she saw. After seeing the exterior, anything on the inside seemed possible.

The foyer was over two stories tall, with two large chandeliers hanging from the ceiling. The floor was made up of an intricate pattern of pristine and polished marble tiles. A white spiral staircase arched its way down the curved right wall, spilling onto the first floor with a broad, inviting base. From the second floor, Nicole could see the beginnings of a wide hallway, with a smaller chandelier accenting the midway. Back on the first floor, a deep purple velvet lounge chair sat by the wall opposite the stairs, where a middle-aged man lounged, his grey hair in a tight crew cut, his shirt unbuttoned at the top.

"And how're all y'all!" Sue-Anne's voice sang as she gave Nicole's mom an emphatic hug.

"We're great," said Mrs. Winger. "Flew in last night."

Sue-Anne held Mrs. Winger at arm's length before looking over at Uncle Pete.

"And I don't believe we've met," Sue-Anne cooed, her hand lightly touching her processed hair.

"I'm Pete, Sue-Anne." Uncle Pete stepped forward and jutted out his right hand. "I'm Andrew's uncle."

Sue-Anne bypassed his hand completely and gave Uncle Pete a long, tight hug.

"Well, aren't you something!" Sue-Anne said when she stepped back. "I usually don't find yanks attractive, but – my! – aren't you are something, indeed!"

Uncle Pete grinned awkwardly as he jutted his hands into his pockets.

"And I'm Barbara, Andrew's aunt." Aunt Barbara stepped in between Uncle Pete and Sue-Anne with an impossibly bright smile on her face.

"Oooh, his aunt!" Sue-Anne exclaimed and gave Aunt Barbara an equally emphatic hug. "So lovely y'all could make it to the weddin'!"

"We wouldn't miss it for the world," said Aunt Barbara, retreating back a bit after the hug.

"Well, come in, come in!" Sue-Anne trotted back over to the man in the velvet lounge chair. "Annette, you met Dan, but the rest of y'all haven't. Y'all, this is my wonderful husband Dan."

Dan gave a sardonic smile and a half-hearted salute as a greeting.

"Nicole, was it?" Sue-Anne turned and stared at Nicole.

Nicole did her best not to immediately cast her eyes to the floor.

"Yeah?"

"You didn't meet my husband either, if I remember. He couldn't make it to the Chicago engagement party.

Had business to attend to. One of the many, many, many reasons why we just *had* to have a Florida party."

"Oh, what do you do for a living?" Uncle Pete asked.

Dan shrugged his shoulders, sighed, and briefly closed his eyes.

"Imports. Exports."

Nicole looked over and locked eyes with Ella. Both had to press their lips together to keep their expressions somewhat neutral.

"You have a beautiful house, Mrs. Bachman," said Laura.

"Oh, thank you, darlin'. You're too kind." Sue-Anne patted her husband's shoulder before rubbing it with her thumb. She looked back at Laura and sighed. "Oh, honey, forgive me. I can't for the life of me remember your name."

"It's, uh, Laura," she said, her eyes darting from side to side as she gave a sheepish grin. Nicole stared at Laura, wishing she'd look over, but was secretly relieved when she didn't.

"Oooh, yes! You're Nicole's best girl friend." Sue-Anne tapped her temple and rolled her eyes. "How silly of me. So glad you could make it! The more, the merrier!"

"No problem, Mrs. Bachman. Thank you for having me."

"Oh, please! Call me Sue-Anne," she said with a flip of her hair. "To be fully honest, you're an inspiration to me."

"Really?"

"Of course!" Sue-Anne exclaimed. "You and Nicole. From now on, no matter what party or weddin' I'm goin' to, even if my best girl friends aren't invited, I'm bringing them along with me! Those who are hosting will just have to understand. A girl is nothing without her ladies!"

Kevin looked back at Nicole with a look of equal amusement and disbelief. Nicole bit her lip and shrugged her shoulders.

"Oh, and you must be..." Sue-Anne started with full enthusiasm before immediately trailing off.

"Kevin," he finished, giving a small wave. "And that's Ella. We're Andrew's cousins."

"Oh, cousins!" Sue-Anne responded with the same enthusiasm as before. "Well, welcome, welcome! Cora and Andrew are out with everyone else, enjoying a nice weddin' party brunch and getting a few weddin'-related errands done. Please, let me show y'all around!"

Sue-Anne led the way as she waltzed out of the foyer and down the hall. With a lazy sigh, Dan got up and joined the pack.

"Don't let the quiet fool you." Sue-Anne bounced when she walked, to the point that it affected how she spoke. Her words jolted from her lips with every step, as if someone had given the words a series of quick shoves. "This place has been a madhouse since the engagement."

Sue-Anne walked down to the end of the hall, which opened up to a large, open living room. The ceiling was two stories up, with another large, crystal chandelier in the center. Large bay windows displayed part of the vast backyard. Sue-Anne hung a sharp right and continued down another hall.

"It's only gotten worse now that the weddin' party is here," Sue-Anne continued. "Karen flew in last night, which gives us a complete set. They're all staying in the guesthouse until the weddin'. Best to keep them in one place! You have to keep an eye on your weddin' party. One lazy bridesmaid and the entire day is ruined!"

Sue-Anne continued on, passing by a large dining area with French doors and vaulted ceilings. The dining room table inside was covered with stacks and stacks of papers, books, and binders. Two or three laptops teetered precariously by the table's edges. There were at least three or four whiteboards by the walls with jibberish scrawled across them. Two women with black headsets paced around the room, talking at a fevered pace. Nicole couldn't tell if they were talking to each other or into their respective mouthpieces.

"Who are they?" Nicole asked, her head careening behind her as they walked past the dining room.

Sue-Anne paused and looked back at the French doors, as if inspecting a car crash from far away.

"Oh, those are just the weddin' planners," Sue-Anne dismissed.

"Are they here full-time?" Kevin asked, looking back as well.

"Well, of course, silly!" Sue-Anne replied. "How else are they going to get everything done?"

"I know startups that are run less efficiently," Kevin noted.

"That's because this is more important than a startup. It's a weddin'!" Sue-Anne exclaimed. "It's been quite the sacrifice for all of us. Since the weddin' planners have been here, I haven't been able to have my Sunday afternoon, post-church celebration luncheons. That dinin' room is the perfect size for our luncheons. Dan loves those luncheons."

Nicole looked back at Dan, who casually shrugged his shoulders.

"And, between you and me." Sue-Anne's voice dropped to a whisper. "If I had to do it all over again, I'd hire different planners. These women have no idea what they're doin'. Honestly, it's like I have to do their job for 'em sometimes."

Nicole looked through the doors again. The shorter, stout lady opened up a 2-inch binder and began flipping madly through it.

"Well, so long as they clean up their little – heh – *operation*, before the festivities, then I guess I can't be *too* upset," said Sue-Anne, before adding: "Always important to keep a positive attitude!"

Sue-Anne turned and continued down the hallway as it looped to the right.

"You have an incredible house," said Aunt Barbara, her eyes slowly moving from one side of the hallway to the other.

"Of course!" Sue-Anne replied. "Dan had just bought the place when we started datin'. It wasn't this nice at first, of course. Much, much smaller. Dan hired construction workers from the very beginnin' of our courtship, and I guess we never stopped!"

"That had to have been expensive," said Uncle Pete.

Aunt Barbara turned and gave Uncle Pete a stern look.

"Wasn't too bad," Dan said matter-of-factly. "I know people."

Ella and Nicole exchanged looks again, but not before surreptitiously checking to make sure Dan wasn't looking at them.

"You yanks are always so concerned with money!" Sue-Anne declared. "But, yes, not *everyone* can have a house like this. Now, let me show you the west wing."

The tour of the first floor continued on, Sue-Anne weaving in and out of rooms and down hallways. The house was as impressive on the inside as it was on the outside. From the antique furniture to the intricate framework and the massive paintings and sculptures, Nicole felt like she was floating around a museum. A museum lead by a woman in a bright pink jogging suit.

After what felt like hours, Sue-Anne brought the group into a small octagonal parlor in the back corner of the house. The room jutted out towards the backyard and had floor-to-ceiling windows on seven of the sides. Sue-Anne and the rest entered from the eighth side, through a glass-paneled door.

"Please, find a seat."

Sue-Anne gestured to the white iron chairs that sat against the windows. Ella sat in a chair facing the door on the side opposite of the room. Nicole sat next to her, with Laura picking the seat next to Nicole.

Sue-Anne fished out a small flip phone, popped it open with her thumb, and pressed a button.

"Hi there, Jennifer? Yes, if you could bring us some tea, that would great."

Sue-Anne snapped the phone shut, pushed it back into her jacket pocket, and cast a broad smile at everyone in the room.

"So, how are y'all likin' Florida so far?" Sue-Anne asked, taking a seat by the entrance.

"It's very nice," said Aunt Barbara. "Actually, Pete and I, we've vacationed a few times in Florida."

"Oh really," said Sue-Anne. "Where?"

"Key West."

"Well," Sue-Anne laughed. "Everyone knows that's not *really* Florida. That's not the South; that's just a tourist destination."

Aunt Barbara smiled a crooked smile in response.

"And how about y'all?" Sue-Anne asked, turning to Nicole and the rest.

"I love Florida," said Laura.

"Really, now?"

"My grandparents actually live just north of Tallahassee," Laura continued. "In Havana."

"Oh, I see," said Sue-Anne. "By Georgia. Y'know, Karen is from Georgia. It's more north than, say, Florida is, so it can never really be as southern as us, but I don't hold that against her."

Laura's eyebrows flickered up before nodding slowly.

The young woman who had valeted the rental van came into the room with a large tray. The tray held a delicate teapot, with ten teacups lined up side by side, nearly filling up the tray.

"Oh thank you, sugar." Sue-Anne's eyes followed the tray as Jennifer set it on one of the glass and cast iron tables.

"You're welcome, Mrs. Bachman."

"No, I mean you forgot the sugar."

"Oh, I'm so sorry ma'am." Jennifer's face dropped. "I'll be right back."

The young girl with darted from the room. Within seconds, she returned with a bowl full of sugar cubes.

"Thank you. That will be all for now," said Sue-Anne. "But check in with the weddin' planners. Their lunch break is due soon. See what they'd like to have."

"Of course, Mrs. Bachman," said Jennifer. "Right away."

Sue-Anne watched the girl leave the room before turning back to the group.

"Always need sugar with your sweet tea." Sue-Anne picked up teapot and poured herself a cup, the steam rising in a thick mist. She placed the teapot down and dropped four sugar cubes into her cup. "I don't know how you yanks do it with your unsweetened teas."

"Isn't sweet tea typically served cold?" Kevin asked.

Sue-Anne let out a laugh.

"Oh, you yanks!" Sue-Anne punctuated her words with another laugh and a long sip of her tea. "So! What are y'all's plans in Florida?"

"Aside from the wedding, I'm afraid not much else," said Mrs. Winger. "We fly out Sunday morning."

"No time for vacation." Sue-Anne *tsked*.

"Most of us have work on Monday," said Aunt Barbara. "But Florida is a beautiful state. Hopefully we'll be back soon."

Sue-Anne turned to Laura.

"Do you work, too?" Sue-Anne asked.

"Um, yes. Yes I do," Laura responded. "I work in project management at an advertising firm."

"Oh." Sue-Anne sighed and gazed at her cup. "I guess the workin' world is the fate of all women until they catch a husband."

Laura's eyes went wide. She looked over at Nicole, who mirrored the same facial expression.

"Well, when y'all do come back, y'all'll have to make sure y'all arrive in time for our kite festival," Sue-Anne went on. "They have it every July, right after Independence Day. It's the pride of East Braedonton. That, and our beauty pageants in the winter."

"It sure is a lovely town," said Mrs. Winger with a hopeful look on her face.

"Oh, yes, yes, but you don't have to tell me," Sue-Anne giggled. "Oh, hold on a sec. I have the best idea."

Sue-Anne pulled out a second phone and danced her fingers around the screen. She pursed her lips and put an index finger up as she brought the phone to her ear.

"Hi there, sugar-daughter," Sue-Anne cooed. "Are y'all done with brunch? Well, when y'all finish, y'all should come to the house before runnin' y'all's errands. Mhmm, Andrew's mom and family are here and they're just dyin' to meet y'all. Mhmm. Alright, darlin'."

Sue-Anne pushed the phone into her other jacket pocket.

"They're just finishin' up brunch and will be right over," Sue-Anne told everyone.

"We just went out for breakfast as well, actually, right on Main Street," said Uncle Pete. "I'm surprised we didn't see them."

"We have more than one restaurant in this town, silly!" Sue-Anne laughed. "Our other restaurant is on the outskirts of town. A lovely establishment, a real upgrade from the little hole-in-the-wall tavern that used to be there..."

"Must've been a literal hole in the wall." Ella turned to Nicole, muttering softly as she brought her teacup to her lips.

"Come again, honey?" Sue-Anne asked.

"Oh, nothing," Ella lowered her cup and smiled. "I was just thinking out loud. It sounds like a great restaurant. We'll have to check it out sometime."

Sue-Anne gave a tight grin before pouring herself some more tea and popping five sugar cubes into it.

***

The Winger family was getting a tour of the second floor when Cora and the rest arrived.

"Mama?" Cora's voice echoed through the house.

"Oh, darlin'-daughter, you're home!" Sue-Anne sang as she danced down the stairs. Nicole followed the rest as they descended the spiral staircase.

Nicole stopped on one of the steps and looked down. Suddenly, the foyer didn't feel so massive anymore. Now, the foyer felt cramped and suffocating. Twenty or so people stood by the stairs, all looking up as Sue-Anne came down. Nicole looked out at the group, a smattering of familiar faces but a sea of unfamiliar ones staring back.

"There you are, Mama!" Cora called out, weaving her way to the front before throwing her arms around her mother. Sue-Anne wobbled as she embraced her daughter before stepping a foot against the edge of the step behind her.

"Let's get everyone into the entertainin' room before we all get squished," said Sue-Anne, planting a kiss on Cora's cheek. "There's no room down here even for Andrew's family."

Cora moved to the side and stared at Nicole and the rest, who were waiting awkwardly on the stairs. Laura gave a small wave.

"Oh, hi y'all!" Cora yelped, her accent suddenly thicker. "Glad y'all could make it!" Cora moved back in front of her mother. "Great idea, Mama. Let's go to the entertainin' room." Cora turned a full 180 degrees and faced the crowd. Nicole finally spotted Andrew, who was standing on the outskirts of the group by the door.

"Come on y'all! Follow me!"

The sea of people parted as Cora walked down the hallway, her mom right beside her, hand in hand. The wedding party crowd soon followed. Aunt Barbara and Uncle Pete started down the stairs, with Mrs. Winger and Kevin right behind them.

"What. The actual. Fuck." Ella looked back at Nicole before going down the stairs as well.

Nicole stood still, one hand on the handrail by the wall. It wasn't until Laura slipped her hand into Nicole's free hand did Nicole start moving.

Together, Nicole and Laura walked down the hallway, trailing behind the crowd as they made their way past the living room, looping past the entranceway for the octagonal parlor, and ending in what appeared to be an entire hunting lodge wedged into one room. Sue-Anne had merely walked by it during their tour, mentioning in passing that it was their "entertainin' room". But what Nicole had seen from the doorframe that morning was nothing compared to what she saw once she was inside.

In one corner was a set of leather couches and armchairs circled around a glass and wood coffee table. In another corner was a long dining room table with rocking chairs pushed into it. There was a pool table to the left of Nicole and a large, flat screen TV to the right. On the opposite end of the room was a redbrick fireplace with a fire already roaring in it.

Nicole stared at the fire with a bemused smirk on her face.

Today's weather definitely calls for nice, warm fire.

The wedding party divided off into distinct groups as soon as they entered the room. Jacob, Andrew's hometown friend, stood by the pool table and in somewhat close vicinity to two other men – one of them Nicole recognized as Evan, Andrew's friend since they were freshmen in college, and the other a complete stranger to Nicole. Cora's sorority sisters, whose names escaped Nicole at that moment, were already sitting in the leather chairs. Everyone else was standing in a large circle, already chatting idly. Andrew was nowhere in sight.

"Cora, Cora, we need to introduce everyone!" Sue-Anne called out, her voice projecting in a way to grab everyone's attention as well as Cora's.

"Of course, Mama," said Cora, stepping forward to Uncle Pete and Aunt Barbara. "Hi y'all. I'm Cora, Andrew's fiancée. I'm so happy y'all could make it!"

"Thank you – and thank you for inviting us," said Aunt Barbara with an unsure smile. "I'm Andrew's Aunt Barbara, and this is his uncle, Pete."

"So great to meet y'all!" Cora sang. She looked at Kevin and Ella and said: "And you two must be..."

"Cousins," said Kevin. "I'm Kevin. And this is my sister, Ella."

"Oh, wonderful," said Cora. "So glad to see his cousins could make it. I know just how important family can be."

Nicole's mouth twitched as she stared at the ground.

"Mama Winger, how are you." Cora gave Nicole's mom a hug that was startlingly gentler than the one she had given her own mother. "You fly in just fine?"

"Yes, the flight was fine," Mrs. Winger replied with the type of ultra-soft voice she typically saved for her children. "No issues or complications, thankfully."

"That's always wonderful to hear. And – Nicole!"

Nicole's head darted up.

"How are you!"

Nicole reflexively moved her hands – one of which had originally been holding onto Laura's – in front of her and gripped them together.

"I'm good," she replied, wondering what else to say next.

"And Laura, how are you, sugar?" Cora asked without missing a beat.

"Great," Laura said, with a look over at Nicole. Nicole glanced back before looking at the ground. "Thanks for asking."

Cora practically danced over to the large group in the center of the room. She placed her hands on the shoulders of the tall, slender girl with black hair. The last time Nicole had seen her, she was carrying a clipboard and barking out orders.

"Y'all, this is Rachel, my maid of honor," said Cora. "But you'd've already known that if y'all'd read the invitation packet!"

Polite laughter wafted throughout the room. Nicole gripped her hands tighter.

Cora shifted over to a brunette who appeared to be around Andrew's age.

"And this is Susanna, my second maid of honor." Cora lifted up Susanna's right hand. "And my sister! And the mother of my adorable little niece!"

"A niece who is already 10 months old," Sue-Anne remarked.

"They grow up so fast," said Mrs. Winger.

"Ten months and Susanna still can't get rid of the baby fat," Sue-Anne sighed out just loud enough for everyone to hear. Susanna pressed her lips together and looked to the floor.

"It's not as easy as it looks, Mama," Susanna replied.

"Well, it's not like the baby was planned or anything..." Sue-Anne continued.

"Mama!" Susanna yelped.

"What? I'm just sayin' that it wasn't like you were plannin' for it or anything," Sue-Anne defended. "Plus, ain't we lucky that this is the week the baby daddy has her? Frees you up to be there for your sister... and get a little extra exercise in."

Cora, apparently oblivious of the previous conversation, shifted over to a tall, blonde girl.

"And this is Meredith. I've known her since kindergarten!"

"Hi y'all," she called out, her eyes moving around the room to everyone, including the members of the wedding party standing off to the sides.

"And this is Sarah." Cora presented Sarah with her arms outstretched, as if Cora were a model at a trade show. Sarah smiled and waved her left hand, before collapsing her fingers into her palm and turning her wrist, showing off the same flashy ring that she had shown

Nicole at the engagement party.

"This is Mandy-Lee, my cousin and junior bridesmaid," said Cora, pointing to the ten-year-old. "And that one is Alexandra, my other cousin, and my flower girl."

The second young girl, who couldn't have been any older than 5, responded to Cora's introduction by looking at the fireplace and going, "Having a fire and running the AC at the same time doesn't make any sense."

"Out of the mouths of babes!" Sue-Anne laughed shrilly.

"Over here is Kyle, our little ring bearer," Cora continued without reacting to Alexandra's observation. "And, of course, my little nephew, to boot."

Cora patted the top of Kyle's head. Kyle responded by batting away Cora's hand and fixing his hair.

Cora took another step over and placed both hands on a tall, brown-haired man's shoulders.

"This is Fred, Kyle's dad, *my* brother and..." Cora paused her emphasis. "Andrew's best man."

As if on cue, everyone in the room applauded.

"Where is Andrew, anyway?" Aunt Barbara asked.

"Oh, I imagine just checkin' in with the weddin' planners," Sue-Anne answered. "He's so hands on like that."

Nicole turned from the room and stared out the doorway, wishing she could see through the walls and into the dining room on the other end of the house.

"And these three are Sam, Luke, and George, my three of my favoritest cousins in the whole wide world." Cora wedged herself in between two of the men, wrapped an arm around each man's waist, and gave them a tight squeeze. She exited the group and pointed toward the couches. "Over there is Karen and Ashley. We were in Kappa Kappa Kappa together at Northwestern." Cora turned and pointed at the men by the pool table. "And over there is Aaron, my neighbor. And those two are Jacob and Evan, Andrew's buddies from Illinois!"

Jacob waved and said a quick, "Hello." Evan smiled awkwardly.

"There'll be a quiz at the end of the day," said Uncle

Pete. "Hope everyone was taking notes."

A few chuckles emanated from the group.

"So, what were y'all fixin' to do after brunch?" Sue-Anne asked.

Cora sighed loudly and looked up toward the ceiling.

"Well, we were gonna go off into our groups and pick up the bridesmaids' dresses and groomsmen's tuxes," said Cora. "Then we were gonna get a few last minute supplies n' such."

Sue-Anne paused for a moment, before her entire face lit up.

"I've got the best idea, honeybun," Sue-Anne exclaimed. "Why don't you take along Andrew's family to run the errands with you? We'll entertain the adults and you can take the kids."

"Are we being called kids?" Kevin asked Ella with a soft, flat voice.

"Kevin, was it? You can go with the men to the tailor's," Sue-Anne continued. "I'm sure you have a ton to catch up on with Andrew. And, Nicole? Laura? Ell-lah? Y'all can go with the girls."

"I don't know..." Nicole began.

"It'll be a great bondin' experience." Sue-Anne's words toppled over Nicole's. "Unless, of course, you already have plans..."

Nicole looked at her mom with quiet, pleading eyes.

"I think it sounds like a great idea," Mrs. Winger agreed. "It can give everyone time to get to know each other better." Mrs. Winger looked over at Nicole as she said the last bit.

"So what do y'all say, girls?" Sue-Anne stared at Nicole, her eyes making Nicole shift her weight from one foot to the other. "Are y'all ready?"

Nicole looked over at Laura, then down at her hands, then over at Ella. Ella surreptitiously rolled her eyes before turning to Sue-Anne.

"Sounds great," Ella said with a big, broad smile.

Abby Rosmarin

Chapter Eight

ENGRAVED INVITATION, PT. 2

"I think I'll just wait until college."

Nicky dangled her feet off the back porch. *Her eyes followed the movement of her legs as one foot disappeared underneath the porch's edge and another reappeared.*

"You do whatever you feel comfortable with," said Andrew. *"I'm behind you 100%, no matter what."*

"Which is better than Mom's, like..." Nicky rolled her head back. *"Sixty-five percent."*

"You know Mom supports you just as much as I do," said Andrew. *"I think it's just something she wasn't expecting. She doesn't know what exactly to do to show support. That's all."*

"She can stop being so weird about it, for one," Nicky muttered.

"That's Mom for you." Andrew leaned back and pressed his palms into the wood. *"I'd be more worried if she* wasn't *acting like a spaz."*

"She's always nervous about something," said Nicky.

"Give her time," said Andrew. *"Before you know it, she'll be too focused on things like teaching you how to drive to really care about this."*

Nicky stared up at the stars. *If she concentrated hard enough, she could see the edges of the Milky Way.*

"Do you think she'll tell anybody?" Nicky asked. *"I mean, before I do?"*

"Mom?" Andrew sat up. "Never. In fact, she'll probably ask you four or five times if it's okay to talk about it before she even says a word."

"Maybe I'll wait until I'm far, far away from Hampshire," said Nicky. "Like, New York, or something. So no one can do anything if they hate me."

"I will make sure no one does anything, regardless," said Andrew with such an authority that Nicky shivered. "And I must've gone wrong somewhere if anyone in this town still thinks they can mess with you without having to deal with me."

"Yeah, but you're in Chicago now," said Nicky.

"And I have no issues coming back at the slightest hint of an issue," said Andrew.

Nicky went silent. She lowered her eyes, hunched over her knees, and tucked her chin into her chest.

"Why are you being so chill about this?" Nicky asked.

"Because you're my baby sister." Andrew wrapped an arm around Nicky and hugged her to his side. "Because there is absolutely nothing you could do that would make me wig out on you." Andrew let go of Nicky, propped his hands against his knees, leaned forward, and looked at her. "Besides, I knew you were gay since you were, like, five."

Nicky stared at Andrew, her eyes wide.

"What?"

"Yeah," said Andrew. "If anything, I was shocked it took you an additional ten years to tell me."

"But... what..." Nicky stammered. "How did you know?"

"Because you never paired up your dolls boys with girls," said Andrew. "Because you always married your princess doll whenever you played 'wedding'. Because I never once heard any rumor that you had a crush on a boy at school. Because... I don't know, I just knew. Brotherly intuition."

Nicky released the air in her lungs with one incredulous laugh.

"Don't tell Mom that I never paired up my dolls right," said Nicky. "She'll swear that it's all because Dad died."

Andrew looked away and towards the ground, his eyelids drooping. He hunched forward and lowered his body towards his lap.

"She's always worried about stuff like that," Andrew said, smiling weakly at his feet.

Nicky followed his gaze, staring at Andrew's feet as they began to swing back and forth. After a moment, Nicky looked back up.

"Do you think he would've been okay?" she asked. "Okay with me being gay, that is?"

"Dad was really cool," Andrew said softly. "He probably would've realized it before I did. Heck, he probably would've realized it before even you did." Andrew sighed and pushed his hands against his knees, lifting himself up slightly. "Dad was just that type of guy. He was... he was really great."

Nicky nodded, staring at her big brother as he stared off into the forest that bordered their backyard. She wanted nothing more than to say exactly what Andrew needed to hear in order to feel better. She wished she knew the perfect combination of words and hugs to get Andrew smiling again. She stared just a little while longer, before looking away and up.

"Do you see this many stars in the city?" Nicky asked.

Andrew let out a quiet laugh and shook his head.

"Not in the least. Too much light pollution."

"I'll have to keep that in mind when I apply to schools in Chicago," said Nicky.

"You're way too young to be thinking about college."

"You're never too young to be thinking about college," said Nicky. "Just ask the new guidance counselor."

"That's what happens when some west coast grad student gets a job in a town like Hampshire," said Andrew. "Assumes we're all hicks itching to take to the plow the second we graduate middle school."

Nicky shrugged her shoulders.

"She means well, I guess," she said, before adding: "Maybe I should tell her I'm gay. Watch her write her memoir in her head as I admit it. Chapter One: how I was the savior to my one gay student..."

Andrew laughed so hard and so suddenly that he snorted. He pulled Nicky in and kissed her on the temple.

"You're ridiculous," he said.

"I learn from the best," she said.

Nicky stared at her feet again, following each foot as it swung down and out of sight.

"But yeah, college," she said after a while. "That seems like a good time. Not like I'll find a girlfriend while I'm in high *school, anyway."*

***

Nicole started going weeks at a time without hearing anything from Andrew. Every once in a while, she'd get a call, a casual conversation while Andrew was running a test at school. Every once in a while, Nicole would call Andrew while she waited for the L. Every once in a while, they'd touch base, checking in with each other.

They talked about work and school and the weather. They kept it topical and under 15 minutes. No plans were made to see each other, even for a quick lunch. Cora's name was never brought up. It was almost as if Andrew had become single again. Because of it, Nicole could pretend that their terse phone calls were due to things like finals or a project deadline. Nicole could pretend that Andrew was just knee-deep in his PhD research and all she needed to do was wait until the semester was over before she could have her brother back again.

She received a large package on the first day of spring. She came home one Wednesday night to a pink box at her doorstep. White, sparkly lines were painted up and down the sides, mimicking a ribbon and bow. Her name and address were written in calligraphy on a sticker situated by inside corner of the painted bow, as if it were a tag on a Christmas present. Nicole unlocked her door, propped the door open with her hip, and carried the box through the doorframe.

Nicole took a few steps inside, allowing the front door to slam shut. She shrugged off her bag, dropped it to the floor, and lowered the box onto her kitchen counter. She attempted to pull apart the wrapping, only to realize that there was none. The box itself had been painted pink and white. She grabbed a steak knife from the knife rack and gently poked around the taped edges.

It quickly became clear to Nicole that the box had been expertly taped up before being painted over. Every flap edge had been secured down tightly. After a few tries, she was able to free one of the flaps. Nicole pulled it back, fed the knife around the remaining flap and opened it all the way.

At first, all Nicole could see was glitter. Glitter mixed with glitter on top of glitter. She put a cautious hand into the box and watched it disappear. She fished out a little plastic kite with the words "East Braedonton Kite Festival", followed by a plastic mini orange. Below that was a figurine couple that looked just like Andrew and Cora, followed by a noisemaker, a hole punch, and a magnet in the shape of an antique sign with, "Welcome to East Braedonton!" printed across it. Underneath the print, someone had written, "y'all!" in black marker.

There was an additional package at the bottom: an 8 x 11 envelope in matching pink and white paint. Nicole pulled the envelope out, causing a cascade of glitter to fall onto the kitchen floor and turn her pants into a wearable disco ball.

She instinctively took a step back, her arms swinging out to her sides, her right hand now clenching the envelope – which made the remaining glitter on the envelope to go airborne, spreading across her kitchen in one effortless arc.

With a defeatist shake of her pants and the envelope, Nicole moved to the other side of the counter and opened the packet.

Inside was a thick pile of multi-colored paper. The first was an intricate invitation, where Mr. and Mrs. Dan Bachman formally invited Nicole to attend the wedding of Cora Bachman and Andrew Winger. Underneath that was an RSVP card, where guests had to indicate whether or not they were going by punching a hole in a designated spot (using the hole punch from the box, assumedly). The RSVP card was followed by a "brief history" of East Braedonton: a bound paperback with a picture of the downtown area on the cover.

A piece of paper separated the history book from the rest of the pile: a tea-stained piece of thin cardstock with the words "Meet the Bride & Groom!" typed in big, bold ink. Beneath that were two packets: one for Cora, one for Andrew. Underneath that was a second piece of paper, identical in every way to the first one, except for the words, "Meet the Wedding Party!" written on it. Beneath that was a set of loose-leaf papers, each one for a member of the wedding party.

Nicole briefly flipped through the wedding party papers. When she reached the end of the pile, she spread the papers across her counter and looked at them all at once. There were so many people in the wedding party – so many individual pieces of paper detailing every single person who would be taking part in the wedding – that Nicole had to cover the entire counter, placing some of the papers on top of the stove and on the edge of the sink. Aside from a childhood neighbor and an old college friend, Nicole recognized none of them. Especially not the guy with the title "BEST MAN", which was noted with a circular silver sticker with serrated edges, as if he had won second place in the "best man" contest.

Nicole stared at everything in front of her. The pink box. The knick-knacks. The piles of paper and glitter everywhere. She looked at everything, concentrating – as if, just by looking at it, somehow it would all make sense to her. She scanned the counter, the floor, her own pants and shoes. With a slow, defeated sigh, Nicole placed everything back into the box and went to the closet to grab her broom.

***

Andrew called the next day, late in the evening. Nicole was sitting on Laura's couch, watching a movie, already nodding off, when her back pocket started jingling. She pulled out her phone and looked down at the screen and wished that this had been one of the weeks that Andrew didn't call. She briefly considered ignoring it, but found herself accepting the call before she knew what was happening.

"Hey there, Nicky," said Andrew. "How are you doing?"

"Oh, y'know." Nicole sat up. Laura stopped the movie. The apartment filled with a weird silence. "I'm doing."

Nicole got up and began pacing around the room.

"Am I interrupting anything?" Andrew asked.

Nicole looked back at Laura and continued walking around.

"Oh, no, no. Not at all," Nicole said. "What's up with you?"

Andrew sighed into the phone.

"Waiting for my stupid test to finish for the fiftieth time. Figured I'd call you up and see how you were doing."

"Oh, you know..." Nicole looped around and into the kitchen, her free hand lightly brushing against the counter. "Just hanging out... I, uh, I got the wedding invitation."

"Those went out already?" Andrew responded. "How about that. I'm assuming you'll be coming, of course."

Andrew said the last bit in his usual, joking voice, the melody of his words dipping low and slowly climbing back up. He sounded more like a master of ceremonies than regular, old Andrew. But Nicole still paused, as if she were genuinely considering whether or not she'd go.

"Hey, just because a question is facetious doesn't mean you don't respond with anything," Andrew jibed. "That is, of course, unless you're *not* coming..."

That time, Andrew's voice didn't dip and rise. His voice didn't change. Instead, he spoke the last sentence with a type of sternness that caught Nicole off guard.

"No, no – of course I am." Nicole shook her head at the wall in front of her. "I'm just distracted, is all. It was just, uh... that was quite the get-up. The invitation and everything."

"Really?" said Andrew. "I have to admit, I haven't even seen the invitations. What were they like?"

Nicole laughed and nodded her head from side to side.

"Well, for starters, it's not a normal invitation," Nicole said.

"Really." Andrew's tone dropped slightly. "How is that?"

"It's a box. A four-pound box with glitter and souvenirs and, like, a history of her hometown."

"That's a cute idea, though," said Andrew, responding so quickly that he almost interrupted Nicole. "I'm sure that took them a lot of time to create."

"There's a full-out biography on every single person in the wedding party. Right down to what their favorite color is," Nicole continued, her own voice growing more defensive.

"That takes a lot of time and care and effort. I think that was very sweet of her."

Nicole looked over at the TV. Two comedy actors were suspended in time, their faces slightly contorted as they attempted to finish the remaining words in their conversation.

"I guess so," Nicole relented. "I mean, in the end I needed those biographies. I didn't even know most of the people on that list."

"Well, you wouldn't, because you don't know any of Cora's bridesmaids." Andrew said the last words the same way a parent responds to a child who gets a stomachache after eating too many marshmallows: *Well, duh. That's what you get.*

"Who's Fred, then?" Nicole spat out, blood rushing to her face.

"Come again?"

"Fred," Nicole continued, licking the tops of her teeth with irate force. "Your *best man*?"

"Yeah? That's Cora's big brother. He means a lot to her."

"So you're letting Cora's family basically take over your side of the wedding party?"

A stinging sensation in her left palm forced her to look down and realize that she was clenching her free hand into so tight of a fist that her nails were starting to pierce the skin. "Like, how many of these guys are actually your friends?"

"It's not like I kept in touch with every guy from high school or undergrad," Andrew shot back. "It's not a big deal."

"Did you even ask Kevin if he wanted to be a groomsman?" Nicole asked. She thought she had more to say, but found herself suddenly silent. It shocked her that her cousin's name was so readily in the forefront of her mind. "You didn't even think to ask your own family? I assumed he'd be your best man."

The line went silent on Andrew's side. Nicole licked her lips and closed her eyes, regretting everything she had said. She wanted nothing more than to rewind time, collect every word she had uttered, and stuff them away so that she'd never say them a second time around.

"I get it," Andrew finally said. "You're upset you're not in the wedding party."

"What? I..." Nicole searched for what to say next and found nothing but the carpet in front of her.

"No, I get it," Andrew continued. "I'm sorry, Nicole, but this is a traditional wedding. Only men on the groom's side, and only women on the bride's."

"Wait, are you..." Nicole began.

"You would've been a kickass groomsman... or, maid. Groomsmaid. But it wouldn't work for this wedding."

Nicole sighed out her last remaining thoughts. She closed her eyes and pressed the side of her head into the phone.

"That's okay. Really, it's okay."

"I could ask if you could be a bridesmaid, though," Andrew offered. "Well, no, because Cora wants symmetry in her wedding party. Having you on her side would tip the scales."

"What about Kevin?" Nicole offered before she knew what she was offering. "Really, you guys have always been so close. Can't he be a groomsman?"

"Huh. I never thought about that," said Andrew. "Y'know, I'll ask Cora what she thinks and I'll get back to you on that."

"No rush." Nicole smiled weakly at nothing, her eyes still cast to the ground.

"But hey, I think my test finished a little while back. I'll talk to you soon, okay?"

"Sure."

"Later, Nicky."

Nicole moved the phone away from her face.

"Later."

Nicole took a moment, holding her phone tentatively in her hand before putting it back in her pocket. She took a few slow, deliberate steps, and returned to the couch.

"What was that?" Laura asked. "Aside from a call

from Andrew."

Nicole sat down and placed her head in her hands.

"A disaster," Nicole mumbled into her palms.

"So, it involved Cora, I'm guessing?"

"When does it not?"

Laura inched in closer and began rubbing Nicole's back.

"What happened?"

Nicole rubbed her eyes.

"It's stupid. Really, really, really stupid."

"So, it was really stupid, and it somehow involved that box invitation and your cousin Kevin?" Laura pieced together.

"More or less."

"And some dude named Fred," Laura continued. "Who is also Andrew's best man?"

"Looks like I don't even need to explain what happened."

"Who is Fred, anyway?"

Nicole turned to Laura and paused for emphasis.

"Cora's brother."

Laura moved her head back and cocked an eyebrow.

"Really? Sheesh."

"I mean, who does that?" Nicole went on. "That's *his* best man. Shouldn't *he* get to pick?"

"Maybe he *did* pick Fred," said Laura.

Nicole's shoulders drooped as she rolled her eyes.

"Like that would ever happen," she said. "From the sounds of it, Andrew has absolutely no say in this wedding."

Laura shrugged.

"Weddings are kinda the bride's deal, anyway."

Nicole reflexively pulled away.

"Whose side are you on?" she snapped.

"No, c'mon. I didn't mean it like that," Laura backtracked. "It's just that, usually guys don't care about things like invitations or flowers."

"But a guy *should* care about who his best man is." Nicole leaned against the couch and dropped her head back. "I shouldn't have said anything. Nothing good came of it. Now I might be one of Cora's bridesmaids because I couldn't keep my stupid mouth shut."

"But I like your stupid mouth," Laura said with a puppyish smile.

"Well, I don't, 'cause it's stupid," Nicole mumbled. "The whole thing was stupid. I shouldn't have brought it up."

"It bothered you, and you said something," said Laura. "That's how communication works."

"Well, communication is stupid, too." Nicole pressed a palm into the center of her forehead. With a shake of her head, she sat up and reached for the remote. "Besides, I've taken too much time away from this movie, anyway."

***

Andrew called the next day while Nicole was on the train. She stared at her phone until the "Missed Call" message popped on her screen. Her phone pinged a minute or so later, letting her know she had voicemail. When she got off at her stop and made her way back to street level, she took her phone out again and listened to the message.

"Hey, Nicky. So, I talked with Cora. She said she loved the idea, but unfortunately it wouldn't work. Cora says that if she added Kevin and you to the wedding party, she'd have to send out wedding party biographies again. It makes sense if you think about it. Anyway, I figured I'd let you know. Hope the day's going pretty well for you. Talk to you later."

Nicole listened to the message a few more times before deleting it and putting away her phone. She walked the length of street from the train stop to her neighborhood in deafening, buzzing silence. She listened to the sound of her footsteps until her thoughts overwhelmed all outside noise.

What was there for her to say? How was she supposed to react? She felt relieved, but also disappointed. At first, she swore the disappointment was because Kevin wasn't a groomsman. She told herself that she had lucked out: bridesmaids dresses are expensive and tacky and being a bridesmaid meant that she'd have to spend more time around Cora and Cora's family.

But she kept going back to Cora's excuse as to why it wouldn't work out. She repeated it over and over in her head, waiting for it to actually make sense. By the time she hooked a right onto her street, she realized she was actually angry that Cora dismissed the idea with such weak reasoning. She was angry and frustrated and it wasn't just because Kevin couldn't be a groomsman and she couldn't fully understand why.

Nicole checked the road before darting across the street to her apartment complex: a U-shaped building with bay windows and delicate window trim. Grey cement lines jutted down from the roof and the undersides of windows, creating a simple, horizontal pattern in the redbrick. The building looked like it couldn't decide between Victorian or Gothic styles and had settled on a nice hybrid between the two.

She loved this building. Her studio apartment was nondescript, and certainly did not have any of the bay windows she saw from the outside, but it was the exterior architecture that drew her in. She signed a lease even when there were cheaper studios available because she wanted to live in *that* building, with *that* design.

Nicole stood at the base of the apartment's walkway and stared at the complex. She remembered how Andrew had helped her move in after graduation. Nicole and her mom would shuffle up all the small, breakable boxes, while Aunt Barbara and Ella carried suitcases and plastic storage bins. Andrew and Kevin and Uncle Pete lugged up furniture, coordinating their movement like they were docking an aircraft carrier. Andrew was knee-deep in exams to grade at that time, but he spared nothing to be with her as she said good-bye to college life.

The sun had long set, the only light coming from the lampposts on the edges of the walkway. Everything was so still now. Nicole continued down the walkway and into her apartment. She let the door slam shut, her bag drop to the floor, and her body collapse onto the bed.

She wasn't sure how long she stayed like that. All she knew was that a beep from her back pocket forced her to move. Nicole rolled to one side, fished out her phone, and checked the screen.

"Feel like doing something tonight?" A message from Laura read.

Nicole looked at her screen to the point that the world started blurring and the words stopped making sense. She closed her eyes, sat up in her bed, and wrote:

"Not tonight. Work was exhausting today."

She hit send, paused, and added, "Maybe tomorrow?" in a second message. Before she could get a return message, Nicole tossed her phone to the other side of the bed and plopped back, her arms spread out, her eyes on the ceiling.

Abby Rosmarin

Chapter Nine

BELLE OF THE BALL

Nicole pressed her head against the side window. She couldn't help but smirk: for this car ride, at least, she wasn't sitting in the middle.

The wedding party – plus Nicole, Laura, and Ella – had piled into two minivans. Rachel – the maid of honor – was driving one, and Susanna – Cora's big sister and second maid of honor – drove the other. Cora sat alongside Rachel in the first van while Nicole, Laura, and Ella were pressed in the back row of Susanna's. The flower girl sat passenger side while Sarah and Meredith sat in the middle.

"I'm so excited, finally taking home our bridesmaids' dresses," Meredith cooed, her accent making Nicole grimace. It sounded like an impression of a southern accent that, halfway through, the person had given up on. "I haven't been this excited since they updated the cheerleadin' uniforms at East Braedonton High!"

"Well, *I* for one wouldn't be waiting until last minute to pick up *my* wedding dresses." Sarah twisted her ring and stared down longingly at it. "I would make sure all my wedding plans were finalized weeks beforehand."

"Don't you need to be, like, *engaged* first, before you plan a wedding?" said Alexandra, the flower girl.

Sarah huffed and brought her ring closer to her face.

"Don't you need to, like, graduate high school before you have opinions that matter?" Sarah snapped back.

"Y'all, no fighting," said Susanna. "This is Cora's day."

"Cora's day isn't until Saturday," Sarah replied. "Besides, why is it just *her* day? Shouldn't we get some recognition?"

"Hey, Meredith, isn't that where you work?" Alexandra called out as they drove past a grocery store.

"Y-y-yes," Meredith stammered out. "For now, at least."

"Cool," Alexandra responded. "Aunt Sue-Anne was talking about how you went from head cheerleader to a grocery store bagger without any hope of getting a good husband. I thought it was this place, but I wasn't sure."

Meredith stared at the back of Alexandra's seat before slumping into her own.

"So!" Susanna piped in with such force that her voice broke. "Y'all in the back. Andrew's sister! Michelle, was it?"

"Nicole."

"Oh my, so sorry!" Susanna said, a little bit louder and with more force. "How are y'all liking Florida so far?"

Nicole shrugged her shoulders.

"It's nice," said Laura. "I actually love Florida. I have family here."

"Oh, that's wonderful," Susanna replied. "It's always nice to hear of a yank who loves the Great State of Florida. And not the fake kinds of Florida, like Miami or Key West."

"'Great State of Florida'?" Ella leaned over and whispered in Nicole's ear. "Please tell me they think the state nickname is the Lone Orange Juice State."

Nicole pressed her lips together to hide a smile.

Susanna turned left onto the main street. The bridal boutique stood at the very end of the downtown area, a handful of buildings down from the diner Nicole and her family had brunch at. A large front window took up the majority of the shop's exterior, with a small white door located off to the side. The top center of the storefront read "Angel's Angelic Brides" in silver, glittering swirls. The main window hosted four mannequins, dressed to the nines in wedding gowns, each gown fluffier than the one to the right of it.

"When *my* wedding happens, I'm not going to use this place," Sarah said as she unbuckled her seatbelt. "I'll research the top designers and fly one in to privately create my perfect wedding dress."

The rest of the van's passengers slowly made their way out. Ella paused to roll her eyes at Nicole before shuffling out of her seat.

Rachel was waiting for them inside the front door, her clipboard back in her hand.

"Alright, do we have everyone here?" Rachel tapped against her clipboard before scanning down the sheet of paper attached to it. "Yup, yup, and yup."

Rachel looked up and smacked her palm against the sheet. The noise made Nicole jump.

"Angel is bringing out the bridesmaids' dresses," said Rachel. "Each and every one of you—" Rachel stopped and looked at Nicole. "—each and every one of you who is part of the wedding party *must* try on their dress. There will be no more alterations done to your dresses, so if your dress is tight, you have two and a half days to lose weight. If your dress is loose, you have two and a half days to gain weight. Failure is not an option. Do I make myself clear?"

"Could you tell my mama the part about not losing weight?" Susanna piped in meagerly.

"I could tell her that you drive like an old person and you're lucky I'm patient," Rachel replied.

"So long as you add in the part about not losing weight, I don't care." Susanna gave a broad smile to indicate she was joking, but her voice sounded too desperate to deliver the punch line properly.

Rachel rolled her eyes and walked away.

The interior of the boutique was a sea of white and beige. White walls and off-white carpets, dresses in every variety of white (or cream, or champagne) imaginable. The only color came from the golden hangers and hanger rods that kept the dresses up, as well as the silver outlines on the three-way mirror. Cora and the girls from Rachel's minivan were sitting on white leather couches surrounding the white felt platform by the mirror. Down the hall hosted a long line of dressing rooms with white doors and white handles. Everyone was effortlessly chatting, as if they had been there all day as part of a ladies' night out. The junior bridesmaid fidgeted in her seat and Karen surreptitiously checked her phone, but everyone else looked right at home.

Susanna, Sarah, and the rest found a seat on the white leather couches. Everyone but Nicole, Laura, and Ella flowed into the seating area and found a spot to sit without so much as a second glance. Nicole took a few hesitant steps forward before retreating back, finding a spot to stand behind the first couch, next to a set of lace wedding gowns. Ella quickly fell into step and stood next to her. Laura looked at Nicole and Ella, glanced at one of the free spots on a couch, and took a seat.

"Here we go, y'all!" A super peppy – assumedly Angel's – voice called from the back before pulling out a rolling rack. Aside from a pastel pink dress in the front, the rolling rack held seven bright orange dresses. Each dress had one thick, diagonal shoulder strap with a fluffy yellow rose on top. The dresses stood out like traffic lights in the sea of white and beige and champagne.

"Oh my goodness!" Meredith squealed. "I cannot believe they're here and ready!"

"Those are the ugliest togas I have ever seen in my entire life," Ella whispered to Nicole.

Nicole stared at the dresses as the rolling rack shifted into place next to the felt platform. They were long, flowing dresses, the fabric so shiny it almost glittered. The yellow rose on the shoulder was easily the size of her fist, if not bigger. For a brief second, she imagined herself walking down the aisle in that dress. She imagined herself in a bright orange bridesmaid gown, linking arms with a groomsman, carrying a bouquet, and smiling wildly at her brother as the processional music played on. She pressed her tongue to the roof her mouth and grinned a crooked grin.

"Forcing someone to wear that is like the ultimate betrayal," Nicole whispered back. "*Et tu, Brute?*"

Ella snorted out a laugh so loud that the girls on the

couch turned toward Ella.

"Sorry." Ella held up a palm and grinned sheepishly. "Held in a sneeze."

Nicole looked over at Laura. Laura looked back, her elbows on her thighs, her hands clasped together in a tight ball by her knees, her brown eyes wide and wild. Nicole looked down at the ground before looking back over at the bridesmaids' dresses.

"Okay, dress one? Karen." Rachel held her clipboard in one hand and lifted dresses from the rack with the other. "Dress two, Ashley. Dress three, Meredith. Dress four, Sarah. Dress five, Susanna. Dress six is mine. Mandy-Lee? Here is your dress. And the flower girl dress for little Alexandra." Rachel pressed her clipboard to her chest after giving the flower girl dress to Alexandra. "Are you going to be okay putting that on by yourself?"

"I'm already five and a half," Alexandra scoffed. "A little dress will not faze me."

Each of the girls disappeared into their respective dressing rooms. The main area was empty – aside from Angel and Cora, who were standing at the entranceway of the dressing room hallway, looking directly at the dressing room doors as if either of them could see what was going on. And Laura, who looked intensely isolated and out of place, the lone person on the white couch. Nicole pressed her palms into the edge of the couch in front of her and leaned forward.

"So, uh..." Laura cleared her throat and turned to Cora. "Did you pick up your wedding dress already?"

"Of course not!" Cora giggled back, her eyes still on the dressing rooms. "That will be kept in a locked room here until the big day. One of the wedding planners will escort it over when it's time. Don't want to dirty it up by putting it in any old closet!"

"Ah." Laura's mouth twisted as she looked away from Cora. She glanced up at Nicole again. Nicole caught her eye for just a moment before Laura looked over at the changing rooms as well.

Within minutes, the wedding party flooded out into the hall and fanned out, filling up the area gated off by the couches. A cacophony of voices filled the room as each girl turned and complimented the girl next to her, touching each other's dresses and twirling around in their own. Cora wove around the girls, touching and smiling and talking in quick, unintelligible sound bites.

Rachel hiked up her dress, stepped onto the felt platform, and cleared her throat.

"Alright, everyone!" she called out, her arms spread wide. "Good to see that everyone's dresses are fitting nicely. How do the dresses feel?"

"I still don't think this dress is right for me," Sarah immediately piped up.

Rachel sighed and rolled her eyes.

"What is wrong with your dress, Sarah?"

"It's just not *me*." Sarah picked up the edges and dropped them with extra force. "I need something that really demonstrates who *I* am as a person. Something like..." Sarah walked past the white couches to the other end of the room and held one side of a gown. "Something like this!"

"For the tenth time: that's a wedding gown," Rachel said, her eyes lowering.

"Yeah, but it's so *me*, isn't it?" Sarah held the fabric closer to her face. "Can't I just try it on, so you guys can see what I'm talking about?"

"For the tenth time: no."

Sarah let go of the wedding dress with a sour look on her face and stomped over to the couches.

"So, aside from Sarah's color commentary, does anyone have any issues with their dresses?"

"Aside from the fact they look like oranges?" Ella whispered to Nicole.

"*Florida* oranges," Nicole whispered back.

"Colors match, lengths match, roses match..." Rachel squinted her eyes as she scanned the group. "If there are no objections, then I need everyone to change out of their dresses. I will bring them to the Bachman estate in the back of my van. They will be hung up in the guesthouse's dining room, which means no one will be allowed to eat, drink, or socialize in that room until *after* the wedding day. Do I make myself clear?"

A small murmur permeated through the crowd of

bridesmaids.

"Alright, then," said Rachel. "Let's change back into our day clothes. Carefully. Very carefully."

The group of girls disappeared again, leaving Angel and Cora with Nicole and the rest.

"Weren't those just lovely dresses?" said Cora, her accent shifting to something more sing-songy.

"You have such a wonderful eye for fashion and beauty," Angel responded. "I think those are the prettiest bridesmaids' dresses I ever saw."

"What do you think?" Cora asked, looking at Nicole.

"What?" Nicole yelped.

"The bridesmaids' dresses. What do you think?"

"Uh..." Nicole looked to the ground. "They were... bold."

Cora laughed.

"'Bold'. You yanks have funny ways of complimenting people!"

"Are you celebrating Florida oranges with your dresses?" said Ella.

Cora tilted her head.

"Beg your pardon?"

"I mean, why else would you have orange dresses..." Ella's brows lowered. "...if you were not celebrating oranges?"

"You certainly are clever!" Cora responded with a broad smile. "That's *exactly* where I was going with that. Oranges are a source of pride for us Florida belles. I wanted my weddin' to represent that."

Ella's jaw went slack. She glanced sideways at Nicole before pursing her lips.

"What did *you* think, Laura?" Cora turned.

"They're nice. Really nice," Laura said with an unsure nod. "They are, uh, really, um, eye-catching."

Cora laughed again.

"I'll never get you yanks."

Eventually the wedding party came back, hanging up the dresses on the rolling rack one last time.

"Let me put these in garment bags for y'all and they'll be ready to go," Angel said with a huge smile before pulling the rack down the hallway and into the back room.

Within minutes, Angel came out with the rolling rack again, this time with three garment bags consolidating the row of dresses.

"Let me roll this outside for y'all and y'all can load it from there," Angel said, pulling the rack behind her as she exited her store.

The rest followed suit, with Nicole hanging as far back as she could. Sarah lingered behind as well, detouring over to a second row of wedding gowns, touching them gingerly as she passed.

"I still don't get why Cora is the only one who gets to wear one of these on her wedding day," she muttered to no one in particular. "I mean, what makes *her* so special?"

***

"Who the hell has that many bridesmaids?"

Ella barely spoke above a whisper, but forced out her words with such gusto that they felt ten times louder.

"I think a lot of women have 7 or 8 bridesmaids. It's not that uncommon," Kevin responded, his voice lacking any of the venom Ella's had. "And – besides – why have bridesmaids in the first place? The whole thing is silly when you think about it. So why fuss over the details?"

Nicole pressed her back against the warm redbrick of the house. They had returned from Cora's errands about an hour ago. Before coming back, they had gone from the dress store to a jewelry shop to a crafts store, collecting the last items that needed collecting, fussing about for no apparent reason. Now everyone was outside in the backyard, sitting around and talking while dinner was being prepared. Some were gathered by the guesthouse, chatting lightly as they stood in a circle with cocktails in hand. Others were by the pool. A few were daring enough dip their feet into the water. The children – namely, Mandy-Lee, Alexandra, and the ring bearer whose name Nicole couldn't remember – were splashing around in the pool, climbing out only to jump back in. Andrew was sitting by Cora with their respective parents on the patio, sitting by a round, white table. The heat was stifling, but it didn't seem to affect anyone but Nicole.

Ella had found a small nook by the side of the house when they went outside. Nicole had followed close behind, feeling like she could finally breathe the second she separated from the clan of bridesmaids. After a while, Laura and Kevin found them and joined in on their discussion.

"Nothing is wrong with bridesmaids," Ella countered. "Having your closest friends or family by your side when you get married is beautiful. But that's it: *closest*. Not an entire clan of people from all walks of life."

Kevin just shrugged and took a sip from his glass.

"How was bonding time with the groomsmen, by the way?" Ella asked.

Kevin shrugged again.

"It was all right. They tried on their suits and I hung out," Kevin replied.

"Did Andrew say anything?" Nicole blurted out, her eyes still locked on the patio.

"About what?"

Now it was Nicole's turn to shrug, only hers was forced and stiff.

"About the whole groomsman thing." Nicole tried to sound nonchalant, but came off sounding whining instead. "You two were so close growing up. You'da thought…"

Nicole trailed off, letting her words dissipate. Off on the patio, Sue-Anne said something that made Cora burst into laughter and Andrew smile broadly.

"I never gave it much thought, to be honest," Kevin replied, sounding every bit as nonchalant as Nicole wished she had been. "I know this comes as a shock, but guys don't really care about stuff like that."

Nicole tried to smile in response. Instead, the corners of her mouth pulled back in a straight line.

"Please tell me the tuxes were orange," Ella added in her gusto-whisper.

Kevin's brow furrowed just slightly as he shook his head.

"Just black," he said.

"Well, you should've seen the dresses Cora is making her bridesmaids wear." Ella cocked her head with a sly grin. "It was like an orange grove threw up on them."

Nicole snorted before covering her mouth with her fingers.

Kevin stayed silent for a second, looking at his sister as if analyzing her.

"Ella, why do you care so much?" he asked after a moment.

Ella's face went blank.

"What?"

"Why do you care so much about this wedding?" Kevin repeated.

"I *don't* care," said Ella. "There's just a lot of stupid stuff going on. The invitations came in the form of a five-pound box. The wedding party is, like, twenty people long. This whole town is something out of the Twilight Zone. All of it deserves some commentary."

"And this has nothing to do with the fact that you had to cancel your own wedding plans and elope?"

Ella rolled her eyes so hard that her head moved in the same direction.

"No it doesn't," Ella shot back. "Besides, it's now the 'in' thing to do house parties instead of receptions anyways. I'm shocked Cora isn't having a second reception just for that."

Kevin looked at Ella one more time before shaking his head and tilting his glass towards his face.

"Believe what you want," Ella added. "I am *not* jealous."

"Who said you were jealous?" Kevin said, glass poised at his lips. He closed his eyes and took a long sip.

Ella opened her mouth to say something before clamping it shut and rolling her eyes again.

"So, is that Sarah chick for real?" Ella turned toward Nicole, her shoulder now pressed against the redbrick, her voice a schoolgirl's whisper. "Does she seriously think she could've worn a wedding gown to someone else's wedding?"

"You should've seen her at the engagement party," Nicole replied, mimicking Ella's whisper. "Walking around, showing everyone her fake engagement ring, talking about what she would do with her hypothetical wedding."

"Now if anyone is jealous, it's *that* crazy chick," Ella countered. "I mean, all bridesmaids are supposed to resent the friend getting married a little bit, but – *come on*. I can see her interrupting the service to tell everyone how she'd be doing it better."

"Ahem! Excuse me, everyone?" Nicole started in her best impersonation of Sarah, her left hand framing her face. "Just so you know, when I get married, I'm not gonna have these vows. I'm going to have something way cooler. And my minister will be cooler. And my dress will be prettier. That is all. *Y'all* can exchange rings now."

Nicole fluttered her left hand away from her face. Ella let out a loud, grateful laugh.

"Laura, you've been pretty silent today," Kevin said, just loud enough to stop Ella and Nicole's conversation. "How's the day treating you?"

"Oh, you know…" Laura smiled awkwardly, glancing over at Nicole before redirecting her gaze up at the sky. "It's been busy." Laura pressed her lips together before quickly adding: "Anything's better than work, though."

"Weddings are kind of the perfect vacation excuse," Kevin replied. "Because what heartless boss is going to deny you time off for a wedding? In a way I wish everyone got married, all the time. It's a good gig, if you ignore the part where you have to pay for airfare and hotels and presents."

Laura laughed quietly and nodded her head.

"You have a point."

"Y'know, I just realized I'm the only one with a drink here," said Kevin. "Any of you guys want a drink, or something?"

"If I start drinking, I won't stop until I'm too drunk to remember that I'm in the Twilight Zone," said Ella.

Kevin gave a skewed head nod.

"Alright, water for my little sis. Anyone else?"

"I guess I could see what they have," said Laura, before looking over at Nicole. "Do you want anything?"

"I think I'm set," said Nicole.

"We'll be back, then," said Kevin.

Kevin lead the way as Laura walked away from nook beside the house. They continued down the small hill before taking a left, walking up the patio, and disappearing into the house.

Ella sighed and got up.

"Well, if everyone else is drinking, I am drinking," she said. "Might as well get some free booze out of the situation, right?"

Nicole drew her lips into a smile.

"Right."

Ella took two steps down the small hill before turning back.

"You sure you don't want anything?" Ella asked.

"I'll be fine," said Nicole. "I'll just hang here for a bit."

"Suit yourself," said Ella as she walked to the pathway and up toward the house.

Nicole watched with her back still against the brick wall. Laughter and chatter filled the entire backyard. Part of her wanted to wander down the hill as well. She wanted to snake her way down the grey-brick walkways, past the swimming pool, past the guesthouse, and past all the flowers and statues and neatly trimmed shrubbery. She wanted to make her way to the acres and acres of manicured grass that lay just beyond all that. She wanted to walk to where the tree line was – so far removed from the people chatting and laughing – and just lay down and stare at the sky and watch the clouds roll by.

Up on the patio, Uncle Pete said something that made Sue-Anne laugh and Dan smile. Cora giggled and Andrew shook his head with a grin.

With a sigh, Nicole removed herself from the nook and circled around the house and away from the patio. She walked in through the front door, finding herself in the foyer once again – only this time the only things greeting her were the chandeliers and the arcing staircase. She wandered down one of the side hallways, passing the two wedding planners in the dining room.

The two ladies – both in their late 30s, one with a short, brunette bob and the other with long, blonde hair in a high ponytail – were still as busy as they were when Sue-Anne first gave everyone the house tour. The one with the ponytail was typing away furiously at one of the laptops while the one with a bob was scribbling what looked like gibberish on a white board.

Nicole continued down the hallway, stopping just short of the kitchen. Bridesmaid Karen was leaning against one of the counters, her head buried in her phone again. She typed something, received a ding, smiled, and resumed typing. Nicole hung a sharp left and found herself in the front foyer again. She eyed the stairs before taking a right and walking down the opposite hallway.

As she approached the entertain' room, Kevin came out of a bathroom and into the hallway, gently closing the door behind him.

"Fancy seeing you in these parts," he said.

"Hey," said Nicole, slowing to a stop.

"Laura's back outside if you're looking for her," said Kevin.

"Oh," Nicole replied. A momentary wave of guilt washed over her, followed by a weird, numb sensation. "Good to know."

Kevin became silent, looking at Nicole the same way he had looked at Ella.

"Is everything all right?" Kevin asked.

Nicole shrugged, looked towards the ceiling, and settled her eyes on the wall next to her.

"Yeah, of course."

Kevin remained silent for a moment longer.

"I know this is probably a complicated time for you," Kevin began.

"Why would it be?" Nicole snapped more than she meant to. "My brother is getting married. That's a happy time. A happy time for everyone."

"So you react to happy times by completely withdrawing?" Kevin asked. His words sounded neutral, but felt incriminating.

"I'm not withdrawing," Nicole defended. "I'm just..." Nicole shook her head and rubbed the back of her neck. "I just have a lot on my mind."

Kevin sighed and briefly glanced over his shoulder before turning back to Nicole.

"You know, I wasn't joking when I said that about Ella," he said, his voice suddenly softer.

"What?"

"About Ella," Kevin repeated. "I mean it when I said that she is acting this way because she had to elope. Cora is getting the big wedding that Ella had always wanted and I think that really bothers her."

"Why would it bother her?" asked Nicole. "She would never want a wedding like this."

"You mean a huge wedding that has two wedding planners and no budget limit?" Kevin asked. "There are few things that get under Ella's skin like a lack of time and a lack of money. And she got both right when she was supposed to start hiring vendors. She'll never admit it, but she still resents having to throw out all of her plans. And – even more than that – I think she resents women who get to have an abundance of both time and money."

Nicole shrugged her shoulders and licked her lips.

"Maybe I should find Laura now," she said finally.

"Maybe you should," Kevin said with a touch of finality in his voice.

Nicole grinned awkwardly and walked around Kevin. She continued down the hall, her feet going faster than she was comfortable with.

"Laura's a good woman, you know," Kevin called down.

Nicole stopped midstride. She had a sudden urge to make herself as small as possible.

"Better than you realize," he added.

Nicole turned around.

"Come again?"

"She came to Florida for you," Kevin continued from where he was standing. "Don't forget that."

Nicole started walking back towards her cousin.

"What is that supposed to mean?"

"Nothing, nothing," Kevin replied. "Just... nothing. Nothing at all."

Nicole stared at her cousin for a beat longer before turning back, walking down the hall, through the kitchen, and out to the backyard.

Out on the patio was her family, still sitting with Cora and her own family, with Laura standing next to the table. Off to the side, Ella was laying in a cushioned lounge chair under a pergola, sipping on what looked like a piña colada.

"Nicole, there you are!" Sue-Anne sang out, reaching for Nicole when Nicole was still in the doorway.

Nicole took a few tentative steps over, stopping just short of the patio furniture.

"Sugar, how are you?" Sue-Anne cooed. "Have y'all been enjoying yourself today?"

"Yeah, sure," Nicole answered.

"Laura was tellin' me how you two met," Sue-Anne continued.

Nicole's jaw went slack as she stared at Laura. Laura stared back before averting her eyes.

"You know how the old sayin' goes: you don't go to college to find a husband; you go to college to find your bridesmaids," Sue-Anne mused. "Although, really, y'all should try to find both."

***

The first thing Nicole did when they returned to the hotel was collapse on her bed.

"Today couldn't have sucked anymore if it tried," Nicole said into the pillow.

When Laura said nothing, Nicole lifted up her head, peering over her shoulder.

"And nothing from the peanut gallery?" Nicole quipped. "Not even a statement of agreement?"

Laura shrugged, looking down at her own bed.

"Sure."

Nicole sat up, legs dangling off the side of the bed.

"What's up?" she asked.

"Oh, *now* you're aware of me," Laura muttered, turning down the sheets on her bed.

"Okay, back up," Nicole said, holding her hands up. "What is going on? You were just fine, like, a minute ago."

"Was I?" Laura glanced up before walking across the room. "You are horrible at detecting emotions if you actually think I was."

Nicole stood up, arms folded across her chest.

"If something is up, just say it," she said. "I don't do this passive-aggressive, passive-whatever shit."

"You could've fooled me."

"I'm only asking you this one more time: what the hell is up."

Laura faced Nicole with her hands on her hips.

"You don't see it yourself? Look at how you're acting just now," said Laura, her voice soft yet reproachful. "And it's just been more of the same since we've landed."

Nicole hugged her arms tighter into herself.

"Well, you can keep explaining, then."

"I don't like who you've become," said Laura, this time with more authority. "This is not the Nicole I know and love."

Nicole huffed and threw her hands in the air.

"Well, *sorry* if my emotions are cramping your style," Nicole shot back. "I thought you were here to support me."

"I *am*," said Laura. "But you're not exactly making it easy for me to do that."

"Yeah, because you're too busy being best friends with Sue-Anne and the rest," Nicole accused. "Too busy being buddy-buddy with the wedding party to actually be my girlfriend."

"Don't make me out to be the bad guy just because I'm being friendly," Laura responded. "And it's not like I can even *be* your girlfriend. You've thrown yourself so far into the closet you're hitting your head on Christmas presents!"

"What are you even *talking* about?"

"You're ashamed to tell them I'm your girlfriend," said Laura. "And not in the 'girl friends' way Cora's mother thinks I am."

"That's bullshit," said Nicole. "I'm not ashamed."

"You barely say a word to me, you hang out as far away from me as you can…"

"Sorry I'm spending a little time with my cousin," Nicole interrupted. "That doesn't mean I'm—"

"You let go of my hand the second you thought anyone might see it," Laura interrupted back.

"What?"

"In the entertaining room," said Laura. "You just let go of my hand. I tried to give you support and you denied it the second anyone from Florida could see you."

"You have it all wrong. Completely wrong."

"Really?" Laura scowled. "Because, as I see it, you let go of my hand so nobody would find out just how *gay* you are."

"That's not why I let go," said Nicole. "I wasn't ashamed and I wasn't trying to hide anything from them."

"Then why?" Laura demanded, her voice starting to tremble.

And, just like that, the venom drained out of Nicole, leaving her exhausted and powerless. Her heart was telling her brain things that she couldn't really translate, and she didn't have the energy to even try. She rubbed her eyes and sighed.

"I'm not ashamed that you're my girlfriend. I'm not like that. You know me."

"'I know you'...?" Laura began.

Laura swayed, her lips tightly pressed together. Eventually she stopped and placed her hand on her head. Her mouth opened into a flickering smile. She gave a defeated laugh as she looked away and around the room.

"Forget it," Laura said. "I'm just tired. I'm overreacting."

Nicole looked to the floor, her shoulders drooping forward.

"I forgot how much this wedding bothers you," Laura continued. "And it's unfair of me to expect you to act a certain way. I'm sorry."

Nicole shrugged.

"It's okay," she mumbled, looking to the ground.

"I don't want to fight."

"We won't fight, then," said Nicole, shrugging her shoulders again.

"This wedding stuff is exhausting. Maybe we just need to do something together, just to reset our brains." Laura paused for a moment before adding: "Do you want to go swimming?"

"Swimming?"

"Yeah," Laura replied. "We haven't used that pool yet. Maybe it would be nice to go for a dip."

Nicole went silent.

"We can wait if anyone is out there right now. We can wait until it's deserted," Laura added. "It can be just the two of us if you'd like."

Nicole uncrossed her arms, her right hand finding the surface of the hotel desk. She felt her palm press into the lacquered oak as she leaned dangerously on it.

"I'm really tired," Nicole said at last. "Maybe tomorrow?"

Laura gave a small, fatigued smile.

"Sure," said Laura. "Tomorrow."

Chapter Ten

IT'S ALL TENTATIVE

"*Columbus Day Weekend,*" *Andrew reassured.* "*I'll make sure to visit home Columbus Day Weekend. And hey, you guys are always welcome to come up. Make a day out of it or something.*"

"*I wouldn't want to intrude.*" *Andrew and Nicky's mom unfolded a long-sleeved t-shirt from the bureau and studied it. "Besides, you're going to meet so many interesting new people and find so many interesting things to do.*"

"*Then you could just come up for a lunch or something,*" *Andrew suggested. He swiveled in his desk chair until he faced Nicky, who was standing at his doorframe with her arms crossed. "Weekends only. No skipping school.*"

Nicky rolled her eyes and stared down at the ground.

Their mom gave the t-shirt a quick snap before inspecting it again.

"*Are you sure you don't want me to run these through the wash one last time?*" *she offered. "Some of your winter stuff is probably getting a little musty. Couldn't hurt to freshen them up a bit, right?*"

"*I'll be fine, Mom.*" *Andrew stacked CD cases on his desk and then transferred each tower into a plastic bin by his feet. "They have washers and dryers in every dorm.*"

"*Yes, but it's always nicer when it's from home, isn't it?*" *Their mom hugged the shirt to her chest.*

Andrew laughed and shook his head.

"Tell you what: I'll make sure to save up all my laundry and bring it with me when I visit," he said. "From the goodness of my heart, I will let you do my laundry instead of me doing laundry at the dorm."

Their mom grinned and pushed Andrew's shoulder a little.

"You can be such a stinker sometimes."

Andrew turned his palms up.

"Keeps things interesting."

Their mom whipped the shirt into the air with both hands one last time before folding it and placing it in one of Andrew's suitcases.   Andrew continued to shuffle through his CD collection, his fingers dancing over a myriad of artists before deciding to pack all of the ones in his hand.

"You know, normal people don't do CDs anymore." Nicky pressed her shoulder into the doorframe, leaning more and more towards it.

"Ah, but the sound is so much better," said Andrew. "It's vintage."

"Vintage?" Their mom piped in. "You know, people used to say that about records. I didn't realize the shift was now on CDs."

"Times are changing." Andrew closed the lid to the CD bin. "And, then, someday we'll reminisce about a time when music was simply digital. Granted, we'll probably be too busy working for our robot overlords, but, on the off chance we have down time…"

"I swear." Their mom shook her head. "You have your father's sense of humor."

"And I wear it like a badge of honor."

Their mom patted down the shirt in the luggage.

"Well, I think now is as good of a time as any to start lunch," she said. "Are sandwiches okay?"

"Sandwiches are always okay," said Andrew.

Their mom looked down at the clothing one last time and exited the room. Nicky moved to the side just enough for her mom to pass through before she resumed her station at the entranceway.

"I know it's, like, totally uncool to actually be in rooms," said Andrew, "but you are welcome to actually step inside."

Nicky rolled her eyes again.

"I'm fine."

"Except for the part that you've barely said a word all day." Andrew pushed himself back in his chair, scooting across the room until he was by the door. "What's up? Are the mean girls in school acting up again?"

Nicky sighed and looked up at the ceiling.

"No, they're fine."

"Trouble in love?" asked Andrew. "Any crushes I should know about? Anybody I need to beat up?"

Nicky blushed fiercely and rolled her eyes again.

"I'm joking. You don't need to tell me about any crushes," Andrew offered in a soft tone. "Not unless you want to."

"I have no crushes," Nicky insisted.

"The day a 13-year-old doesn't have a crush on someone is the day I find swimming gophers in my bathtub," said Andrew. "But, again, seriously: you don't have to tell me anything you don't want to."

"Like I said: I have no crushes."

"And I believe you, then," said Andrew. "But there's still something the matter."

Nicky hugged herself tighter. Her arms started to ache where they crossed.

"Nothing's the matter. I'm fine."

Andrew shuffled his feet out to the side, scooting himself and his chair closer to Nicky.

"Now that I refuse to believe." Andrew took a small spin in his seat, traveling 360 degrees and stopping right where he started. "C'mon, you can tell me: I'm a dude in a chair. Everyone loves dudes in a chair."

Andrew spun around again. Nicky couldn't help but laugh. She closed her eyes and allowed the laugh to die down into a contented smile.

"It's because I'm leaving soon, isn't it," said Andrew.

"No..." Nicky started. She found herself hunching over where she stood, attempting in vain to make herself smaller.

"You're a terrible liar, just for the record," said Andrew.

"I'm not lying." Nicky shifted her weight from her heels to the balls of her feet.

"Evidence number two."

Nicky huffed and slung her head back. She avoided her brother's gaze and opted to stare at his ceiling instead.

Andrew scooted closer with his chair.

"Hey, I get it," he said. "It's all right. It's a huge change. You can be upset about it."

"I'm not upset about it."

"If it walks like a duck and talks like a duck... it really doesn't matter if it says it's not a duck."

Nicky broke out into a sudden laugh.

"What does that even mean?"

"It means that you can pretend all you want, but it won't make the feelings disappear," he said.

Nicky uncrossed her arms, only to grab her right wrist with her left hand.

"It's only an hour drive to the city, anyway," said Nicky. "It's not a big deal."

"Except for that part where it is a big deal," Andrew countered. After a moment, he added: "Hey, it'll be fine. I'll visit a ton. I'll call all the time. It'll be like I never even left."

"Except for that part where you did."

"I told you it bothers you," Andrew said with a gentle smirk.

Nicky shook her head and pushed her back against the doorframe.

"Whatever."

"It's going to be an adjustment, but you're a tough kid. And, really, this changes nothing," said Andrew. "No matter what, I'm always going to be there for you. I'm always going to be just a phone call away. Say the word and I'll be here."

Nicky said nothing and instead stared at the floor.

"And I'm going to check in. Make sure you're not getting into trouble," Andrew warned. "Mom's going to be my eyes and ears. If anything is off, I'll be back here in a heartbeat."

"Sure, whatever."

"And I need you to be my eyes and ears for Mom. Make sure she's on the straight and narrow, too. Do you think you can do that?"

"Because Mom really needs me looking after her," Nicky mocked.

"Hey, this is a big job," said Andrew. "I can understand if you're not up for it."

"I am up for it," said Nicky. "I just think it's a bogus job."

"Please, we all know this house would collapse into chaos

without me." Andrew *pushed himself backwards in his chair, his arms open wide.* "It's *going to take at least a team of two to pick up where I leave off."*

"Yeah, we're *all here purely because of you," Nicky jibed.*

"Prove *it otherwise and I'll believe you. Until then..."* Andrew *stood up and walked to his chest of drawers. Nicky found herself smiling, to the point that her cheeks were starting to hurt. Somewhere during that time, Nicky also found that she had started to cry as well.*

Without missing a beat, Andrew stepped over and wrapped Nicky in his arms. Nicky held onto her own torso as Andrew drew her in, but her head instinctively rested against Andrew's chest.

"You're *going to be okay, kiddo. You're going to be a-okay."*

"You *sound like that guy on that stupid crime show,"* Nicky *said half into his shirt.*

Andrew burst into a fit of hearty laughter. Nicky could hear his laugh ring in the air; she could hear it gather in his chest, and she could feel it as his belly moved along with the laughter.

"Yeah, you're *going to be just fine." Andrew took a step back and held Nicky's shoulders with his hands.* "And I mean it: *say the word and I'm here. Kids at school giving you trouble. Problems with homework. You can just want me to come over and watch TV with you, and I'll be here."*

"Promise?" Nicky *let her hands drop by her sides.*

"I promise," said Andrew. "Pinky *swear and everything."*

"It's *not a pinky swear unless you actually pinky swear."* Nicky *held one of her hands out, her pinky finger out and hooked.*

"Ah, c'mon, do I have *to?" Andrew asked with an exaggerated whine.* "C'mon, I can be the guy who invents the verbal pinky swear. I'll make millions."

"Fine," said Nicky. "But *only if you give me some of the millions."*

"You'll *be the first person I write a check to when that happens," said Andrew.* "Now, if there are any CDs you want to keep, you need to let me know now, because this entire collection is coming with me."

Andrew grabbed his chair and pushed it back to the desk.

"You are so weird," said Nicky, entering the room for the first time that afternoon.

***

"Maybe you should try inviting both of them out to do something," Laura suggested.

It was nearing May and Chicago was just starting to realize what season it was in. The tulips were in full bloom in Millennium Park. The lines for the Skydeck were picking back up. After months of prolonged cold and endless rain, the sidewalks were again walkable. Nicole wasn't isolated to the inside of her apartment or her cubicle or a train car anymore. She could wander the streets once more if she wanted to.

Andrew never brought up the bridesmaid debacle after that day in March. He also never brought up Cora's name, either. Conversations that were once simply tentative and timid were now strained and forced. Both parties talked to each other like they were counting down the seconds until the conversation was over. Phone calls were getting less and less frequent and more and more pragmatic. At some point, they started discussing things like the weather, like two acquaintances making small talk to fill the time.

"Maybe I should try getting a lobotomy," said Nicole, grinning sardonically to Laura. "Seems a lot easier."

"C'mon now," said Laura. "I know this has been a strange year, but you never know. I mean, what do you know about Cora?"

"Aside from the fact that she's read one too many bridal magazines?" Nicole replied.

"The engagement party was over the top, there's no doubt about that."

"The engagement party rivaled most people's weddings," Nicole clarified.

"I guess you haven't *really* lived until you've seen a pre-wedding bouquet toss," said Laura, mimicking Nicole's grin.

"Or a 'first dance as an engaged couple'," Nicole added.

"So, that was insane. No question about that," said Laura. "But, you've seen Cora, like, twice: that party and at the coffee shop – and that's about it. Maybe things would be less awkward if you got to know her a little better."

"What is there to know? She's all about her lavish wedding, she has no plans for the future..." Nicole moved the end of her straw around, stirring up the sugar at the bottom of her iced coffee. "And she wears head-to-toe fur."

"She owns at least one fur coat, yes," Laura countered. "I don't know, maybe it won't change anything. But at least you can say you tried, right?"

"I don't know." Nicole sat back in her seat and drummed the table. "I'm just exhausted by the whole thing. It still doesn't feel real."

"And if you start spending time with Cora, it might actually start feeling real?"

"Is it too much to hope for a break-up at the eleventh hour?" Nicole asked. "Or, like, a hurricane to touch down and force a wedding cancelation? Isn't hurricane season in the summer, anyway?"

"It was just a suggestion," said Laura. "I mean, you can do whatever it is that you feel is right. I just think a lot of this has been made worse by the fact that you haven't spent any time with Cora."

"No, no, you're right." Nicole sighed. "Unfortunately."

"It can always be a double date, like last time. No one's asking you to join Cora on a nail appointment. At least not yet."

"I refuse to pay someone $20 so they can put my hands in a bowl of water and then paint my nails when I can do that on my own," said Nicole. "I'd rather walk the streets in a full-length mink coat than pay good money to get a manicure."

"Spoken like the woman I love."

***

Nicole meant to call that evening and make plans with Andrew. She meant to call that next evening as well. And the next. And the next. And the next. Nicole returned to her phone time and time again, ready to call up Andrew and see what he wanted to do. But each time, she'd put her phone back down and find any excuse as to why the next day would be better suited for the phone call.

It wasn't until two weeks later, when her train was delayed due to traffic on the rails, that she finally attempted calling. It was early morning and her train had been stopped a few stories above street level. On impulse, she pulled out her phone and dialed Andrew's number. She didn't even realize that she had done it until she heard the ringing in her ear.

Part of her hoped that Andrew was sleeping in, or in class, or doing something – anything – that would keep him away from his phone. Suddenly, the idea of making plans to a voice messaging system seemed so desirable that she pressed her phone into her ear, praying she'd hear Andrew's automated message instead of his voice in real time.

"Hey there. How have you been?"

Nicole felt her heart sink. She twisted her body to face the window and ran a nervous hand through her hair.

"I'm good, I'm good. Uh, how about you?"

"Oh, you know, grading term papers," Andrew replied. "Been doing this nonstop since last Monday. Almost finished, though, so there's at least that. How about you?"

"Just going to work," said Nicole, twisting around so much she could almost see the people behind her. "My train's going nowhere, though."

"I can't tell you how happy I am that I don't have to take the train on a daily basis," he said. "Amazing weather we've been having, though, right? Finally stopped raining?"

"Yeah, finally stopped," Nicole repeated. "Hey, um, I wanted to ask if you were free this weekend or something."

"Um, I should be," said Andrew. "Why do you ask?"

"I, uh, was curious if you wanted to do something. Maybe go down to the Ohio Street Beach like we used to?"

"Yeah, that would be fun," said Andrew. "We haven't

hung out in ages."

Nicole smiled for a fleeting second before the corners of her mouth started to quiver.

"I figured it could be, like, a nice outing or something," Nicole continued. "You could bring Cora, I could bring Laura..."

"Heh, I just realized their names rhyme," said Andrew.

"Yeah, how about that." Nicole took a hard swallow and scratched the back of her neck. "And, I don't know, we could have, like, a barbecue, or something? Or maybe even just a walk, nothing big."

"Yeah, yeah, that would be fun, except..." Andrew trailed off.

"Except what?"

"Sorry, I tried to multi-task just now and it didn't work out." Andrew paused for a moment. "It's just that Cora is back in Florida right now."

"Why is she in Florida?" Nicole asked a little more abruptly than she would've liked.

"Because that's where she lives? Finals week is over for her, so she went back home."

"Oh," Nicole replied. She felt a sudden lurch as the train started moving forward. "When will she be back?"

"Not until her graduation ceremony, and that's in June," said Andrew, his voice suddenly more tense.

"Well, maybe we could plan for something around then?"

"Uh, I don't know, maybe," said Andrew. "I mean, she's coming up for the graduation ceremony and then flying right back to Florida for her graduation party."

"Will there be a red carpet and pink glitter for this party, too?" Nicole teased.

"Care to say that again?"

There was something in Andrew's voice – something angry and assertive – that made Nicole clamp her mouth shut. She had never heard Andrew talk like that before and it scared her to hear it.

"Nothing, just a bad joke," Nicole backtracked, her palms sweaty. "Um, but – hey – maybe I could go to the graduation ceremony with you, then. Keep you company while she gets her diploma. Maybe we'll have dinner or something?"

"There's already a dinner planned," Andrew replied with a chilled voice. "And tickets have already been purchased. Between the two of us, we were barely able to get enough tickets for her family. I was this close to not being able to attend."

"Wow, I'm sorry. Sorry I asked. Forget about it." Nicole stared out the window and at the rushing streets below and desperately wished she could be somewhere – anywhere – on those streets instead of where she was now. "I didn't realize Northwestern was so stingy about their tickets."

"That's not important. And even if they weren't, it's important for Cora's family to be there. All of them."

Nicole wanted to say something. She wanted to call out Andrew on how he was talking to her. She wanted to tell him how hard it was for her to even suggest an outing in the first place. There were so many different emotions welling up inside her that it was all she could do to not start crying on the phone and in the middle of her commute.

"That's okay. Fine. Perfectly fine," Nicole said, shaking her head to the beat of her own words. "I hope you guys have a good time at the ceremony. And uh... tell Cora I said congratulations?"

Andrew sighed in the phone and became silent. For a moment, Nicole thought she had lost the call.

"Will do," he said finally. "But, hey I really need to get back to these papers. I've been up since 6 and I'll probably be here until midnight. I'll talk to you later, okay?"

Nicole let her head rest against the window and closed her eyes.

"Okay. I'll talk with you later."

The weekend came and went. Plans to have a barbecue were dropped before they could be created. Nicole made it a point to go to the Ohio Street Beach by herself, walking around alone, listening to the waves crashing lightly onto the shore.

Chapter Eleven

PRE-WEDDING, PRE-REHEARSAL, PRE-CEREMONY PARTY

For a few precious seconds, Nicole thought she had woken up in Chicago. The bed under her felt exactly like her bed. The sheets and blankets felt exactly like her sheets and blankets. She blinked open her eyes into the darkness and swore she could even see her desk and her closet.

Reality settled in like a thick fog when Nicole sat up. Suddenly, she was back in the outskirts of Miami, on a flimsy mattress, in a motel room, her back facing the shabby metal door. Behind her, Laura was sleeping soundly in her own bed. One of her arms was tucked under the covers, while the other lay above her head, its fingers gently touching the headboard. The modest light coming in from around the window shade draped across Laura's body, making a perfect, slim rectangle that started at Laura's collarbone and ended just above her knees. The light from under the door sprawled across the carpet, ending just before it got to Nicole's bed. Nicole quietly crept out of the room, down the stairs, and back to the pool area.

Nicole went through to the gate entrance and found Ella by the corner's edge of the pool, her PJ pants rolled up to her thighs and her legs in the water.

"Well, good morning," said Ella, slowly kicking her legs back and forth. The water bubbled up over the edge of the pool, soaking the bottom of Ella's pajamas.

"And good morning to you, too." Nicole walked over to her cousin. She slipped off her flip-flops and dipped a toe in the water.

"Don't be hesitant. Just dive right in," Ella goaded. "And by 'dive' I mean 'sit down and put your feet in'."

Nicole placed her hands on the concrete and slowly sat herself down before inching her legs into the water.

"Shockingly cool, given how hot it is," Ella remarked.

"I'm not too concerned," Nicole said more to the water than to Ella.

"Any idea as to what's in store for today?" Ella asked.

"Vaguely," said Nicole. "I'm sure there's a written itinerary somewhere."

"On pink paper, with glitter," Ella added.

Nicole's lips drew back into a tense smile. She sat in silence, kicking the water in beat with Ella, welcoming the intermittent chills as the water lapped up onto her dry legs.

"You had a fun time at *my* reception, right?" Ella asked suddenly.

Nicole stopped moving her legs and crossed them at the ankles.

"Yeah, of course," Nicole answered, the water still rippling across her skin.

"Kevin's wrong about everything, by the way," Ella asserted. "Absolutely wrong. But still, even if he were right, I think I'd have a right to think this whole thing is unfair. Right?"

"Right," said Nicole.

"I've been working my *ass* off since high school. I've paid for *everything* myself. Of *all* the people in the world, those who work like dogs should be allowed to have something great, even if it's just for one day." Ella sighed, leaned over, and dipped her hands in the water. "I wasn't asking to ride in on an elephant or anything – just a break from the world, just for a second. And instead I got a town hall ceremony and a backyard reception in Long Island."

"I really did have fun at the reception," said Nicole.

"Yeah, but, like, *backyard barbecue* fun," Ella countered. "Not *wedding* fun. And the whole time I was stressed because I still had to sort out the issues with my student loans and I couldn't find a new job and I had all this stupid coursework still to do…" Ella pulled her hands out of the water and leaned back. "I never even got a honeymoon. And now Daddy's Little Rich Girl is having the wedding of her dreams without a care in the world. I'm sorry if it makes me sound bitter, but that's just not fair."

"I'm sorry," was all Nicole could say.

"And even if I *did* have a huge wedding – even if I *did* rely on Daddy's money all the time – I would still be speaking up about this circus," Ella continued. "Just because she's marrying Andrew, it doesn't mean that we all have to pretend that we like her. I don't even *know* her. And, from what I see, I am *glad* I don't. I'm not going to act like everything is perfectly normal when *obviously* it's not."

"I hear you," said Nicole. "I really, really do."

"I mean…" Ella turned to Nicole. "Do *you* like her?"

"Cora?" Nicole asked.

"No, the waitress from the restaurant," said Ella. "Of *course* Cora."

"I don't know," said Nicole, watching her toes wiggle through the water. "I mean, like you said: I don't really even know her. But then again, she hasn't given me any *reason* to. And, I mean, it's very clear that this is her wedding, not Andrew's."

"The best man is *Cora's brother*, for crying out loud." Ella rolled her eyes. "Who doesn't let the groom pick his best man?"

Nicole huffed slightly and smiled.

"To be honest, I thought it was going to be Kevin. For best man, I mean," said Nicole. "They were thick as thieves before you guys moved to New York. And even then."

"Honestly?" Ella turned to Nicole. "I thought it was going to be you."

Nicole pressed her lips together and said nothing.

"And who has a *two* maids of honor?" Ella continued. "There is no way Cora is at all close to all of those bridesmaids."

"And yet I wasn't even considered to be one," Nicole replied, before reflexively grimacing.

"Well, like I said before: you dodged a bullet, there. God knows what hoops they've had to jump through as bridesmaids," said Ella.

Nicole clamped her fingers around the edge of the pool and tilted her head further down toward the water.

"I once had a friend in undergrad who got married just like Cora," Ella continued. "Even forced the groom to have her own *dad* be the best man. I saw the pictures of the ceremony; it looked horrifying. All that was missing was a shotgun in the dad's hands. I was asked to be a bridesmaid, but I declined because of school." Ella huffed and rolled her eyes. "I decline *everything* because of school. But, anyway: the wrath that I incurred from her because I said, 'no,' was insane. Made me feel terrible. But *apparently* it was nothing compared to what she put her bridesmaids through. From 'planning parties', where – no lie – all they did was sit around helping her come up with wedding ideas, to weekly weigh-ins, to making her bridesmaids swear that they'd run everything from a tattoo to a haircut by her first. Absolute bridezilla."

Ella lifted one of her feet out of the water before immediately splashing it back under.

"Then she had the audacity to denounce bridezillas after her wedding and swear that she was never like *those* crazy bitches."

Nicole laughed.

"Well, I guess things could be worse," Nicole said.

"Things could *always* be worse," said Ella. Ella leaned back further, craning her neck as she stared up and over and into the parking lot. She tilted her head away from Nicole and took in a slow breath.

"Y'know, that street looks busy enough," she said, her voice half as loud as it was before. "I bet we could hail a taxi pretty easily."

"Why would we hail a taxi?" Nicole asked.

Ella sat up and brought her face close to Nicole's.

"Why *wouldn't* we?" she asked. "We're in Miami, and instead of going east to the beach, we're going west to

Crazy Town, USA. And to do what, exactly? Stand around awkwardly while Sue-Anne makes a spectacle out of herself?" Ella looked around before adding: "What if we played hooky today? Go downtown, go shopping. Go to the *beach*. The Atlantic Ocean is right there, for crying out loud."

Nicole watched her toes wiggle faster. She thought about Sue-Anne parading around. She thought about Rachel barking orders at everyone. She thought about Sarah showing off her fake engagement ring and trying on wedding dresses. She thought about the sea of people she barely knew or didn't know at all. She thought about the fact that she hadn't had a chance to say a single word to the people she *did* know. She thought about another day cornered off while everyone else stood around and talked about absolutely nothing and acted like they had never been happier in their entire lives.

"Isn't there a party we need to go to or something?" Nicole said finally.

Ella scoffed.

"Yeah, like some pre-rehearsal, pre-pre-wedding, post-bridal shower extravaganza." Ella rolled her eyes. "I doubt we'd miss much."

Nicole looked up at the sky. A pale shade of green stretched across the horizon before fading into blue. Aside from a few wisps directly above, there was barely a cloud in the sky.

"I don't know if we should miss it," Nicole said slowly. "I feel like we'd piss off a lot of people."

Ella shrugged.

"Then we get back in time for it. Even if we just go until lunch, that's like, what, five hours where we don't have to watch the wedding madness unfold?" Ella argued. "I think we deserve at least that."

Nicole pulled her legs out of the water and hugged them to her chest. Water rolled onto her PJ shorts as her hands touched her wet shins. She closed her eyes and imagined getting breakfast again at the Jasonson diner in East Braedonton. She thought about the waitress finding ways to call her a "yank". She thought about spending the morning sitting around while Andrew continued to avoid her.

"I'm in," Nicole said at last.

"What, really?" Ella coughed. "You're in?"

Now it was Nicole's turn to shrug.

"Just as long as we're back in time for that party thing," said Nicole. "I mean, what's the harm? It's not like there are any set plans before then, anyway."

Ella smiled so broadly that her upper lip curled into her gums.

"I like the way you think." Ella hopped out of the water with such a force that it splashed Nicole. "We should probably get ready before anyone else gets up."

Nicole nodded and stood.

"And maybe change into actual clothes," Nicole added. "I doubt we'd be allowed in any stores with PJs that smell like chlorine."

"It *is* Miami," Ella said with a smirk.

Together, they left the pool area, went up the stairs, and traveled down the second-floor walkway.

"Meet you in ten?" Ella asked, her voice now in a whisper.

"Works for me," Nicole answered. As if on cue, both slowly turned their respective doorknobs and quietly opened their doors.

Nicole stepped into the same dark room as before. The light from the doorway spilled onto Laura's bed, turning the tiny sliver into a spotlight. For a brief second, Nicole considered gently nudging her awake. Maybe they'd get ready together and sneak out onto the main street. She stared at her girlfriend for a little while longer, before imagining Laura's hesitant face, before imagining Laura telling Nicole not to go, before imagining the case Laura would make for staying around to deal with Cora and her mother and everyone else.

Nicole closed the door behind her and changed in the darkness.

***

It didn't take too much work to catch a cab. While the road wasn't as busy as Ella had thought, they were eventually able to flag down an empty cab traveling down their road.

"You know you can just call a cab?" the driver said as the girls got in the back seat. "It's a lot faster in neighborhoods like this, especially at this time of day."

"Oh, yeah." Ella gave a sheepish, embarrassed smile. She scratched the back of her neck. "I guess I didn't think of that."

"Where to?" the cabbie asked, not missing a beat.

"Downtown," Ella answered.

"Any street? Building? Store?" The cab driver wrapped his arm around the back of the passenger side seat, his knuckles resting gently against the glass dividing the front seats from the back. "Any place in particular?"

"Uh, just downtown," said Ella. "We'll figure it out from there."

***

Ella and Nicole wandered the streets of Miami before stopping inside a café. They ate a quick breakfast inside and ordered coffees to go. With their hands wrapped around their disposable coffee cups, they strolled around some more before hailing another taxi.

"Where to?" the cabbie asked.

"The beach," Ella asked.

"Like… South Beach?" The cabbie turned and stared at Ella.

"Whatever beach in Miami, sure," Ella countered.

The cabbie laughed and shook his head.

"Not from around here, are you?"

"Um… what makes you say that?" Ella asked slowly.

The cabbie laughed again and flipped the switch on his fare box.

"I'll take you to Miami Beach," he said, pulling out onto the road. "Different town than Miami. But I'll take you there. No problems."

Nicole kept her eyes on the road as they drove across a long stretch of bridge. The Miami skyline slowly shifted away from them as they crossed over into Miami Beach. The cab driver dropped them off at a park across the street from a long strip of restaurants. Ella paid the fare and grabbed Nicole's hand as they made their way through the park and to the shoreline.

As the rest of the world started to wake up, Nicole and Ella dipped their toes in the warm Atlantic water and stared off into the horizon. To their left was a string of high-rise apartments. A few people were already out on their balconies, sitting in patio furniture and sipping from ceramic mugs. Nicole wiggled her toes into the sand, sinking them in.

Nicole thought she could fall asleep standing up, watching the waves come in. She closed her eyes, took in a deep breath, and smiled. Within moments, a beeping noise went off in Nicole's purse.

"They've figured out we're gone," said Nicole, glancing sideways at Ella.

"They can deal," Ella dismissed.

Nicole smiled and stared lazily out at the water. Her phone dinged at her again before playing out its ringtone in full.

"That's going to get annoying," said Nicole, her eyes on the water.

"Then turn off your phone," said Ella. "In fact, before Mom can get on my butt, I'm going to do the same."

"Good idea." Nicole reached into her bag and fished out her phone. She stared at her screen: two text messages and a missed call from Laura. She glanced surreptitiously at Ella before moving her phone to her hip. Nicole looked down at the screen just long enough to type out a message to Laura that read: "In Miami. Be back in time for the party."

Nicole glanced one last time at Ella before hitting send, turning off her phone, and shoving it to the bottom of her purse.

***

For the first time in a long while, Nicole was walking around with a smile on her face. She strolled down the beach with Ella, humming along to the songs pouring out of passing cars, before catching a taxi back to downtown

Miami. They wandered the streets before stepping into a boutique, trying on overpriced outfits and holding up overpriced purses.

Ever since she had touched down in Florida, Nicole had felt weightless, like she was barely there, like she could blow away at any moment. In Miami, shopping with her cousin – as if the entire trip were nothing more than a girl's weekend in Florida – she felt like her feet were finally planted on the ground.

"I wish we had brought our bathing suits," said Ella as they browsed through the boutique. "That water is *so warm*. You just don't get that in the northeast."

"Lake Michigan's no better," Nicole responded. "That's definitely one thing the South has over us."

"Please." Ella pulled out a dress from the rack and surveyed it. "For the last time: this is not the South. This is Miami. And East Braedonton is in the Twilight Zone."

Nicole rubbed her finger and thumb across the fabric of one shirt. Her smile slowly flattened out.

"We should probably head back soon," Nicole said, looking down at the shirt.

Ella threw her head back and made a face.

"Five more minutes, Mom," Ella whined. "Please?"

"We're probably in enough trouble as it is," said Nicole. "It's only going to get worse if we miss the party."

"But we'll have to hear about it for a longer period of time if we get back early," said Ella. Ella held the dress to her torso, spinning around with it before placing it back on the rack. "Tell you what: we can finish up at this store, grab lunch, and hail a taxi back. We can even take the taxi straight to Cora's house. No harm, no foul."

Nicole unhooked the shirt she had been touching from its hanger and held it up above her head.

"I guess another hour couldn't hurt."

Ella smiled and continued to browse through the clothing, tenderly picking out various dresses. After trying a few on, Ella took a dress to the front. Nicole raised an eyebrow.

"What? Given what we've had to put up with, I think I've earned it," Ella said, handing her credit card to the cashier. "It's nice to live like the other half from time to time."

"Makes sense," said Nicole, as she watched the cashier neatly fold the dress and place it in its bag.

After Ella's purchase, they went across the street to an Argentinian steakhouse, where Ella pretended to agonize over the different meats and dishes before settling on a salad and water. Nicole order the same and nibbled tentatively. Ella paid for lunch with the same credit card and they both went back out into the street.

Ella had no problems flagging down another taxi. As the taxi pulled up in front of the steakhouse, Nicole walked around to the opposite door, her hands trailing across the cab as she moved.

"14 Richmond Boulevard, East Braedonton," Ella instructed to the driver.

The cab driver turned around and cocked an eyebrow at Ella.

"Come again, lady?"

"That's the address, right, Nicole?" Ella asked. "14 Richmond Boulevard? I remember that because, hello, rich-man. Cora's daddy is obviously loaded if he can afford a house like that."

Nicole shrugged her shoulders.

"Sure, yeah."

Ella tilted her head back to the cab driver.

"Yeah, 14 Richmond Boulevard in East Braedonton," Ella repeated.

"Lady, we don't go to East Braedonton."

"But, it's like, *right there*." Ella pointed to the right with both hands, as if East Braedonton was in the steakhouse.

"I can take you anywhere else – Coral Springs, Hialeah – hell, if you want Fort Lauderdale, we'll go to Fort Lauderdale. But no cabbie is going to take you to East Braedonton. No matter what."

"Are you guys scared of the town or something?" Ella asked mockingly. Nicole shot Ella a look that went completely ignored.

The cabbie laughed.

"I ain't afraid of East Braedonton. Wouldn't catch me dead there unless you paid me, but I ain't afraid of it. Nah, it's against the law in that town. Says it goes against their overall 'look' or whatever."

"So there is no way I can get you to go to East Braedonton," said Ella. "What if I paid you double?"

"Ain't worth the fines, ma'am," said the cab driver. "Ain't worth the fines."

"Well, this is going to be awkward." Ella sat back in her seat. "Then drive us to the Oasis Motel."

"Whatever you say." The cab driver flicked his blinker and pulled into traffic.

"Thank you, sir," Nicole added quietly.

"No problem, ma'am," the cab driver muttered.

Ella reached into her bag and pulled out her phone. She turned it back on and immediately started calling someone. She crossed her legs, hooked her free hand into the cook of her elbow, and tilted her head back.

"Hey, Kevin?" she said. "Yeah, yeah, yeah, I get it. Okay, yeah. Whatever. You can berate me all you want later. Listen, I need you to pick me up at the motel soon. Can you do that?"

***

"I hope you have your explanations ready."

Kevin looked back at the two girls. Both were looking down at their seats and seatbelt straps, as if buckling themselves in required all of their concentration. Even after she was set, Nicole kept her eyes down, avoiding Laura's stare from the passenger side.

"We just wanted to have some fun," said Ella.

"Dad thought you had gotten kidnapped," Kevin continued, pulling out from the parking lot. "If Nicole hadn't said anything to Laura, he probably would've called the police."

Ella shot a bewildered look at Nicole.

"I didn't want them to worry," said Nicole.

"Well, it didn't work. Everyone's still worried," said Kevin. "We did everything we could to minimize your absence." At a stop sign, Kevin turned his body all the way around so he could lock eyes with Ella. "It's time to realize this week is not and will not be about you."

"I'm not trying to make it about me," Ella snapped. "I just wanted to have some fun. If I'm going to use vacation time, I should be allowed to at least have *some* vacation, right?"

"By completely going AWOL?"

"By actually enjoying the city we're in," Ella corrected. "Sorry for not alerting the presses first."

Kevin went silent, his knuckles turning white as he throttled the steering wheel. Nicole looked over to see Laura staring out the passenger side window, her body leaning against the door.

"We told the Bachmans that you slept in," Kevin said at last. "That all the excitement from yesterday wore you out and you were feeling a little sick."

"You got the 'sick' part right," Ella replied.

"Enough." The volume of Kevin's voice stayed the same, but the force behind his words was enough to clamp Ella's mouth shut. They drove in silence, past the fields, past the orange groves, past the downtown area, and into Cora's neighborhood. The next time Kevin spoke, it was to the intercom system at the front gate.

As he eased into the cul de sac, Jennifer came out to meet them with her eerie, formal smile.

"They're out back," she said. "Would y'all like me to show y'all before I park y'all's car?"

"We'll be fine." Kevin flashed her a warm smile and handed her the keys.

Ella slid open the side door and poured herself onto the driveway. Nicole followed suit, stepping out of the van before locking eyes with Laura, who was slowly closing the passenger door behind her.

"What?" Nicole said, instinctively leaning back.

Laura pressed her lips together and scanned the ground. She looked up and opened her mouth, but nothing came out. After a moment, Laura just shook her head, turned, and walked towards the backyard.

"Oh, come on," said Nicole, catching up to Laura. "It's no big deal. Ella thought it would be fun to sneak out and have a morning in Miami. In *actual* Miami."

"You snuck out," Laura paraphrased. "And you see nothing wrong with that? How is that not a big deal to you?"

"If it's because I didn't invite you, then I'm sorry." Nicole huffed slightly, going at a near jog to keep up with Laura. "Next time I'll wake you up or something."

"That's not it," Laura said softly. "That's not it at all."

"Then what is it?"

"There's the sleepyheads!" Uncle Pete said with too much gusto. "How are you guys feeling?"

As if on cue, Laura immediately fell back, walking at half the speed she had been doing before.

"Better," Nicole replied with a weak smile. "Thanks for asking."

Nicole could see her mom and Aunt Barbara – along with Sue-Anne – bringing up the rear behind Uncle Pete.

"You missed out on a wonderful brunch," Uncle Pete went on. "Lovely brunch, right out here on the patio. Everything you could've imagined. Very delicious."

"Sorry we missed out," said Nicole, staring at her uncle's shirt instead of his eyes.

"Oh, no harm, no foul, right?" Uncle Pete asked, his voice slightly pleading, as if he was genuinely curious if there had been no harm and no foul. Nicole looked over at Ella, whose arms were crossed and eyes locked on the ground.

"Of course," Nicole replied.

"There y'all are!" Sue-Anne sang, her arms wide. She pulled Nicole in for a tight embrace and immediately pushed her back before going over to hug Ella. "Your daddy said y'all were feelin' under the weather. Nothin' contagious I hope, right?"

"Just some jet lag," said Ella.

"Well, it's a long flight from – where did y'all come from again?"

"New York," Ella said flatly. "A lot to adjust to, flying from New York to here."

"Well, we're just happy you're here now," Nicole's mom said from behind Sue-Anne. Aunt Barbara said nothing and instead crossed her arms in the same fashion as Ella.

"Well, enough living in the past." Sue-Anne clapped her hands and motioned towards the porch. "Y'all're just in time to help with decorations."

"Decorations?" Nicole repeated.

"For the pre-wedding, rehearsal eve party," Sue-Anne answered. "Didn't you read your invitation packet?"

"Cover to cover," Ella muttered with a smirk.

"Come again, darlin'?" Sue-Anne asked.

Ella's head snapped up towards Sue-Anne. She immediately put on a broad, insincere smile.

"I said: 'how can we help?'"

"Well, come this way, then." Sue-Anne twirled, turning her back to the girls and facing the backyard again. "I'm sure we can find use for y'all."

Nicole glanced back at Laura, who had stationed herself next to Kevin. Laura returned Nicole's gaze with a look that made Nicole want to crawl inside herself. It wasn't a look of anger, it wasn't a look of sadness... Nicole couldn't put her finger on it, but it cut her to the core. She turned back around and walked down the gravel path.

Nicole had prepared herself for the group in the backyard to go silent at her arrival, giving her the stink eye before turning back to their conversations. What she wasn't prepared for was the complete apathy. Jacob and Evan were chatting by themselves, with Karen off to the side, texting away with her back to the two. Rachel was dragging the two wedding planners around the pool, pointing to different corners and barking unintelligible orders at them. Sarah was sitting by herself, twisting her fake engagement ring and starring longingly at her hand. The rest of the wedding party was standing in a circle, holding onto stemware and laughing loudly. In the midst of that group stood Andrew and Cora. Cora laughed and touched Andrew's arm. Andrew smiled absently as he looked just above her.

"I know it seems in poor taste, what with making y'all help and all," Sue-Anne said as she walked up the porch steps. "It wasn't our first choice, believe you me. The weddin' planners hadn't anticipated the rehearsal eve party and forgot to book the decorators for today. We considered firin' 'em based on that gross bit of incompetence, but then we decided that it was a blessin' in disguise. I mean, why not make it a family effort? What's a party if you don't personally have a hand in it?"

Nicole stared at Andrew, hoping he'd look her way. When it was obvious that he was going to look at everything *but* her, Nicole found a seat under the pergola and sat down. Ella followed suit and sat on the lounge chair next to her.

"I'm not trying to say I told you so, but we would've been better off just staying out the whole day," Ella said quietly.

Nicole sighed.

"You're not wrong."

***

Everyone was designated to a different area of the house to decorate, with very specific instructions by Rachel. Nicole was paired with Karen and Ashley – the two girls from Cora's sorority – and Susanna – Cora's older sister – to decorate the octagonal parlor room, which was currently filled with stacks upon stacks of cardboard boxes.

Rachel opened the boxes and inspected each before giving directions.

"The garlands need to be hung from every corner at *exactly* the same height, which is *exactly* 13.35 inches," said Rachel, her fast-talk turning her accent into something unrecognizable. "Is that clear?"

"Makes sense to me," said Susanna.

"When it comes to the hanging pom-poms, they *need* to be equidistant from each other on the ceiling. But make sure to mix up sizes. I don't want to see a single large pom-pom next to another large pom-pom," Rachel continued. She pulled out a roll of clear tape from her pocket and thrusted it at Susanna. "This is the *only* tape you're allowed to use. I don't want to see anything else. No packing tape, no wrapping tape, and certainly no duct tape. Use small squares and make sure you press out any air bubbles. You destroy the magic if you make the tape visible. Is that clear?"

"I got it," Susanna said.

Rachel immediately stepped forward to Ashley and

Karen. Karen hid her phone behind her back and gave Rachel a nervous smile.

"I'm sorry, but are my orders interrupting your constant texting?" Rachel cocked her head to one side.

"No, no. I heard everything you said," Karen replied, her voice oddly airy and ethereal.

"Then what did I say?" Rachel asked, her eyes narrowed.

"Um, hang up the garlands... and the pom-poms... um..." Karen looked around and swallowed hard. "I got the gist of it. I really did."

"The 'gist' is for mediocre people and mediocre weddings. *This* is neither," said Rachel. "What the hell is so important that you have to glue your nose to your cellphone?"

"Just – just my boyfriend," Karen explained. "He went abroad this year and—"

"I don't care if he's a spy for the American government," Rachel snapped. "Put your phone away or I'll take it away."

Karen dropped her eyes to the ground and slipped her phone into her back pocket.

"So, let's see..." Rachel pulled out her clipboard from under her arm and scanned the paper again. "I've discussed the garlands, the pom-poms – oh, and every table needs a white tablecloth with a crystal centerpiece in the center. Understand me? Equidistant from every edge. Hence the 'center' in centerpiece. I want the tablecloths put on right and I want the centerpieces in the actual center. If anything is off, I'll have everyone's head."

"We got this, hon," Ashley added, her genuine country-western accent a welcomed change. "If we have any questions, I'm sure we can find you."

"There's a lot of rooms, a lot of preparation, and the party is in five hours. I'll be too busy with catering to hold your hand as you hang up a decoration." Rachel hugged her clipboard to her chest and started pointing at various things in the room. "Garlands, pom-poms, tablecloths, centerpieces. Oh – and those tablecloths better be wrinkle- and fold-free. If they're not, use the steamer, which we're keeping in the laundry room. And bring the tablecloths there. Do *not* take the steamer out of the laundry room. I will decapitate the first person who does. Got it?"

Nicole pursed her lips together as her eyes darted towards the door.

"Alright. Get to it and I'll be back in a few to make sure everything hasn't gone completely to hell."

Rachel spun on her heels and marched out of the room.

The four of them just stood there at first, surveying the room as if a tornado had gone through it. Eventually Susanna stepped forward, opened the flaps of the first box, and picked up a garland.

"Who wants to help me with this?" she asked, the garland hanging limply in her hand. Karen snuck out her phone, typed wildly, and pushed the phone back into her pocket.

Nicole grabbed a handful of the pom-poms and dragged a chair into the center of the room. She cut a few squares of tape and began sticking the strings to the ceiling.

"I wish we all could go the same speed as you," Ashley remarked, holding a pom-pom as Karen stepped up onto a chair. "We'd be done with time to spare."

"Heh, I guess," Nicole mumbled with a sheepish grin. "I figured the sooner we're done, the better."

"Oh, it's tedious work, no doubt, but it's for a good cause."

"A pre-rehearsal party is a good cause?" Nicole found herself saying.

"Cora's gettin' married. This is her week." Ashley steadied the chair as Karen secured the pom-pom to the ceiling. "Tradition is important, especially to Kappa Kappa Kappa sisters. We'd do everything in our power to protect that."

Nicole made a noise that sounded a bit like, "Huh," as she pressed out the air bubbles in the tape.

"I can only hope that my K-cubed gals will do the same for me when it's my time to get married," Ashley continued. "It's hard and thankless work, but it's worth it."

"Well, Darrell might propose when he comes back

from Spain," said Karen. "And you and Cora will obviously be bridesmaids."

"I hope he does, hon, I really do." Ashley stepped away from the chair and picked up a garland at one end. "Just be careful. Hopefully all that time in Spain won't be a bad influence on him."

Karen took the opportunity to check her phone again before stepping down for more pom-poms.

Nicole pressed her last pom-pom string into the ceiling before walking over to the box of linens. She pulled out the first tablecloth, hugged it to her chest, and – with it still folded – made her way to where the steamer was. She vaguely remembered seeing the laundry room during Sue-Anne's tour.

But, really: if she got lost and found herself wandering around for hours instead, then all the better.

Nicole kept her eyes on the ground as she walked through the house, hoping to avoid establishing eye contact or catching the attention of anyone. Out of the corner of her eye, Nicole could see the crowds of people putting up decorations throughout the house. Streamers were twirled and taped into corners. The kids who were part of the wedding party (flower girls? Junior bridesmaids? Ringbearers? Junior groomsmen?) were in one corner polishing silver with fluffy white cloths. Nicole turned down another hallway and the laundry room soon came into view. With a surreptitious glance at the festivities going on behind her, Nicole stepped into the room.

"Fancy meeting you here."

Andrew stood in front of the dryer, his back to Nicole, a dress shirt held tautly in both hands. Once he established eye contact with Nicole, Andrew turned back around to the shirt.

"And likewise," Nicole replied, hugging the linen closer to her chest. "What brings you to the laundry room?"

"I have a bit of a dress shirt emergency," Andrew said, looking at the shirt. "I'm learning the hard way that there's a reason why I only wear t-shirts." Andrew let go of the shirt with one hand and batted at the ends of the shirt, which, as Nicole now saw, were starting to curl up. "Honestly, who makes clothing dry clean only? It's just unfair."

"It's all a scam," said Nicole with a shrug and a smile. "I'm sure all the high-end stores get a kickback or something. It's a conspiracy created by Big Laundromat."

"I think you might be onto something," said Andrew with a slight chuckle, brushing at the ends of the shirt one more time before shaking it out and setting it on top of the dryer. "What about you? What brings you in here?"

Nicole loosened her grip on the linen, letting all but one corner topple to the ground.

"I'm on steamer duty," she answered, gesturing with the linen.

Andrew stepped back.

"Well, don't let me interrupt the steaming duties."

"Did you just say 'steaming doody'?" Nicole asked, a wicked grin on her face.

"Oh wow. How did I miss that?" Andrew said with a laugh. He shook his head and laughed some more. "If that's the case I *really* don't want to interrupt your steaming duties."

Nicole laughed as well. She took another step into the laundry room and scanned the area.

"So this might not be as embarrassing as a steaming doody, but I have no idea where the steamer is."

Andrew looked around.

"I don't even know what a steamer is supposed to look like, to be perfectly honest," said Andrew.

"Well, if I find it, I'll let you know," Nicole replied. "I don't know much about dry clean only clothing, but a steamer might help you with your shirt."

"Crisis potentially averted, then. I appreciate that."

Nicole sighed and smiled and glanced down at the tablecloth. Now unfolded, the linen was practically crease- and wrinkle-free.

"It's become quite the madhouse here," said Nicole.

"There's a lot to get done before the rehearsal eve party," Andrew answered.

Nicole shook her head.

"Rehearsal eve party," she muttered and rolled her

eyes.

"Care to elaborate?" Andrew asked.

"C'mon, you have to admit that the whole concept of a 'rehearsal eve party' is a little silly," said Nicole.

"It's a big deal to Cora, and to Cora's family," Andrew replied, his voice sharp. "And it's important to me."

Nicole bit her tongue and cast her eyes to the floor. Part of her wanted to apologize; another part of her wanted to shake Andrew.

"I think the steamer is that thing in the corner," Nicole said finally.

Andrew stepped to the side and looked into the back corner.

"Well! Now I know what a steamer looks like," he said, his hands in his back pockets. "I'll give you space to steam. I think I need some time away from that shirt, anyway."

"I'm sure there are bigger things to get done right now, anyway," Nicole replied, trying in vain to keep her tone neutral.

"Well, that's the shirt I'm wearing tonight, so it *is* a pretty big deal," said Andrew. Nicole couldn't be sure, but she thought she could detect venom in his voice.

Nicole shuffled to the side, away from Andrew, the linen bunching in her hands, before walking over to the steamer.

"I'm sure it'll be fine," Nicole said finally, draping the tablecloth over the bent metal that ran alongside the steamer's stand. "Do you want me to find you when I'm done with the steamer?"

"Ah, I'll be fine," Andrew answered. "You're right: there's a lot to get done right now. I'm sure I can be of service somewhere."

Nicole turned to the steamer and cringed.

"Have fun, then," she answered, turning on the machine.

And like that, Nicole was alone in the room. She stared at the machine, waiting for the steam to come out of the handheld. It wasn't until the steamer sputtered at her that she realized there wasn't even any water in the machine in the first place.

***

The van ride back to the motel was tense, filled with a suffocating silence. They had left the house after decorating to change into more formal wear for the night. Nicole stared at the road, the houses, the passing trees, doing her best to avoid eye contact. She didn't want to look at anyone – not her mom, not Ella, and certainly not Laura. She sat in place and gripped her knees, feeling like she could barely stay in her own skin.

"I hope that was the worst of it," Aunt Barbara said after they passed the East Braedonton border. "I don't know what has gotten into you and I'm not a fan of it."

Ella sighed and continued to look out the window.

"And Nicole, I expected better from you," she continued.

"I'm sorry, Aunt Barbara," Nicole mumbled into her lap.

"At least you're apologizing," said Aunt Barbara. "Can't say the same for my own daughter."

Ella rolled her eyes and shook her head.

"Y'know, I might've expected that behavior from you 10 years ago," Aunt Barbara continued, her eyes fixed on Ella through the rearview mirror. "But you're an adult now. Act like it."

"Whatever," Ella breathed out.

"And if you're going to start acting like a teenager again, I can start treating you like one," Aunt Barbara said, her voice startlingly cold. "You're not too old to get grounded."

Ella crossed her arms and tilted her head away from the window.

"Look around you. I'm already grounded," she said, echoing her mom's icy tone.

Nicole kept her eyes fixed on the motel as it gracefully came into view. She bit the inside of her lip as Aunt Barbara parked the van and she waited until everyone was already out before undoing her seatbelt. In silence, she followed Laura up the stairs and into their room. Nicole took two steps in and gently closed the door behind her,

her hand still clasped around the doorknob, as if she was preparing for a quick escape.

"What was that all about?" Laura asked as soon as the door to their room latched.

Nicole caught her breath before looking away. She removed her hand from the doorknob.

"It's not that big of a deal," she said. "We just wanted to enjoy Miami. We've been spending all this time in the outskirts of it, so we figured, 'why not?'"

"So... you snuck off, ignored my calls, ignored my texts... so you could go to the beach?" Laura slowly drew out.

Nicole licked her lips and found that her mouth had gone dry.

"It was spur of the moment. We didn't mean any harm by it."

"Your brother is getting married in two days and you decide to go *missing*?" Laura paused and pressed her lips together. "I don't get why you felt like you had to hide from me like that."

"I wasn't hiding. I was just..." Nicole wracked her mind for what to say next. "It was just a... a thing."

"Did you think I was going to hold you hostage, or something?" Laura asked. "If you really needed to go do something with your cousin, I wouldn't have been offended. You know I'm not that type of girlfriend." Laura paused again and shook her head. "I get it. This isn't exactly the most relaxing situation. But you snuck away. You ignored me. Do you have any idea how that makes me feel?"

"It wasn't like I was trying to hurt you," Nicole said. "I just... I don't know. I wasn't thinking. I just wanted to get away."

"That seems to be the common theme as of late," Laura muttered.

Nicole felt her face get hot.

"What's that supposed to mean?" Nicole snapped.

"Nothing. Nothing at all," Laura quickly retracted. "That was a snarky and unnecessary comment and I'm sorry."

Nicole rubbed her eyes. She felt a sudden wave of

exhaustion, a weariness that rested in her bones.

"It's okay," she said. "I'm sorry, too. I shouldn't have snuck off like that."

Laura let out a smile that seemed to match the fatigue Nicole felt.

"We can always change our flights and spend an extra day here, after the wedding," Laura offered. "Then we can actually enjoy Miami, guilt-free. No one in East Braedonton has to know."

"I like your thinking," said Nicole. "But I think I'm in enough trouble at work. We'll have to save it for another time."

"Then we save it for another time," said Laura. "Or, maybe tonight after the party we can ask to borrow the van and drive in for the evening."

"And the ideas just keep on coming," Nicole said.

"Mama always said: when it comes to good ideas, I'm full of it."

Nicole snorted out a laugh.

"Call me crazy, but I doubt your mom ever said that."

"She could've," Laura reasoned. "In between all those, 'why won't you take ballet like your sisters,' or, 'can't you just find a nice boy to date?'"

Laura dramatically clasped her hands together as she drooped her shoulders and shook her head and looked up at the ceiling. Nicole broke into a huge smile. Laura dropped her act and gazed at Nicole, her lips slowly moving into a warm grin.

"I think we better get ready for the rehearsal eve party," Laura added after a moment. "It would be a pity if we were late, especially after all that hard work we put into decorating the house."

"Oh, don't remind me." Nicole grimaced, feigning a wound to the heart. "I'm going to have nightmares of paper machete pom-poms for years to come."

"At least you weren't stuck on dusting duty," Laura offered. "Speaking of, I definitely need a shower before we leave this room." Laura turned and started walking to the bathroom. "There's always room for one more, if you're interested."

Nicole looked over, past Laura, at the mirror in the

bathroom, at her own reflection, before shaking her head.

"Tempting, but I'll have to take a rain check," Nicole answered. "I might try to take a quick nap instead."

"Well, if this isn't a sign we've become that old married couple, I don't know what is," Laura chided with a smirk before walking into the bathroom and closing the door behind her.

Nicole sat down on the bed and closed her eyes, listening to the muffled sound of water from the showerhead hitting the porcelain tub. Her body softened for a brief moment, her eyelids drooping as she let out a long exhale. She glanced over to the left, her eyes falling on her suitcase. She immediately tensed up, and did her best to stifle the compulsion to call up the taxi service and have dinner in Miami Beach instead.

***

Dusk had already settled and the house was brilliantly lit up when they returned to Cora's family's estate. They looped around the small cul de sac in front of the house, this time greeted by a team of young men in suits. One man politely asked for the keys and drove off with the van while another ushered them around to the backyard.

Nicole was shocked by how many people now littered the lot. There had been an overcrowded feeling in the yard when it was just the wedding party and family. Now the area felt outright overpopulated. She was surrounded by hordes and hordes of people, all standing around in small circles, chatting and laughing idly as another set of men in suits drifted from group to group, presenting trays of all sorts of h'ors deuvres. A few of the faces looked familiar – Nicole vaguely recognized them from the Chicago engagement party – but, for the most part, everyone was completely alien to her.

The entire backyard was drenched in white crepe paper. Streamers twisted and crisscrossed above the pool while paper roses adorned everything from the bushes to the tables. White Christmas lights raveled their way around pedestals and trees, gently looping from one treetop to another. A round white table now accented the center of the patio. On top was a vast assortment of foods surrounding a large ice sculpture of a swan.

"How is that not melting in the heat?" Ella asked, looking at the ice swan.

"Let's see if we can find Andrew," Mrs. Winger said as she was accepting a mini sandwich from one of the boys in a suit.

"How are *they* not melting in the heat?" Ella added, staring at the catering guy.

"He's probably somewhere inside, I imagine," said Aunt Barbara.

The inside of the house was even louder and busier, to the point that it made Nicole wish she could retreat back out. There was barely a free inch of space. Everything felt squished. The kitchen had been redone into a makeshift bar, with a long white tablecloth covering the kitchen island and bottles of all sorts of hard liquors and fine wines lining the windows behind the counter. If Nicole hadn't known any better, she would've thought that she had found herself at the lower level of a swanky restaurant.

"I'm going to go grab a drink," Ella called out.

"So long as that drink isn't in Miami," Kevin replied.

"Okay, that's totally uncalled for," Ella snapped.

"Children." Aunt Barbara stopped and turned back. "Kevin, that was uncalled for. But, Ella, he wouldn't be able to say it if you had actually stayed with your family."

Ella rolled her eyes and shook her head.

"I'm not trying to sneak off," she said. "I just want to get a drink."

"And we'll know who to call if we find the minivan missing," Kevin added.

Ella huffed again.

"Would it make everyone happy if I promised I'd grab my drink and tag along with Mom and Dad like a puppy all night?" she asked.

"You don't have to stay with us all night, sweetie," said Uncle Pete. "You're a grown woman. I trust you'll stay on the premises for the whole duration of the party."

"Oh my God, you make one mistake..." Ella trailed off before hanging a left and maneuvering around the people in the kitchen. Nicole continued to follow her family, weaving around and bumping into the hordes of people.

"Oh, there y'all are!" Sue-Anne called out, effortlessly brushing by a group to give Mrs. Winger a hug. "Have y'all been havin' a good time?"

"Of course, of course," Mrs. Winger replied with a smile. "It's incredible. This place has been transformed."

"With y'all's help, it did!" Sue-Anne beamed. "If it weren't for Cora's weddin' this weekend, this would've been the most excitin' party all summer for East Braedonton."

"Oh, I'm sorry, could you say that again?" Aunt Barbara interjected.

"Come again, darlin'?"

"Just, your town's name. The pronunciation," Aunt Barbara said. "I guess I had assumed it was pronounced 'bridin-ton'. Not 'bread-en-tin'."

"That's how I've heard it, too," Nicole added, thinking of the cab driver who wouldn't bring his cab near East Bride-in-ton.

"Oh, bless your heart. Of course we're not 'briding-town'," Sue-Anne responded, intentionally over-pronouncing the word. "Why on Earth would anyone think it's anything other than 'bread-en-tin'?"

Aunt Barbara clicked slightly out of the side of her mouth.

"Well, because, in Latin, an 'a' and an 'e' together like that usually make an 'I' sound," she said.

"Oh honey, ain't that a dead language?" Sue-Anne let out a shrill laugh. "I don't remember much from school, but I do remember that! My, my, that must be a yankee thing."

Aunt Barbara crossed her arms and cocked an eyebrow, seemingly nonplussed.

"Well, enough of *that* borin' history lesson," Sue-Anne continued on obliviously. "Let me introduce y'all to everyone. So many people who couldn't make it to Chicago this past winter..."

Sue-Anne walked through the middle of the Winger family group, dividing them clear down the middle as she walked back towards the kitchen. Everyone turned and began following Sue-Anne. Nicole instinctively took a step back from the group.

"Everything okay?" Laura stopped and looked back.

"I think I might wander, actually," Nicole answered. "Maybe grab a drink like Ella did."

"Well, the kitchen is back this way, anyway," said Laura. "I can always grab a drink and wander with you."

Nicole faltered. Something about what Laura said didn't sit right, and Nicole couldn't put her finger on why.

"Um…" Nicole tilted her head to the side and looked away. "Is it okay if I go by myself? I can meet up with you later."

Laura looked behind her, towards the Winger family as they slowly walked away down the hall. She looked back at Nicole, sighed, and nodded her head.

"Sure. Sure thing," Laura replied, before adding with a little more energy: "You're lucky I like your mom so much. You're lucky I like *you* so much."

Something in Nicole softened, only to ping with pain immediately after. She closed her eyes and let out a slow breath.

"I know," was all she could say in response.

As Laura turned away, Nicole took one last long look before turning around as well and disappearing down the hallway, snaking around people with her head kept low. By the time she reached the front foyer, Nicole hung a sharp right and tiptoed up the stairs.

By contrast, the upstairs area was remarkably quieter. The doors to most of the rooms were shut, aside from the bathroom at the very end of the hallway. With the exception of a few people talking by one of the shut doors, Nicole was alone. Nicole walked hesitantly down the hall and into the bathroom, closing to the door behind her cautiously, like she was afraid of rigging a booby trap.

It wasn't until the door was latched behind her that Nicole realized that she had never turned on the lights to the room. She was encased in darkness, aside from a muted light coming through the small window. She slid her hands along the wall by the sink, fumbling over the wallpaper until she found the light switch. She cringed and blinked at the lights, unable to handle the change.

After fluttering her eyes a few more times, Nicole walked over and sat on the edge of the bathtub. She placed her elbows on top of her knees and collapsed her head into her hands.

Ella had received an outright interrogation when she left for a drink, but, really, the focus should've been on Nicole. At that very moment, there was nothing she wanted more than to hijack the minivan, drive back to Miami Beach, and spend the rest of the evening with her toes in the sand. She wanted to look out at the horizon and take in the open air and just let the sound of the waves effortlessly wash over her.

There was no way to describe how she felt in that house, at that party, other than suffocated. She felt closed off, surrounded by people that she didn't know and, frankly, didn't want to know. She remembered how the backyard of the house stretched out past the hedging, a vast expanse of trimmed grass bordering a dense tree line. Part of her thought about sneaking away to that area, even if it could mean crossing paths with a gator in the dark.

In some strange way, stumbling across that hypothetical gator seemed less frightening than stumbling upon Andrew, especially if he were linked arm and arm with Cora. Nicole smirked, rubbing her eyes and her temples. She imagined herself seeing Andrew and Cora and then immediately running into a gator's mouth in response.

Two gentle raps on the door knocked Nicole out of her reverie.

"Um, occupied!" Nicole called out in a wavering voice.

"Oh, sorry, sorry," a muffled but slightly familiar voice responded. As if jolted by a cattle prod, Nicole got up from her spot, flushed the toilet across from her, and let the water run from the sink for a minute. She waited an extra breath before opening the door to a lanky man with jet-black hair leaning against the wall across from the bathroom. Andrew's friend from college.

"Well, fancy seeing you here," Evan said.

"And likewise," said Nicole, a small, relaxed smile creeping up on her face.

"How's Andrew's favorite sister?" Evan asked.

Nicole felt her whole face tense up.

"Oh, I'm good, I'm good," she said absently, before quickly adding: "And how about you? I feel like I haven't talked to you in forever."

"It probably has been," said Evan. "Not since I got my Master's, probably."

"Time flies, then," Nicole replied. "How's life these days, anyway?"

"Work," Evan replied with a laugh. "I do real estate up in the Milwaukee area now. Not exactly what I expected to do with two degrees in chemistry, but, eh, what can you do. The adult world is funny like that."

"Tell me about it."

"And how about you? You're out of college by now, right?"

"Yeah, I graduated last year," said Nicole. "I'm at this design firm right now."

"Oh wow, nice. How's that going?"

"Uh, it's going," Nicole replied, biting her lip to cut off a grimace. "We'll see what happens." Nicole cleared her throat. "So, um, how's the evening going for you?"

"It's going," Evan replied. "I mean, it's not exactly what I had in mind when I heard I'd be in Miami for Andrew's wedding, but – hey – what can you do?"

Nicole shrugged in response.

"Really weird, though," Evan went on. "Like, we're right by Miami, but not we're not going to Miami for Andrew's bachelor party. In fact, Andrew isn't even *having* one, period."

"Really?" said Nicole. "That's... that's really odd."

"Like, at first I tried to convince that Fred guy to throw Andrew one, but then I was like, y'know, maybe it's okay to not press this..." Evan looked around and lowered his voice. "Truth be told, I get the feeling this won't be Andrew's last opportunity to have a bachelor party, if you know what I mean."

Nicole tilted her head to one side.

"I mean, I'm happy for him and all," Evan continued with a sly smirk. "But, man, I hope he's signing a prenup. That's all I'm going to say on this matter." Evan leaned back and scanned the area again. "Although, maybe a lack of a prenup would work in his favor. Looks like her family is loaded. I'm sure he wouldn't have much to offer in the divorce, other than student loan debt."

Nicole looked down at the ground, her face getting hot.

"Oh, wow. I'm sorry," Evan said suddenly.

"You have nothing to be sorry for," Nicole said at the ground.

"No, really, I do. I was totally out of line." Evan took a step back. "That was so uncalled for. That's your brother and I'm sorry."

"No, no, no. It's okay," said Nicole, looking back up. "I appreciate the honesty."

"I really am sorry," Evan continued.

"You really don't have anything to apologize for," said Nicole, closing her eyes. "I mean, I'd be lying if I said that I thought this marriage was a good idea."

Evan sighed and shook his head.

"It's just weird, isn't it?" Evan continued. "Like, you grow up wondering why the divorce rate is so high – how all these people could get married, only to get divorced down the line. Now I'm at that age where all my friends are getting married, and I'm starting to see why."

"And it makes you wish there was something you could say to stop them from making a huge mistake," Nicole added.

"Pretty much," said Evan.

Both let the silence fall between them. Nicole looked down the hall. The two people who had been talking by the door were long gone.

"It is what it is, though," Evan said at last.

"I know," Nicole replied.

"Hey, the next time I'm in Chicago, we all should grab lunch," Evan offered.

"Yeah, that sounds like fun," said Nicole.

Evan sighed again and shook his head.

"Still hard to believe there's a town like this in the Miami area, y'know?" he said. Evan paused, looked around again, and added: "Hopefully his next wedding is in Chicago, am I right?"

Nicole let out a small, relaxed smile.

"Hopefully," she said. She pressed her lips together and stepped to the side, ushering the way to the bathroom. "I'm totally getting in your way. You didn't come up here to talk with me."

"Ah, no worries," said Evan. "Nothing awkward about a chat just outside a bathroom. I'll see you later, all right?"

"Yeah, I'll see you around."

Nicole continued to shuffle to the side as Evan stepped through and closed the door behind him. She thought about slipping into one of the rooms on the second floor, spending her time alone while the party went on in muffled noises below her. She thought about finding her way up to the third floor, or even to that rooftop patio she had seen from the outside. Something in her ached and, for a brief moment, she let that feeling come to the surface. But before it could flourish, she tamped it back down and forced herself back down the hall and down the stairs towards the foyer.

She was about to hang a left at the bottom of the stairwell when she saw Cora standing in the left-hand hallway by one of the front bay windows. Nicole stopped and gripped the stairwell banister, surreptitiously peeking into the area.

Cora gingerly held a drink in one hand as she laughed uproariously. Andrew stood next to her, the wrinkled shirt he was once fussing over now pressed and buttoned into place. He stood and smiled, one of his hands resting on the side of Cora's waist. Cora wore a gray-and-yellow sequined mini-dress that bunched where Andrew's hand lay.

Cora's bridesmaids surrounded her: from Rachel, who looked surprisingly at ease in the moment, to Sarah, who twirled her fake engagement ring around her finger. To the left of Sarah stood Laura, laughing along with Cora, contributing something to the conversation that sounded nothing more than garbled noise to Nicole.

Nicole stared at Laura, her grip on the bannister tightening. With a sharp exhale, Nicole swung to the right around the bannister and fled down the center hall until it opened into the kitchen. She moved straight towards the kitchen island and stared at all the various liquors in front of her when she got there.

"Can I help you with anything, miss?" a voice from behind her said.

Nicole swiveled around and caught her breath, her pulse quickening as if someone had just caught her stealing.

"Um, uh – come again?" she asked.

"With your drink, miss. Is there anything I can help you with?" A young man stood in front of her in a suit identical to the caterers' and valet parkers', his hands gently clasped together in front of him. His accent was sweet and vaguely Georgian, as if he had just walked off the set of *Gone with the Wind*.

"I'm fine," Nicole said, her face tight and hot. "But, thank you, though."

"My pleasure, miss. If you need anything, I'll be right over there." The young man pointed to the table across the kitchen, where an assortment of cups, as well as a tip jar, sat.

"Good to know," said Nicole.

She waited until the young man turned away from her before she returned to the alcohol selection. She stared at the bottles as if her thoughts could bounce off of them. She thought about Evan predicting Andrew's divorce. She thought about seeing Laura chatting with Cora as if nothing could be more natural. After letting the rest of the day play through her mind, Nicole grabbed a handle of whiskey, held it down by her side, and slipped outside. She traced the redbrick exterior with her eyes cast down until she turned a corner and found the isolated section that Ella had discovered the day before.

"Well, look what the cat dragged in!"

Nicole looked down to see Ella sitting by the wall. Ella zeroed in on the whiskey bottle poking out from behind Nicole and laughed.

"Great minds think alike," said Ella, holding up a wine glass, filled a third of the way up with a clear liquid. "It's gin. I wasn't as badass as you, taking the whole friggen thing."

Nicole sat down next to Ella, propping her elbows against her knees and letting the handle of whiskey dangle from her fingertips.

"Was this your plan all along?" Nicole asked, the bottle slowly swaying back and forth.

Ella shrugged.

"Not really," she said. "I mean, I planned on getting drunk, if that's what you mean. But after getting cornered by some old lady – I think it was Cora's grandma or great aunt or great-great cousin, whatever – I decided this was my only option. Bunker down and booze it up."

"You mean 'hunker'?"

"I know what I said."

Ella lifted up her glass, nodded it towards Nicole as if she were making a toast, and took a large sip.

"The lady wouldn't let it go about how 'us yanks' do things in 'the North'," Ella continued. "Saw my wedding band and suddenly I'm getting grilled about my husband, my wedding, my livelihood." Ella took another large sip. "The good news? I'm very kind for a yank, as I so have learned. And I did. Over and over and over again, I've learned *that* vital piece of knowledge."

"Obviously, she was trying to test your kindness," said Nicole, grabbing her bottle with her free hand and unscrewing the cap.

"Testing my sobriety is more like it," Ella mumbled, taking a large gulp before wincing and pressing her lips together. "You should've seen the look she gave me when she found out how I got married. Like, you would've thought I'd gotten married in a barn, or something."

Nicole took a swig of whiskey and felt her entire body warm up.

"Actually, people do that now," Nicole said with a chuckle. "People actually find barns to have their weddings in. It's, like, a thing."

Ella groaned, closed her eyes, and finished her glass.

"So now the town clerk is even worse than a barn," Ella muttered. "Go me."

Nicole lifted the bottle up, this time taking as long of a swig as she could before her throat instinctively closed off from the burn.

"You know what I don't get?" Ella put down her empty glass and stared off into the darkness. "I've worked so hard to get where I am. I didn't beg Daddy for money or hope I'd marry rich. I didn't skate by in school. I've worked my ass off. I've desperately worked my ass off. I've made sacrifice after sacrifice after sacrifice to be where I am now, and – still – I'm not where I want to be. And then there are people like Cora, who..."

"Get everything?" Nicole offered.

"Get everything for nothing, and then some." Ella motioned for the bottle. Nicole handed it over and watched as Ella took two powerful gulps. "Like, what has she done to deserve all this? Her *pre-rehearsal* party is nicer than my wedding and reception put together. Times, like, a hundred, too." Ella passed the bottle back to Nicole, who responded by taking an identical set of swallows. "It's all luck. Stupid, stupid, unfair luck."

"It's not fair," said Nicole, closing her eyes. "Not fair at all."

She could tell the alcohol was already getting to her. The ground was starting to sway underneath her. She let her head move from side to side along with the sensation before opening her eyes again.

"I just keep waiting for this to be all some weird joke," said Nicole. "How can any of this be real? How can Andrew actually be getting married under these circumstances?"

"I think grad school has fried his brains," said Ella. "There really is no other explanation."

Nicole raised the bottle to her lips, letting the whiskey burn her tongue. Nicole moved the bottle over to Ella. Ella clasped the bottle with both hands, tapping the glass with her rings before taking another swig. Nicole closed her eyes, taking in the distant sounds of the party. She opened them again to stare at her feet, which were starting to burrow into the ground.

"Can I tell you something?" Nicole said after a moment. "And you gotta promise not to tell anyone?"

"You're one of the few sane minds in this absurd outing. Anything you say is safe with me," said Ella.

"I ran into Andrew's friend – y'know, one of the few

groomsmen he actually chose? – just a moment or so ago," she said. "And he basically said that he thinks Andrew and Cora are going to get divorced."

Ella let out a loud laugh and nursed the bottle in response.

"Do you think that, as well?" Nicole asked, slightly cocking an eyebrow.

"Oh, that's just an inevitability," Ella said with a shrug. "Like, what, 60% of marriages fail? I doubt this one will magically find itself in that elusive 40." Ella wiped her mouth and hung her head back. "Plus, isn't there a thing about, y'know, the more elaborate a wedding is, the more likely it will fail?" Ella lifted her head back up and laughed into the bottle. "If that's the case, Roger and I are destined to be together forever."

Nicole motioned for the bottle and took a long gulp, the whiskey now tasting like nothing against her tongue.

"I just don't get it," Nicole murmured. "Like, Andrew's a smart guy. A really, really, really, really, smart guy. A smart guy who has always been really picky about girls. Really, really, really picky. You'da thought he'd never seen a girl in his life with how he is with Cora."

"Maybe he's hoping for a piece of that wealth," Ella said with a smirk. "I can only imagine what Cora's dad does to be this stupidly rich."

"Imports and exports, remember?" Nicole replied, her voice dipping half an octave.

Ella let out a laugh.

"Oh God, I forgot about that," she said. "Well, ignoring the part where Andrew could get whacked, then, it makes sense. He *is* marrying into a *lot* of money."

"Gotta pay those student loans off somehow, huh?" Nicole leaned forward until the ground shifted beneath her heels. She jerked her body back up. Her vision blurred as the world delayed in catching up with her.

Both girls sat there for a while in silence, occasionally passing the bottle back and forth. They were just around the corner from the main party, but it felt like a completely different world. The party lights couldn't really reach this area of the house. No party guests were mingling this far away from the festivities. The sounds were muted and distorted, as if the party was happening on a neighboring property. For a brief second, Nicole felt like she was in college again, sitting just far enough away from the actual party, surrounded by people who actually understood her.

"We've been looking all over for you," said a voice in the bleary distance.

Nicole swung her head around and saw Laura standing right next to her. Or perhaps not – Nicole couldn't tell if Laura was close to her or several yards away. Nicole turned up one corner of her mouth, creating a half-hearted grin.

"Funny, we were doing exactly *not* that," Nicole replied, her head slowly sloping to one side.

"What?" Laura asked, before adding: "Are you drunk?"

"As a skunk on a monk doing a slam-dunk," said Ella. Nicole bit the insides of her cheek to suppress a laugh.

"Andrew and Cora were hoping to open some rehearsal eve presents, and we didn't want to start without you," Laura said with slow deliberateness.

Nicole snorted.

"Rehearsal eve? Do you even hear yourself?" Nicole rolled her eyes so emphatically that her head jerked back. "How can you even say that with a straight face?"

"C'mon, now. I think you've had too much to drink," Laura replied, crossing her arms. Nicole fixated on Laura's forearms as they wove around her elbows. Nicole closed her eyes and felt the world spin.

"Obviously not enough. I'll need a lot more before I start thinking rehearsal eve presents are not the dumbest thing I've ever heard of in my entire life," Nicole said, her eyes still closed, her entire body now leaning to one side. "Apparently I need to be drinking what *you're* drinking to think that."

"This really isn't the time for this," said Laura, her voice a tone that Nicole hadn't heard before. "Your brother is waiting for you. We're all waiting for you."

"Does that make us the center of attention?" Ella piped in. "I'm sure Cora's *thrilled* with that."

Nicole snorted out a laugh. Her shoulders jolted up her neck before shrugging forward, causing her torso to move forward as well.

"I think that's a little unfair," said Laura.

"Wow, when did you become my sister-in-law's keeper?" Nicole jeered. "You're supposed to be on my side."

Laura sighed, placed her hands on her hips, and looked over her shoulder, towards the party.

"You're supposed to be here for *me*, dammit," Nicole muttered, her upper lip still curled in disgust. She paused only to look down at the nearly-empty bottle. "Like, honestly, what the fuck, man."

"I don't want to do this. You're drunk and... I don't want to do this," Laura said, her eyes avoiding Nicole. "Just, come on now. No one's asking you to carry presents or anything. Just... come on. It'll be quick."

Nicole groaned and pushed herself up. She immediately pressed a hand onto the redbrick wall behind her. The world struggled to rise with her. Before Nicole could right herself, she reeled backwards into the wall, feeling like the world had just rocketed above her before crashing back down. Nicole pressed her tongue into the roof of her mouth to keep from throwing up. With one hand still on the redbrick, Nicole jutted her free hand out and helped up Ella.

"Fine, fine, fine. Let's do this stupid rehearsal eve, pre-pre-wedding, look-at-all-the-ways-I-can-get-attention shenanigan-thing," Nicole said, walking past Laura with her eyes locked in on the ground in front of her. "But you owe me. You owe me sooooooo big for this."

Nicole continued her forward momentum until she was around the house and back in the thick of the party again. She bobbed around various social circles, bumping into the occasional guest and mumbling out a, "sorry." She stopped in the middle of the backyard, where she gritted her teeth and tried to fight a sudden onslaught of nausea.

"Ah, there they are!" Uncle Pete's voice sang out. Nicole felt a hearty hand land on her shoulder. "Now we can start."

Uncle Pete led Nicole over toward the pool area with Ella and Laura tagging right behind them. By the side of the pool, Andrew and Cora sat on a bench underneath one of the pergolas, with Sue-Anne and Dan on one side and Nicole's mom on the other.

A spine-chilling rush of air went down Nicole neck. She turned to see Uncle Pete waving one hand in the air.

"Finally!" Sue-Anne's voice rang through a hidden speaker system. "Now that the family is all here: everyone, if y'all haven't already, come by the pool so we can begin!"

Now it was Nicole's turn to get bumped into as the crowd congregated around the pool, closing in every gap, standing shoulder to shoulder and looking forward as if they were all at a concert. It took every bit of strength she had not to let her legs sweep out from under her and go crashing to the floor.

"So, this first gift is from May-May McGuire, who, as you all may know, was Cora's very first Sunday School teacher," Sue-Anne's voice continued to bellow from the speaker system. The sounds echoed in Nicole's skull, forcing up a headache so intense that she forgot where she was for a moment. She tried to watch Cora unwrap her gift, only to realize that even the slightest sway from side to side to see past everyone made her nauseous. She stopped standing on her unbalanced tiptoes, only to realize that standing flat-footed and staring at the backs of people's heads made her feel just as sick.

The air suddenly felt incredibly warm and stale. Nicole's mouth went dry and her skin went cold.

"I'll be back." Nicole turned to who she hoped was Uncle Pete, her eyes locked onto the ground by her feet.

"Is everything all right?" said a bleary voice that somewhat resembled Uncle Pete's.

"Yeah, yeah, yeah. Just... bathroom. I need to use the bathroom. I'll be back."

Nicole inched her way out of the crowd, her eyes on the ground, a constant stream of, "excuse me," and, "pardon me," tumbling out of her throat. She kept scooting past people, all the while terrified that she would never find her way out, that she'd be stuck in this crowd forever. She stepped around fancy shoes and open-toed sandals until she finally made it to the edge of the patio – where, mercifully, only a handful of people stood. She darted up the stairs, opened the patio door, and spilled back inside. The AC hit her with force, making her body break out into goosebumps.

"Can I help you?" A young man's voice – vaguely Georgian, vaguely familiar – echoed in the distance.

The world blurred more and more around her. Nicole ignored the voice and stumbled down the hall until she was at the front stairwell. With one hand grasping the handrail, Nicole climbed up the stairs and returned to the oddly familiar bathroom. She slammed the door behind her, fumbled for the light, and dove at the toilet.

Nicole was barely able to get her arms around the rim of the toilet before she started retching. Her entire body convulsed as everything that could've ever possibly been in her stomach transferred out. She was able to pause just long enough to push her hair to her side before it started up again.

The cold of the porcelain and of the floor tiles sent shivers up her spine. She continued to heave long after there was nothing left to heave out. Her stomach contracted violently, making her wince and sporadically yelp out a cry.

The wincing and yelping soon gave way to pure crying. Nicole held her face in her hands, her elbows locked against the edge of the toilet. Spit and snot and tears hung from her face as her body continued to lurch. She stayed there for a little while, somehow relishing the weird, miserable state she was in, before leaning back and reaching for the box of tissues on the counter.

She grabbed four or five tissues, haphazardly wiped at her face, and then tossed the tissues into the toilet. She grabbed a few more, this time to wipe her nose and the corners of her mouth. She closed the lid and flushed. She pulled herself up and over to the sink and turned on the faucet. She cupped her hands under the cold water and splashed her face a few times. With a shaky hand, Nicole grabbed one of the hand towels and gently padded her skin dry.

Her legs started wobbling. The world still felt heavy and lethargic and disorienting. Nicole made her way back down to the ground and rested against the bathtub. She leaned backed until her head touched the rim.

She shifted her gaze from one end of the bathroom to the other. The bathroom felt surreal and alien to her, as if she had been placed in a funhouse. She had a strangely intimate knowledge of this bathroom now, but it wasn't enough to curb the feeling that she was in an imitation world, the kind your mind creates during a fevered sleep. The world continued to spin madly around her. She closed her eyes and took in a long, slow breath, praying that, when she opened them, she'd realize that this had all just been a dream.

Chapter Twelve

FUTURE GIRLFRIEND

"You should have a girlfriend," Nicky stated, her mouth full of cereal.

Andrew nearly choked on his toast.

"What?"

Nicky twirled her spoon in the air before scooping up another mound of cereal.

"You should have a girlfriend," Nicky repeated. *"I think you should have one by now."*

"I didn't realize there was a deadline," Andrew replied. *"Are your friends bugging you about me again?"*

Nicky swallowed her cereal with a gigantic gulp.

"When are they not?" Nicky said. *"But, no. That's not why I decided."*

"Okay then, shoot." Andrew broke his toast in two and took a large bite out of one half. *"Why do I need a girlfriend?"*

"Because you've never had one before," said Nicky. *"And now you're in college and everyone has a girlfriend in college."* Nicky scraped the edge of the bowl with her spoon. She stopped and added: *"Unless you already have one. Do you already have one?"*

Andrew shook his head.

"No, no…" Andrew tore a piece of his toast and popped it in his mouth. *"If you must know, I've been on a date or two. But nothing more than that. Definitely no girlfriends."*

Nicky tilted her head towards her cereal, staring at it with a strange intensity before looking back up.

"Can I ask you a question?"

"Well, this can't be good." Andrew shoved the rest of his toast into his mouth. "Either way: shoot." Crumbs sputtered out from his mouth and landed on the table.

"Why?"

Andrew grabbed his glass of orange juice and took three large swallows.

"Why what?"

"Why don't you have a girlfriend?"

Andrew placed his cup down and shrugged.

"Because I've yet to meet anyone that I would want to actually call my girlfriend," said Andrew. "I've met a lot of girls who want me to call them my girlfriend, but not the other way around." Andrew shrugged again. "And I figure it's not worth my time if I don't feel the same way."

"But how do you know?" Nicky asked. "When do you know someone should be your girlfriend?"

"I'll just know," Andrew said nonchalantly. "Just because I haven't met someone like that yet doesn't mean I won't."

Nicky nodded, her eyes still on her cereal.

"Do you think that will ever happen with me?" Nicky asked quietly.

"Find someone who wants to call you their girlfriend?" Andrew asked.

"Well, yeah, kind of," said Nicky. "You didn't have any girlfriends in high school. Will it be that way for me, too?"

"First off, you're in junior high. Second off, you don't want to date anyone in high school – or junior high, for that matter," said Andrew. "Trust me on that one." Andrew reached over the table and grabbed another piece of toast. "Besides, I have the utmost faith you'll find someone. Someone who wants to be with you, and someone you want to be with."

"Really?"

"No, I was lying the whole time," said Andrew, cocking an eyebrow. "Of course. You just have to have faith that you'll find the right someone, whoever that someone may be."

Andrew gently eyed his sister for a second before spreading butter over his new piece of toast.

"Do you have faith, then?" Nicky asked, stabbing the cereal

with her spoon, making a tap, tap, tap, *sound against the inside of the bowl.*

"That you'll meet the right someone?"

"That you'll meet the right someone," said Nicky. "I mean, if there's no hope for you, there's definitely no hope for me."

Andrew sighed.

"I figure it will probably happen someday. But, regardless, I'm not too worried. I've got a GPA to maintain and a scholarship I can't afford to lose." Andrew pointed his toast at Nicky. "And you shouldn't be worried, either. For either of us."

Nicky stirred her bowl. The remaining pieces of cereal danced around in slow, circular motions in the milk before scattering off into their own little paths. She gently placed the spoon down and propped her head up on her hand.

"Still think you should get a girlfriend," she said half-heartedly.

***

"You sent out the wrong sample, Ms. Winger."

Cassandra Evans stood behind Nicole, her hands on her hips. It took everything in Nicole's power not to hang her head over her keyboard.

"That's my fault. I'm sorry," she said.

"Obviously it's your fault. You were the one who sent it," said her boss. "So I need you to schedule a carrier to bring the *right* sample out."

"Yes – of, of course," Nicole stammered, looking over at her boss before casting her eyes back down.

"Just be happy we caught this," Cassandra said. "We're already pressed for time. Any delays could completely destroy this project."

"I'm really sorry," Nicole replied, doing her best to not sound like she was pleading. "I'll schedule it right away."

"Just... don't make a pattern out of this, okay?" Cassandra said. She stood there for a moment or two before adding: "Hey, is everything all right?"

Nicole sat up a little straighter and turned her seat until she was facing her boss straight on.

"Of course. Why?"

"You'd been on point with the Anderson project, but as of late you've been off," Cassandra explained. "Making a lot of dumb mistakes. Is there anything going on at home that I should know about?"

"No, no. I'm fine. Really, I am. I'll schedule the carrier and, truly, any other mistake, I'll fix," Nicole promised. "I'm so sorry if I've been messing up lately. It won't happen again."

"Okay, then…" Cassandra said slowly. "Your life is your life. I won't fault you for not wanting to talk about it with me. But I *will* fault you if you let it affect your work anymore than it already has."

"Got it," was all Nicole could say.

Nicole watched Cassandra walk away. When Cassandra was completely out of sight, Nicole went to work attempting to fix her mistake. She prepared the new sample packet and contacted the carrier service, gritting her teeth and taking shallow breaths as she did.

She knew it did no good to be so flustered over losing focus – especially since getting flustered would only cause her to lose focus even more – but she couldn't help herself. She felt flustered and frustrated and she wanted to blame someone – anyone – for why she was messing up her chances of getting hired on as a salaried employee.

She wanted to blame it on the time she had been wasting walking past Cassandra's office twice a day for the past month, working up the courage to ask for time off, only to chicken out and go back to her desk. She wanted to blame it on the fact that she was being forced to take that time off in the first place. But, at the end of the day, she blamed herself for letting everything get to her like it did.

After sending off the right sample, she double-checked every single thing she did, every email she sent, every decision she made, slowing her work to a grinding halt, until she left for lunch. Her mom was in town, and they were going to have lunch together. She left work as quickly and as quietly as she could and she met up with her mom at their usual restaurant. At the restaurant, they sat down at a table by the window. Nicole immediately picked up and scanned the menu, even though she knew what she was going to get.

"How's working going?" Nicole's mom asked.

Nicole shrugged into her menu.

"It's going," Nicole mumbled. "I kinda screwed up today."

"Oh no, sweetheart." Her mom's voice sang across an arc of notes. "What happened?"

Nicole shook her head and shrugged her shoulders again.

"I just messed up some deliveries." Nicole continued to mumble, her eyes still locked on the menu. "It was silly... just a really stupid mistake. Which I need to stop making."

"Has work been tough?" her mom asked.

"No, not that," Nicole answered. "I've just had my mind on other stuff, I guess. Kind of distracted."

"Is everything all right between you and Laura?" Her mom closed her menu and leaned forward. "If you're having relationship problems, you know you can always talk to me, right?"

"No. No, no, no. It's not that. Not that at all," Nicole answered.

"Is it money problems?" Her mom's voice dropped to a whisper. "If you need help with your bills..."

"Mom, really. It's fine."

"Then, sweetheart, what's the matter?"

Nicole sighed and shook her head.

"Nothing. I'm just distracted."

Nicole looked away and out the window as she spoke.

"It's because of Andrew's wedding, isn't it?" Her mom asked after a moment.

"No, Mom. It's not because of Andrew's wedding."

"I know it hasn't been easy," said her mom. "And he's been spending so much time in Florida. I know that doesn't help things."

Nicole said nothing and zeroed in on her menu.

"But the wedding is in a month, and I'm sure things will get better after that," said her mom. "Wedding stress can really affect people. But we'll make sure to do something together after the wedding. Like old times."

Nicole took in a long, slow breath and closed her

menu.

"I'm fine, Mom. I really am," said Nicole. "I'm sure Andrew's having a great time – and I'm not messing up at work because of the wedding. That would be stupid if I were. I'm just... letting myself get caught up in stuff. Work stuff. Employment stuff. That's it."

"Well... you always have a way of landing on your feet," said her mom. "Whatever it is, I'm sure you'll do great. That company would be nuts not to hire you on full-time. Did they give you any grief when you requested the time off?"

Nicole's face flushed.

"I haven't said anything yet," she said, "but... I will. Soon."

"Well, you still have a few weeks, I guess. No harm in that," her mom replied with a reassuring smile.

Both sat in silence. Mrs. Winger gazed out the window while Nicole looked down at the table. Nicole closed her eyes and took in the sounds of idle chatter, chair legs scraping against tiled floors, forks and knives tapping against thick porcelain plates. For a split second, she was lost in the sensations of the moment.

"Hi there, my name is Mandy and I'll be your waiter," a perky voice interrupted. "Can I start you guys off with any drinks?"

"I think we're actually ready to order food as well, if that's all right," Nicole's mom said, her palms resting on her menu.

"Of course. What can I start you off with?"

Nicole's mom gestured toward her daughter.

"Honey, you can order first."

The waitress angled her shoulders towards Nicole.

"And what would you like to have?"

Nicole couldn't help smirk before giving her order.

***

Nicole went straight from work to the Navy Pier that day. It was one of her favorite places to go to, even at the height of tourist season. She stayed away from the attractions and simply spent time by the pier's edges.

When she felt like no one was looking, she'd slip under the gray chain on the East Grand Ave side and sit along the edge and let her feet dangle above the water. Today, she leaned against one of the gray metal postings connecting the chain divider, her knees tucked tightly against her chest.

Her back was to the city and her eyes were fixed on the horizon, staring out at Lake Michigan as if it went on forever. She closed her eyes and felt the warm wind on her face. She took in a slow breath and, for a second, it felt like the wind was blowing directly into her lungs. She slowly breathed out and opened her eyes again. The small, constant, hypnotic waves of the lake put a gentle smile on her face.

God, she loved this city, and she loved that she had places like this to retreat to when she needed to get her head on straight. She sometimes wondered how her mom handled meetings in the city, if the city ever stressed her out, if she ever breathed a sigh of relief driving back to Hampshire. Her mom was better suited for a small town like Hampshire, but Nicole knew that her hometown was not for her anymore. She was a city girl with a city frame of mind. Just like her brother.

A muffled song jingled from inside Nicole's purse. Nicole let the ringtone play out for a bit before she lowered her legs, pulled her bag onto her lap, and pulled out her phone.

"Hello and good evening," she tried to sing-song into her phone, only to find that her voice was flat and monotone.

"Someone's feeling extra silly today," said Laura.

"Eh, something like that," Nicole responded.

"Uh-oh. Is everything okay?" Laura asked.

"Yeah, yeah, no, it's—it's fine," Nicole replied, a nervous hand jutting through her hair. "Just a hectic day at work."

"I can empathize, if it's anything," said Laura.

"Haha, yeah," was all Nicole could muster.

"If you're not feeling up to coming over tonight, I totally get it," said Laura.

"What? No, no, of course not," Nicole blurted. "Why

would you say that?"

"It's no big deal or anything, but you're usually here by now," said Laura. "And if you had a rough day, I'd totally get it if you wanted to nix hanging out."

Nicole pushed herself up and ducked underneath the chain divider.

"No, no, of course not. I just... had to work late, and right now I'm on a walk. Just clearing my head a little, is all. I'll be right there."

"Take your time. No need to cut off your walk just to get here sooner."

"No, no, it's all right. I was heading back anyway," Nicole said, jogging down the road, doing her best to keep her voice steady and her breathing normal. "I'll be right there."

Chapter Thirteen

IN THE EVENT THE FLOWER GIRL EXPLODES

Everything ached when Nicole woke up.

Her muscles ached, her bones ached. Her lungs and her eyes ached. Her head lay heavy on the pillow, as if it had been pushed down by an outside force. Her head pulsated and throbbed. In fact, the only thing that didn't ache was her stomach, which churned violently with nausea.

She attempted to open her eyes, only to be met with a wave of dizziness. She took in a few shallow breaths, winced, and forced her eyes open. Her mouth was dry and sticky. She slowly pushed herself into a sitting position, imagining the glass of water she'd eventually have.

"Good morning. Or, more appropriately: good afternoon."

Nicole winced again, pressed her palms into her temples, and moved her head towards the direction of Laura's voice. She looked over to see Laura hunched next to the lamp by her bed, knees tucked into her chest, a book opened and resting on her legs. Aside from the lamp, the entire room was pitch black. The shades were drawn, with a slight sliver of bright, white light peaking around the sides.

"What time is it?" Nicole asked, her words garbled.

"It's a little after 1," Laura said quietly, her eyes still on her book. "Everyone is at Cora's right now. They're having a pre-rehearsal brunch and luncheon."

"So what I'm hearing here is I'm not missing out on much." Nicole rubbed her eyes and slowly slid her feet out of bed.

Laura sighed loudly and turned a page.

Nicole bit her tongue as a wave of nausea swept over her. She focused on the wall in front of her as she hunched forward, her hands gripping her knees.

"I feel like shit," she mumbled out.

"I can imagine."

Nicole muffled a burp and grimaced again.

"Your uncle should be coming by in a few hours to pick us up for the rehearsal," said Laura.

"Well, if I didn't feel like barfing before..."

Laura sighed again, closed her book, and got up from her bed.

"What?" Nicole asked, turning to face Laura.

Laura crossed her arms and sat against the chest of drawers. Nicole looked past her, at the vanity mirror behind Laura, at the reflection the mirror gave of her back. Laura sat in silence, her mouth slowly contorting with each breath.

"Is this necessary?" Laura eventually said.

"Is what necessary?"

Laura closed her eyes and shook her head.

"I get it, I really do," said Laura. "This isn't easy for you, at all. There's a lot going on, and I don't envy you. But... there's gotta be a better way of handling it..."

"Come again?"

Nicole lowered her forearms onto her thighs, her hands dangling limply from her body.

"I don't want you to get upset or anything. I really don't." Laura looked away from Nicole and shrugged. "Just... the entire time we've been here..." She trailed off and shook her head again.

"If you have something to say, say it," said Nicole. A new type of nausea washed over her. Nicole tried to swallow it down.

"Running off to Miami, getting drunk at the rehearsal eve party, just... I don't know, everything." Laura uncrossed her arms and tossed them defeatedly up in the air. "There's gotta be a better way of dealing with it than what you've been doing."

"Well, sorry if Dr. Phil wouldn't be proud of my coping skills." Nicole rolled her eyes, only to immediately regret doing it. She pressed her tongue into the roof of her mouth to stifle the urge to throw up. "It's not exactly like I've had the best support system to deal with this in the first place."

Laura stayed silent and crossed her arms again. The air between them grew thick and stale. Nicole looked to the door, suddenly craving whatever fresh air was outside of the room.

"I don't know what more I can do," Laura said finally. "I can't help you if you keep pushing me away."

Now it was Nicole's turn to stay silent. All the words that she wanted to say were bottlenecking in her brain. She couldn't sort out her feelings, let alone find the right words to articulate them. Her heart started pounding against her chest. She locked her jaw as an indescribable frustration welled up inside her. She pressed her hands together, desperate to get at least one thought out and in the open. But when she looked up at Laura, and looked her directly in her eyes for the first time that day, everything stopped. And, in an instant, she went from too many words, to no words at all. She went from feeling frustrated to feeling lost. She felt something soften, and, in that softness, something collapsed.

"Forget what I was saying," Nicole murmured, her eyes back on the ground. "It's stupid. It's all so stupid. I'm sorry."

Laura took in a long, sharp breath.

"The wedding is tomorrow. We fly out the next day. I know this isn't exactly easy but..." Laura started to trail off before saying: "Maybe it would be better to just go with the flow for now. By this time on Sunday, we'll be up in the air. Maybe it's time to just focus on that."

"'Go with the flow'?" Nicole repeated slowly, her

cheeks suddenly flushing.

Laura shrugged again.

"There's no point in doing anything else," she said. "I mean, we'll go with the flow, get through the wedding, and get back to our lives. It's not worth it to go against the grain now."

Nicole bit at the inside of her cheek, an acrid taste building up in the back of her throat. She had to choose what she said next very carefully. She knew she risked sounding irrational, or saying something she knew she'd regret.

But she also knew she couldn't quell this feeling of absolute betrayal. Laura didn't get it. Really, nobody got it. And she knew she'd never be able to fully explain why that was so infuriating and so frustrating.

Nicole locked eyes with Laura in her search for what to say next. She wasn't sure what look she gave Laura, but, whatever it was, it struck Laura like a fist to the stomach. Laura's face went slack, her eyes widened, her shoulders hunched forward. Whatever that look was, it conveyed exactly all the anger and repulsion that Nicole was trying to push away in her mind.

"Whatever. I'm too hungover to argue," Nicole said, looking back down at the ground. "What time is Uncle Pete coming to pick us up?"

"Um, uh... around three, I believe?" Laura stammered, turning away from Nicole. "So in an hour and a half, more or less." Laura ran both hands through her hair. "We should probably get ready."

"Um, yeah. We should." Nicole swallowed and pressed her tongue to the roof of her mouth again. "Do you, uh, want the first shower, or anything?"

"I showered this morning. I'll be fine," Laura said, her back still to Nicole. "Showers are good for hangovers, anyway. Take your time."

Nicole took in a shallow breath before pushing herself off the bed. She stood up slowly and meandered over to the bathroom. She closed the bathroom door, turned the water on all the way to hot, shrugged off her clothes with a morose slowness, and stepped into the shower.

Nicole had no idea how long she stayed in the shower,

letting the water hit her face like sharp little pellets. She knew it took her a long while before she could even muster up the gumption to wash her hair. Part of her felt like she could stay in that shower all day. When the water slowly started getting colder and colder, Nicole reluctantly stepped out and dried off.

She opened the bathroom door to see Laura meticulously applying makeup in the vanity mirror. Laura glanced over briefly before returning to her eyeliner. Nicole opened her suitcase and pulled out the black dress she had brought for the rehearsal. Part of her wanted to turn to Laura and make a joke about dressing up like she was going to a funeral, but she knew just how poorly that joke would go. With a soft sigh, Nicole changed into her dress and started brushing out her wet hair.

***

Uncle Pete came just as Nicole had finished putting on her makeup. She heard him knock on their door, his muffled voice asking if they were ready. Nicole moved her gaze from the door to Laura, who had long-since finished getting ready and was back to reading her book by the side of her bed. Nicole watched as Laura closed her book and got up. Laura turned back briefly, looking at Nicole as if to confirm that it was okay to open the door.

Nicole couldn't help but smile: there was her girlfriend, dressed to the nines, sparkling with her pendant necklace and sapphire earrings. She had on a type of ruby red lipstick that Nicole hadn't seen before. For a brief second, she felt the same rush that she got when she met Laura for the very first time. But there was a heaviness that followed the rush. It was like the weight of reality had come crashing down on her spirits at the very moment they had been lifted.

"Hey there, Uncle Pete," Laura said as she opened the door. "Thank you again for coming to get us."

"Oh, no worries, no worries whatsoever," Uncle Pete replied. "Anything I can do to help."

Laura stepped away from the door and grabbed her purse. Uncle Pete, who was holding the door open with his shoulder, tilted his head at Nicole.

"Feeling better, Nicky?" he asked.

Nicole took in a deep breath and grabbed her purse as well.

"Yes, Uncle Pete," she said flatly. "I'm doing fine now."

"The Wingers are notorious lightweights when it comes to alcohol," said Uncle Pete. "I was the same way in college. Made me a huge hit at parties, let me tell you..."

Nicole followed Laura and Uncle Pete out of the room, the stuffy outside heat hitting her hard the second she stepped through the door. She took deep, deliberate breaths as they made their way to the minivan. She watched as Laura opened the side door to the van, only to get into the passenger seat next to Uncle Pete. Nicole's chest tightened as she made her way into the far back and buckled herself in.

"The restaurant we're having the rehearsal dinner at tonight is apparently the nicest restaurant in town," Uncle Pete said as they pulled out onto the road.

Nicole smirked.

Didn't someone say there were only two restaurants in all of East Braedonton?

Nicole leaned against the window, allowing the chill of the glass to numb her forehead. She watched the world transform around her yet again as they crossed the city line into East Braedonton. She closed her eyes and tried one last time to let her mind go blank.

"Here we are: First Church of East Braedonton," said Uncle Pete. Nicole opened her eyes as Uncle Pete pulled into a parking spot. "Although, to be honest, from the looks of the town, I'd say it's the only church, too."

"Joy," Nicole mumbled and reached for the side door.

The church was the same one Nicole saw on their first day in East Braedonton, that towering white structure that marked the end of the downtown area. Cars filled up the parking lot, with people bustling in and around the building. Even from the back parking lot, the church felt massive and imposing. Nicole followed Uncle Pete and Laura through the main entrance, past the lobby, and into the church.

The interior of the church, with its tall, vaulted ceilings and woven columns, left Nicole speechless. Each window hosted a bold stained glass design. Detailed Biblical scenes played out in paintings on the ceiling. It was like someone took the Sistine Chapel and gave it brown wood trimming.

People hurried around church, carrying decorations of all shapes and sizes. Silk streamers danced across the archways, bisecting some of the Biblical scenes. Flower arrangements hung along the window edges. Each corner of the church hosted an iron stand, and each iron stand held a poster-sized portrait of Andrew and Cora. Monogramed cushions and matching tissue boxes adorned every pew. The center aisle entrances into the pews had been cordoned off with shiny ribbon, which drooped down in the center and tied into a complicated bow on the top of the backrests. Below Nicole's feet, a red carpet had been rolled out and pinned down, accented with gold spirals and Andrew and Cora's initials stitched in silver. Row after row after row of flower arrangements in vases lined the sides of the church, culminating in an outright meadow of gardenia and orchids at the front.

Also at the front of the church stood what looked like a combination gazebo and pergola, lined in lace and ribbons and even more flowers. Scattered around the gazebo-pergola stood Andrew and Cora, the bridesmaids, the groomsmen, and family members. Cora's family appeared lost in conversation with each other while Nicole's family stood awkwardly off to the side. Jacob, one of the few groomsmen Andrew actually chose, stood next to Nicole's mom.

"Finally," breathed out an exasperated voice. Rachel rolled her eyes at Nicole before marching out of the gazebo-pergola and into the aisle, where she hollered: "EVERYONE WHO WAS SUPPOSED TO BE HERE IS NOW HERE. PAM! GRETCHEN! TIME FOR YOU TO ACTUALLY DO YOUR JOBS!"

Rachel gave a knowing look to Sue-Anne before rolling her eyes again.

Sue-Anne smiled back before trotting down the aisle, arms extended out.

"Why, welcome back, Pete!" Sue-Anne beamed, embracing Nicole's uncle in a tight hug. "Thank you so much for getting Andrew's sister and her friend."

"No problem, no problem at all," Uncle Pete replied, gingerly breaking from the hug. "The least I can do for family."

Sue-Anne took a step back and looked Nicole up and down.

"Well, last night certainly was interesting for *you*," said Sue-Anne with a huff.

"Um, yeah... I'm, I'm sorry about that..." Nicole mumbled, scratching her neck as she looked away.

"It was quite the sight, you passed out in one of our second floor bathrooms," Sue-Anne went on. "Auntie May found you. Poor lady was just looking for a powder room and what she got instead was a drunk."

Sue-Anne smiled as she talked, delivering her lines in a lighthearted, singsong fashion, but it still made Nicole shrink back in her skin, as if Sue-Anne had just spent the last few minutes yelling at her.

"I'm really, really sorry," said Nicole, enunciating even less than before.

"Well, bless your heart, I always knew yanks couldn't hold their liquor," said Sue-Anne. "I'm just happy that you had Laura to keep you company until you were ready for public again. Every girl needs a friend like that – someone with enough sense to not drink herself silly in the very birthplace of moonshine."

Sue-Anne paused to wave her hand in the air and laugh.

"But, anywho. Now that everyone is here, we can get started with our rehearsal." Sue-Anne turned to the gazebo-pergola, eyeing the two ladies standing nervously beside it, clipboards clasped tightly in their hands. "Grand. *The planners* are ready. Let's see if they can prove their worth for once."

Sue-Anne strode back to the gazebo-pergola. Nicole walked down the aisle and over to where her family stood.

"She lives," Kevin deadpanned as Nicole approached.

"Wait, what's going on?" Jacob asked.

"My daughter and my niece both decided to raid the

liquor cabinet at the rehearsal eve party," Aunt Barbara stated. "Nicole was nearly comatose when we found her."

"Oh, Nicky, wow," Jacob replied, locking eyes with Nicole briefly before looking away. "Sorry. I guess you're forever 10 years old in my eyes. Keep forgetting you're an adult now."

"By some definition," said Kevin.

"Really, Kevin?" Aunt Barbara turned to her son. "Neither the time, nor the place."

Kevin shrugged in response.

"If it's anything, I threw up, like, everything I had ever eaten when we got back," Ella offered with a smirk.

Aunt Barbara rolled her eyes.

"Not helping," she said.

"We were really worried," Nicole's mom said. "I wanted to call an ambulance."

"Thankfully, you were still responsive," said Aunt Barbara.

Nicole felt her whole face get hot. She looked over at Laura, who was now standing next to Jacob, her eyes firmly planted on the ground.

"I'm really sorry, guys," Nicole mumbled once again.

"Hey, the important thing is you're here," said Uncle Pete. "No use dwelling on the past. Right, guys? Right?"

Nicole looked over at the gazebo-pergola and saw four of the bridesmaids and two of the groomsmen looking over at her. All six of them quickly looked away. She looked over at Andrew, silently pleading that he would look at her. His back remained turned to her as he kept a protective arm wrapped around Cora's shoulder.

"Alright, um," said one of the planners. "If everyone could take a seat, that would be great."

Nicole went for the outside edge of the pew, as far from the center aisle and the gazebo-pergola as she could get. She pushed herself up against the edge, her shoulder barely inches from a portrait of Andrew and Cora smiling in front of a gray backdrop. She looked over at the portrait, which was easily four or five feet in height. In the picture, Andrew had his hands on Cora's waist, as if they were posing for a prom picture. Both were smiling from ear to ear.

Within seconds, she felt a rush of air as Ella sat down next to her with a *plop*.

"Well, now," Ella whispered, her hands landing loudly against her thighs. "Still hungover?"

Nicole sighed.

"A little bit."

"I'm impressed, by the way," said Ella. "I didn't think you could outdrink me. But you practically killed that bottle."

"You were drinking from it, too," Nicole replied, crossing her arms.

"Not like *you* were."

"Alright, my name is Pam, and this is Gretchen," the stout lady said after everyone had sat down, pointing to herself and then to the lanky lady next to her. Her fake southern accent was possibly the poorest out of anyone Nicole had met in East Braedonton. "We just want to go over the rundown for the big day tomorrow, including any provisions in the event of any unplanned circumstances."

Nicole leaned back and craned her neck, looking around at everyone in attendance. Her family had somewhat filled up the front pew on the left side of the church, while Cora's entourage had scattered themselves amongst the pews on the right-hand side, filling up a solid third of the entire section. The various men and women who were decorating continued to mill about along the edges of the church.

"So, we'll start with the transportation," said Pam. "The bride will be arriving at the front of the church at 3:10 on the dot by stagecoach. In the event the stagecoach is unavailable or running late, we will have a stretch limo waiting as backup. The lead photographer will be in front of the church to document the arrival. In the event the lead photographer is unable to photograph the arrival, one of his assistants will step in. The photographer will also document when Cora meets with her father before walking down the aisle. In the event that Cora's father is unable to walk Cora down the aisle, we will enlist the help of her Uncle Jebediah."

"Are you saying I won't make it to my own daughter's wedding?" said a low, casual voice. Nicole turned to see Cora's father off to the side, his hands interlaced and behind his head, a contented but ornery smirk on his face.

"No, no, no, of course not," Gretchen stammered, her accent equally as terrible as Pam's. "This is, uh, just provisions. Purely provisions."

"Ah, you worry too much," he said, letting go of his hands and flicking them at the wrist, as if shooing something away. "Anyway, on you go."

"Well, o-okay then." Gretchen shuffled her feet, cleared her throat, and held the clipboard inches from her face. "Well, alright. So, the rest of the wedding party – groom included – should be here no later than 1:30 p.m. Everyone should arrive in the approved attire and, if applicable, hair and makeup ready. In the event anyone is running late, please call me and we will make any necessary arrangements to minimize your tardiness."

"We have…" Pam began, trailing off as she looked down. She flipped through a few pages before continuing. "Kevin, Ella, and Nicole Winger as ushers. The same applies to them: no later than 1:30 p.m. Hair and makeup ready – if applicable – and in proper attire. In the event they are running late, they shall call me and we will see if we can make any necessary arrangements to minimize their tardiness."

"I don't remember signing up for that," Ella whispered to Nicole. "And, seriously: how in the hell are you an usher and not, like, something more important?"

Nicole rolled her eyes and shrugged her shoulders, a slight, cynical smirk forming in the corner of her mouth.

"Now, it's very important – Kevin, Ella, and Nicole – that, as ushers, you *only pass out the approved wedding programs to the guests.*" Gretchen gave an intense stare as she spoke. "This is your *strictly assigned* job. You will not be asking anyone if they are part of the groom's or bride's side. I repeat: *you will not be asking anyone if they are part of the groom's or bride's side.* The professional ushers inside will help escort guests to their seats. In the event one of you are unable to pass out the wedding booklets, we will have one of the professional ushers take your place."

"A professional escort will take my place?" Ella

whispered. Nicole bit down on her tongue and stifled a laugh.

"Doors will be open for guests at 2 p.m. sharp," Gretchen continued. "Ushers – Ella, Kevin, and Nicole – will stand by the doors, greeting everyone with their best southern hospitality before offering a program. In the event the ushers are not able to enact their innate southern hospitality, we will ask that ushers at least attempt a southern accent."

"Well, bless her heart," Ella whispered over to Nicole with the most dramatic southern accent Nicole had ever heard. Nicole pressed her lips together, which did little to stop her satisfied grin.

"Alright, boutonnieres and bouquets will be delivered at 12:35 pm," said Pam. "In the event something happens with the florist, I will be on hand with backup boutonnieres and bouquets.

"In honor of Cora's cheerleading days, we have enlisted the help of the East Braedonton High cheerleading squad to blow bubbles from 1:55 p.m until the end of the wedding. We have a list of backup cheerleaders in the event that any of the original cheerleaders are not able to make it in time. And we will keep a backup stock of bubble solution and at various consistencies in the event that the bubbles made are not up to par."

Gretchen cleared her throat, her eyes down at her clipboard.

"Now, onto the procession," she said, picking up where Pam left off. "All doors will be closed at 3:00 pm sharp, and the procession will start at 3:05. We will first start out with Pastor O'Hara and the groom coming down the aisle, followed by the mothers of the bride and groom. There will be a brief interlude as the harp is played. In the event the harp is broken or the harpist is unable to play, we will have a string quartet waiting on hand. After that, the ring bearer and flower girl will walk down..."

"And in the event the flower girl explodes, a child actor will be ready to replace her," Ella finished, causing Nicole to snort out a laugh. Gretchen stopped what she was saying and stared at Nicole. The rest of the congregation turned towards Nicole in response. Nicole could feel Sue-Anne's glare beating down on her.

"God bless you!" Ella said loudly, sniffling her own nose for emphasis.

"Okay, then. Moving on." Gretchen pushed her glasses closer to her face and flipped the top page over the clipboard. "The procession of bridesmaids and groomsmen will go as followed: Maid of Honor Rachel and Best Man Fred will go first. Then Second Maid of Honor Susanna, coming up on her own."

"Bless her heart, she's big enough to count as a pair, anyway," Sue-Anne added, looking over at her oldest daughter, who reacted by getting red in the face and looking toward the ground.

"After Susanna, we have Meredith and Greg, followed by Karen and Aaron, then Ashley and Jacob, Sarah and Evan..."

"Excuse me, but is there any way I can move up in the procession?" Sarah butted in. "I don't get why I'm so far back. I am, like, Cora's bestest of best friends and I think that earns me a spot at the top. I mean, I'm practically like a maid of honor. Or, technically, *future matron* of honor."

"You are where you are, Sarah," Sue-Anne responded with a paralyzing venom. "There's no changing. Remember: ya git what ya git and ya don't pitch a fit!"

Gretchen paused for an extra beat before looking back down at her clipboard.

"And, at the very end, Mandy-Lee, the junior bridesmaid, will close out the procession. There will be another interlude as the harpist plays, followed by a brief moment of silence. At this point, the stagecoach will arrive just outside of the church. Cora will come out of the stagecoach and meet with her father at the base of the stairs. They will then walk into the church and down the aisle. At this point, the harpist and the organist – or the string quartet in the event either are unable to perform – will both start playing the bridal music. The East Braedonton High cheerleaders will do double time on the bubbles until Cora arrives at the altar, at which point the cheerleaders will resume their normal pace of bubble-blowing."

"Well, this is all good and fun, but what about where

the bridesmaids and groomsmen will go?" said Rachel with furrowed brows. "And what about the pace they will use when walking down the aisle? Honestly, have you been asleep on the job or what?"

Sue-Anne piped in before either Gretchen or Pam could respond.

"Well, darlin', sometimes if want a job done right, you gotta do it yourself," she said, a satisfied smile beaming from her face. "In fact, let's start working on that right now. I'm sure we will have the solution in no time."

Sue-Anne smacked her hands against her knees as she stood up. With Rachel in tow, Sue-Anne roused the rest of the wedding party up and ushered them over to the gazebo-pergola.

For the next two hours, Sue-Anne and Rachel went back and forth about how fast the wedding party should walk and where the wedding party should go once they had reached the altar.

"Um, can we get a sample of the music, please?" Rachel turned to Pam and Gretchen. "Or do you not have it?"

"Oh, no, no. We do," Pam said, fumbling a CD out from one of the bags by the pews and an old boom box from underneath the pew. "Here, let me plug this in."

"Maybe we should have people walk in sync to the rhythm of the song," Rachel mused, tapping her pen against her clipboard as Pam rushed to find an electrical outlet.

"Well, the important thing is timing," Sue-Anne replied. "We don't want the music to change in the middle of a bridesmaid and groomsman coming down the aisle. Can you imagine anything more embarrassin'?"

"*Well, the important thing is* at least *we* don't have to deal with rehearsing how to walk," Ella whispered to Nicole, mimicking Sue-Anne's accent perfectly. "I mean, truly, darlin': can you imagine anything more embarrassin' – aside from being in this joke of a weddin'?"

Nicole sat back with a gratified look on her face. As she did, she couldn't help but notice that Laura had gotten up to help Pam find an outlet. With her mom now with the wedding party and Laura across the church, Nicole became acutely aware of how isolated she and Ella were. Aunt Barbara and Uncle Pete were sitting on the opposite end of the pew, watching the rehearsal events unfold. Kevin's nose was buried in a book – a book he had pulled out of seemingly nowhere.

"I still cannot believe you're not in the wedding party," Ella continued. "I mean, you're Andrew's sister. Forget that – he's more than just your brother. He was, like, second dad to you."

Nicole tried to shrug her shoulders, but found that her joints had locked up. She looked over at Andrew with a new surge of fury.

"Are you surprised?" Nicole said, her eyes locked on Fred, the best man, who was standing next to Andrew by the altar. "The best man is Cora's brother. Half the groomsmen are from Cora's family. This is not Andrew's wedding." Nicole's lips puckered as a new type of rancor weaved its way through her. "I'm shocked I was even invited in the first place."

"I mean, at least you have your girlfriend with you," said Ella. "I'm dealing with this travesty of a wedding without Roger."

"Please," Nicole huffed, crossing her arms. "Look at her. She's as gung-ho for this stupid wedding as everyone else." She sucked the air between her teeth and closed her eyes. "Truth be told, I wish it had been Roger who had come and Laura who had been unavailable. I'm sure he would've seen what's going on for what it actually is."

"I wish he'd been able to come, too," said Ella, turning her heard toward the center aisle, where Sue-Anne was instructing Alexandra, the flower girl, how to move her feet while walking down the aisle. Alexandra responded to the instructions with the flippant wave of her hand.

"It's really not fair, y'know?" Ella continued.

"It really isn't," Nicole agreed.

Nicole watched as the wedding party went up and down the aisle, over, and over, and over again. When they were finally satisfied with the procession, Sue-Anne and Rachel ushered the wedding party to the gazebo-pergola.

"So, do we want to line everyone up in the order they came down the aisle, or…" said Gretchen.

Rachel put up a hand, her palm barely inches from Gretchen's face.

"We got this," she said, and joined the rest of the wedding party.

Nicole slouched back in her seat, breathing through the last bits of her hangover as the wedding party was arranged and rearranged along the gazebo-pergola. Sue-Anne first had them line up outside of the structure, sorting people according to when they came in, then according to ascending order in height, then according to descending order in height.

With a shake of her head, Sue-Anne dismissed the lineup and ushered everyone inside the gazebo-pergola, attempting every possible group combination before moving everyone back out of the gazebo-pergola.

The only people who didn't move were Andrew and Cora, who stood at the base of the steps of the gazebo-pergola. They stood still in the center, facing each other and holding hands as if they were about to get married right then and there.

As the wedding party filed out of the gazebo-pergola, Andrew stretched his arms to the sky and yawned. He then put his hands on his back and twisted, causing him to turn towards where Nicole was sitting. Andrew met Nicole's gaze and gave her a cautious, weary smile. Nicole responded by making a silly face back, crossing her eyes and sticking out her tongue. She brought two fingers to her temple, pretending to shoot herself. She uncrossed her eyes to see that Andrew had turned his back to her again.

With a new heaviness forming in her chest, Nicole watched the rest of the rehearsal unfold. Sue-Anne eventually figured out a line-up that she liked and had everyone rehearse the procession one last time. She had the wedding party walk in sync with the beat, snapping her fingers to cue when a foot should hit the floor. She watched like a hawk as the wedding party outright waltzed down the aisle and made their way to their designated spots. When the junior bridesmaid made her way down the aisle, two men in the back of the church closed the doors leading into the lobby, temporarily cordoning Cora and her father off from the congregation.

Before the doors could reopen, Sue-Anne held up a hand. Pam immediately hit pause on the boom box.

"Should we have the bridesmaids kiss the groomsmen on the cheek when they get to the front?" Sue-Anne pondered, before shaking her head and waving her arms. "No, no, no. Nix that. The only people kissin' will be the bride and groom. Anything else will take the attention away from the real stars of the show." Sue-Anne turned to Pam and shouted: "Alright: here comes the bride!"

Pam hit play on the music. The two men opened the gigantic doors as they took long strides back. In the center of the doorframe stood Cora and her father, Cora's hand resting lightly on her father's arm. Together they walked down the aisle, their feet landing on the floor with every quarter beat. Cora's eyes were locked on Andrew, her lips scrunched together as if she was worried about something. Andrew, on the other hand, was beaming. His smile nearly filled his entire face as he watched Cora come closer and closer to him.

"Now, as we rehearsed back at home," Sue-Anne said as Cora and her father reached the gazebo-pergola. "Andrew, step forward. Shake your new father-in-law's hand and then take Cora's."

Andrew stepped forward, shook Dan's hand, and then slipped his hand under Cora's. Andrew's eyes were wide, staring at Cora like she was the only person in the room – the only person in the world. Nicole looked over at Laura – who had stayed by Pam and the boom box during the procession – and felt something sink further in her chest. What it was, she couldn't figure out. All she knew is that if Ella hadn't turned to Nicole to mimic a gagging gesture at that exact moment, she might've said or done something she would've later regretted.

***

The rehearsal dinner was just as grand as the rehearsal eve party. The decorations were more subdued; fewer ruffles and more crisp linens. The restaurant was teeming with people, the noise of their chatter rising and falling like the ebb and flow of the ocean. At the center of the restaurant stood a gigantic ice sculpture – a swan, just like at the rehearsal eve party.

Off to the side stood a large chalkboard with an ornate frame, held up by an equally ornate stand. The chalkboard read: "They practiced their 'I dos' and now are ready to celebrate with you! The Future Wife & Husband, Cora and Andrew." It took every ounce of self-control she had not to swipe a hand down the chalkboard writing, smudging the perfect calligraphy. Instead, Nicole turned to a caterer, who had walked up to Nicole and her family with a tray of champagne, and politely plucked a glass up by its stem.

"Careful now," Kevin warned, walking next to her as the family made their way toward the center of the restaurant.

"I don't plan on getting drunk," Nicole replied, her grip tightening on the glass. "I just want some champagne."

"You just want alcohol right now?"

Nicole shrugged, trying in vain to look facetious.

"Y'know, helps take the edge off, and all that."

"Much like a bottle of whiskey takes the edge off?" Kevin countered.

Nicole drew in a sharp breath and looked away.

"Hey, I get it. I really do." Kevin reached out and placed a firm palm against his cousin's forearm. "In all seriousness. This can't be easy. But the wedding is tomorrow. It'll all be over soon."

Nicole stopped and turned to Kevin.

"Why does everyone keep saying that?" she hissed. "Everyone is either super excited for this wedding or they just assume that the worst will be over once the wedding is done."

"I wouldn't ever assume it'll be as easy as that," Kevin replied. "But it's not worth it to get so upset over something that's out of your control."

Kevin stared just past Nicole, nudging his nose in the direction of Laura, who was talking to some elderly lady that Nicole had never met.

"Besides, maybe it would be better to focus on more pressing matters," he said.

Nicole gave Laura a once over, rolled her eyes, and

turned back to Kevin.

"I mean it," Kevin pressed.

"What are you getting at?" Nicole asked.

Kevin sighed and looked down.

"I'm not here to lecture," he said. "Hopefully you'll see things differently when you look back on this. Things might make more sense, then, than they do right now."

Now it was Nicole's turn to sigh, bringing the champagne glass to her lips.

"Whatever you say."

Nicole turned and broke away from Kevin. She snaked her way around the tables, looking down at the ground, deliberately avoiding all groups or individual persons. She eventually found her way to a corner, where there was nothing around her but a small table holding a six-tier cupcake stand. Each tier in the stand held a different set of intricately decorated cupcakes. Nicole grabbed a cupcake decorated with a glittering fondant dove and took a large bite.

"Just the person I needed to see!" Sarah's voice boomed as she strutted over.

Nicole reflexively took a step back, her ankle hitting the wall's baseboard. Nicole finished the cupcake bite in her mouth with a hard swallow and chirped out something that sounded like a, "Hello."

"Your mom is way too sweet to interfere, but obviously *you* don't mind doing whatever you want," said Sarah, her right hand twisting the fake engagement ring on her left. "I need you to talk to your brother about the procession."

"What about the procession?" Nicole asked, her back now pressed against the wall.

"Well, I think it's a little unfair to me that I'm so far in the back," said Sarah. "I mean, how is anyone gonna pay attention to me? I have a better idea in mind and I need you to talk to Andrew about it."

"Um, I don't think I'm exactly the right person for the job," Nicole replied slowly.

"Oh, nonsense, you're perfect," said Sarah. "Well, perfect for the job, at least. I mean, very few people are perfect."

Sarah flipped her hair behind her shoulder with a satisfied smile on her face.

"Anyway, what I'm thinking is, we let the best man and maid of honor and second maid of honor do their thing, yadda, yadda, yadda. I'm not thrilled with it but I recognize that compromises must be made in the name of friendship. *But*, after Susanna goes down the aisle, there is a pause in the music. The center doors close. Then they reopen for me, and we get that string quartet that's waiting on standby to start playing as well. I mean, they're already there, so let's use them. Maybe we can pass out rose petals to the people sitting by the aisle so they can throw them in front of me as I come down." Sarah paused before sucking in a loud breath. "Or! Or, we can have everyone *stand*. What do you think? Isn't that perfect? Wouldn't that be *great* for Cora's wedding?"

"Um... why not," Nicole said, bringing her glass to her lips and gulping down the rest of her champagne.

"So, what's keeping you then?" Sarah barked. "Go talk to Andrew already."

Nicole closed her eyes and shook her head.

"I haven't even seen him since we got here," Nicole replied.

"Well, he's totally in the kitchen right now, away from everyone. Perfect time to say something."

Nicole nearly placed her glass down on top of a cupcake.

"Why is he in the kitchen?"

Sarah shrugged.

"How would I know?" Sarah replied. "Either way, you need to get in there, like, *now*, and tell him that I need to be moved up in the procession."

"Yeah, yeah, sure." Nicole turned her head towards the kitchen door. "I'll go do that."

"Oh, you're the best." Sarah stepped back and jutted out her left hand, admiring her ring from afar. "Besides, I just got this beauty cleaned. Everyone needs to see it."

"Of course," Nicole mumbled, sliding past Sarah. Nicole hugged the wall until she was at the kitchen's plushy leather door. With a quick glance around, Nicole pushed the door open and stepped in.

The atmosphere inside the kitchen was electric with its busyness. Cooks and chefs in starched white uniforms darted from one counter to the next, from one saucepan to another, yelling out cooking times and asking for updates on garnishes. Nicole spotted a figure somewhere near the back, sporting a black suit that stood out amongst the sea of white jackets.

"I never took you to be a chef," Nicole said when she felt she had gotten close enough.

Andrew whipped around, nearly knocking over a bottle of olive oil in the process.

"You scared me, there," said Andrew, short of breath.

"Sorry, didn't mean to..." Nicole looked down at the counter, at the teetering bottle of oil. "I heard you were in the kitchen, so I wanted to come in and see what's up."

"Well, I guess 'what's up' is the lack of catfish crab cakes... whatever those might be," said Andrew, his eyes back to scanning the counter. "Sue-Anne had asked me to come in here and get an update and I guess I lost track of time. Have people been asking for me?"

"Um, not that I know of. But then again, I really haven't been talking with people."

"You really should socialize more, Nicole," said Andrew. "I think you'd have more fun if you got to know some people here."

Nicole pressed her lips together and placed a hand on the metal counter.

"Well, I just wanted to make sure everything was okay," she said. "You know, see how you were holding up."

"I'm holding up fine," said Andrew. "It's a little chaotic right now, but I'm doing fine. I mean, I *am* getting married tomorrow, so a little chaos is to be expected."

Nicole could only nod.

"And I'm sure things'll still be crazy after the wedding, too," Andrew continued. "But eventually it'll all die down."

"Well, uh, anything I can do to help after the wedding, I'm here," Nicole offered, a cautious smile forming on her face. "I could even go to Northwestern and stand in as temporary TA until you get back. I'd accidentally fail everyone, but still…"

Andrew's face fell.

"Nicole, who said anything about going back to Chicago?"

Nicole didn't realize her fingers were curling around the edge of the counter until her nails started digging into its underside.

"But, of course you're coming back to Chicago," said Nicole. "Your PhD…"

"I'll get it at FIU," Andrew cut in.

"What?"

"I'll get it at FIU," Andrew repeated. "Or Miami University. Wherever."

"But – wait," said Nicole, thoughts moving through her mind like molasses. "But you…"

"I'm moving to Florida," said Andrew. "Plain and simple."

Nicole felt the blood drain from her face.

"But, no. That can't be," she said. "I mean, you're in the middle of your dissertation and—"

"I'm going to take the fall semester off, get settled, and see if I can transfer in. Simple as that."

"But it's not," said Nicole, her mind started to pick back up speed. "It's not as simple as that. This your *PhD*, Andrew…"

"So?" Andrew retorted. "I'm not worried. Maybe it will set me behind academically, but it's nothing I can't make up. And if they give me grief, I'll just change gears and get my Master's."

Nicole felt her whole face get hot.

"But the PhD is something you wanted since, like, middle school."

"I don't think 10-year-olds know what a PhD is."

"You've always wanted to be a scientist," Nicole pressed. "You wanted to be a professor, you wanted to teach at Northwestern…"

"So I'll teach in Florida instead. Who cares?" Andrew crossed his arms. "Some colleges only require a Master's, anyway. I'll be fine."

"No, you won't be fine."

"Good to know you've developed an ability to see into

the future," Andrew snapped.

"Why are you doing this? Why are you throwing everything away?" Nicole's ears started ringing.

"Why do you care? This is my life," Andrew shot back.

"Because Chicago is your home and it always has been and—"

"Well sometimes you change your homes for the ones you love," Andrew interrupted.

Nicole let go of the counter and pressed both hands to her forehead.

"You can't expect me to believe for a second that you're perfectly okay with throwing away everything you've worked for – that this is 100% your decision," Nicole said, her palms sliding over her temples. She took a sigh and added: "You don't have to go through with this. If you're having any second thoughts about the wedding, you can tell me and we can bolt. Mom will understand."

"...And now I get why you needed to track me down," Andrew replied slowly. "You know, this is so like you. Taking something small and coming to some seriously insane conclusions."

Andrew stared at her, his eyes piercing into her. She stared back with a paralyzing anxiety, like she had just been caught staring at a stranger.

"Can't you see this is all one big mistake?" she blurted out.

Andrew's face went blank.

"Well, at least it's out in the open now," Andrew replied coolly.

Nicole caught her breath, realizing exactly what she had just said. She raked her hands through her hair. It was too late to deny it. No going back now.

"I know there's a part of you that agrees with me. I know it," she said. "But you're too stubborn to admit it."

"No. *You're* too pessimistic to do anything but assume the worst," Andrew snarled. "I'm getting married tomorrow. To Cora. Because I love her. End of story."

"And you're okay with her bringing you away from Chicago, away from everything and everyone in your life," Nicole cried out. "You're so much on her side that you won't even consider your own family."

"It's not a side thing," Andrew replied, his voice suddenly and shockingly calm. "She's going to be my wife. But if there's going to be a side, I *am* going to side with my wife, every time. That's what marriage means."

"Then I hope to God I never get married." Nicole's lower lip trembled. Before the tears could well up, Nicole turned away and barreled out of the kitchen, past the chattering groups, and towards the front door.

"Hey, there you are," Laura called out from a few yards away, surrounded by three of the bridesmaids and Nicole's mom. Laura reached out a hand, touching Nicole on the arm as she walked past. "We'll be sitting down soon, so I was—"

"Leave me alone!" Nicole shouted, jerking away from Laura as she charged towards the exit. Nicole spilled out into the parking lot, realizing with dizzying dread that she had no idea where she was going to go next. Her chest started to tighten up. Her heart was pounding against her ears. The parked cars around her started to blur together as she tried in vain to catch her breath.

"What is going on?" said a once-familiar voice. "What has gotten into you?"

"What has gotten into *you*?" Nicole shouted over her shoulder as she continued to walk away, her back to Laura, her eyes locked on the cars in front of her.

"Do you really think this is the right way of going about this?" Laura continued.

Nicole spun around to see her girlfriend walking towards her, followed closely behind by Meredith, Karen, and Ashley – the three bridesmaids that Laura was laughing along with – as well as Nicole's mother. Behind them, Kevin and Ella were hurrying out of the restaurant and into the parking lot.

"Do *you* really think I brought you to Florida so you could chastise me?" Nicole snapped, taking an aggressive step forward.

"What are you talking about?" Laura responded.

"Oh, you know *exactly* what I'm talking about," Nicole yelled, flinging her arms out. "You're not here so you can be on her side. You got that?"

"You're making a scene," said Laura.

"Oh my God!" Nicole shouted. "Do you hear yourself? If you're so up her ass, why don't you just marry her alongside Andrew?"

"What?"

"Yeah, wow, unnecessary much?" Karen interjected, her eyes sizing up Nicole.

"Oh, do not even start with me about unnecessary," Nicole rolled her eyes so dramatically her head flung back. "Says the girl who can't peel her eyes away from her boyfriend's text messages for more than a minute. Don't even get me *started* on unnecessary."

"Nicole, really, I think you should calm down..." Laura began.

Nicole's hands tightened into fists.

"Do you even *hear* yourself?" Nicole spat out. "Seriously. *Seriously.* Do you even hear yourself? That's all you can do. Tell me to calm down while hanging out with the enemy. If I'd known you were going to be my own personal Benedict Arnold..."

"Goodness, Nicole, what in the world..." said her mom.

"Not now Mom, honestly. Not now." Nicole closed her eyes and jutted out a palm. "I've spent so long going along with everything – just like *everyone* wanted me to – and I've had enough!"

Nicole looked over at Ella, praying that she would say something – do *anything*. But Ella's silence just further proved that Nicole was one person against everyone else.

Nicole clawed her fingers through her hair and took a step back.

"Andrew is about to throw his whole life away! How am I the only one who sees that? How am I the only one who sees how messed up this whole thing is – how messed up this whole stupid town is?"

"Hey!" Meredith shouted. "Do *not* badmouth the great East Braedonton! We're the Gem of the South!"

"Oh shut up!" Nicole rolled her head to Meredith. "You're not even *remotely* the South!"

"You take that back!" Meredith yelped. "Florida fought in the Confederacy! It is SO the South!"

"You do NOT live in the South!" Nicole hollered. "You live in a suburb of Miami! *Miami!* Your entire town pretends they're the South and then overcompensates by living out every single southern stereotype – which is a complete insult to every *actual* southerner, ever!"

"Now, Meredith, don't listen to her," Ashley responded in her thick Nashville accent. "Your town is a very lovely town…"

"And *you!*" Nicole pointed a finger at Ashley, her whole face getting hot. "Don't even get me started on you! You and your stupid sorority. Your Kappa Kappa Kappa. Newsflash! That spells out KKK! Your sorority is the *KKK.* How has that not even passed your mind once? You *moron!*"

Ashley's jaw hung open for a moment, her eyes locked on Nicole.

"Why, I never…"

"Nicole, I don't know what's going on, but you're obviously very angry and lashing out right now," Laura said slowly.

"'*Obviously*'?" Nicole yelled. "Be more condescending, why don't you? This entire trip, that's all you've been. Nothing but condescending. If I had known this was how you were going to be, I never would've invited you."

"Come on now, obviously you don't mean that…" her mom began.

"No, Mom! I do!" Nicole snapped, flashing red over the second use of the world 'obviously'. Everyone *obviously* knew how she felt. Everyone thought Nicole was *obviously* in the wrong.

"I wish I'd never invited you!" Nicole shouted, squeezing her eyes shut. "At least then I would be a little happier!"

"Nicole…" Kevin began.

"Stop it with the condescending tones!" Nicole yelped, turning to Kevin with wide, wild eyes. She turned back to Laura, so furious that she could barely see straight. "I mean it. I wish I had never invited you. I wish I'd made you leave the second I realized how shitty of a girlfriend you are."

The world went silent for a moment. An intense

ringing filled Nicole's ears. Her brain pulsated wickedly in her skull. Her heart lodged in her throat.

Laura closed her eyes and pressed her lips together. She bowed her head forward, opened her eyes, and stared at the ground.

"Fine, then," she said, her voice disarmingly soft. "I'll be gone before the morning."

"Laura, honey..." Mrs. Winger began.

"It's okay," said Laura, already backing up. "It would be awkward if I stayed. Wrong, even."

Mrs. Winger turned to Nicole, her eyes pleading. This time it was Nicole's turn to stay silent, to refuse any type of support. In the distance, Nicole could see Sue-Anne and Rachel hurrying down the restaurant stairs, both saying short snippets to the other in rapid-fire succession.

"I'll be fine, I just..." Laura set her jaw. "If someone could give me a ride back to the hotel..."

"I'll do it," said Kevin, stepping forward.

"Do you really think that's a good idea?" Ella asked her brother. Nicole gritted her teeth. *Now* Ella speaks up...

"Trust me, I know what I'm doing," said Kevin. "Laura, whenever you're ready..."

"Now. I'm ready now," said Laura with her eyes closed.

"Alright. Let me get the keys from my mom," said Kevin.

"I'll meet you at the van," said Laura, her voice cracking. She turned her back on Nicole and disappeared into the parking lot.

Kevin looked at Mrs. Winger reassuringly.

"This is for the best," he said softly, his hand resting on Mrs. Winger's shoulder briefly before walking towards the restaurant, passing Sue-Anne and Rachel without acknowledging them.

"Just what in the blazes happened out here!" Sue-Anne shouted as she approached the group.

"We're *supposed* to be sitting down for the dinner," Rachel barked. "Instead we have everyone wondering what the commotion was all about."

"Nicole just made Laura leave," Meredith tattled.

Nicole's face tightened as Sue-Anne and Rachel both turned to her.

"Now, Nicole." Sue-Anne's voice echoed in Nicole's ears. "I'd figured you were a bit, well, troubled, but I never realized you were *this* troubled! Making such a great friend leave. If I had friends that were even half as loyal..."

"She's not my *friend,* dammit. She's my *girlfriend.*" Nicole threw her hands up. "My *actual* girlfriend. I'm sorry if you can't wrap your head around it but – guess what – I'm *gay.*"

Sue-Anne just stood there for a moment, silent.

"Is that clear enough for you yet?" Nicole took a step forward. "I'm G-A-Y gay. I didn't bring my *friend.* Laura's my girlfriend. Got it? Girl. Friend. She is my *girlfriend.*"

A sudden thought popped into her head, interrupting the whirlwind of emotions going on in Nicole's mind.

Is? Or was?

It was as if someone had just opened the relief valve. Nicole could feel all of her anger and venom – all of her energy in general – leak out of her, until she was just standing there, shoulders drooped, looking around for Laura or Kevin or the van in the parking lot.

"Everyone heard you yell in the restaurant," said Rachel, her voice cold and callous. "It is just luck the whole restaurant didn't come out to watch your little episode. I don't know how we're going to handle this."

"You sure made a mighty mess with this stunt," Sue-Anne added.

Nicole closed her eyes, wondering how in the world she had any energy left to continue standing where she was, to take in even one more breath.

"This is what we're gonna do: we're gonna go inside and pretend like your little blow-up never happened," Sue-Anne explained with a calm authority. "Cora and Andrew do not need to know about this. If anyone asks, I'll tell them that you had too much to drink – *again* – and you needed some fresh air to sober up. We'll deal with explaining Laura's absence if and when we have to. Is that understood?"

Nicole let her head hang down, her eyes on the

ground.

"Sure."

"Good," said Sue-Anne, flashing a toothy smile. "Now let's get inside, and we can *finally* get Cora and Andrew ready for their big rehearsal dinner introduction." Sue-Anne turned away from Nicole, faced the group, and clasped her hands. "You should hear the song we picked out for their rehearsal dinner first dance. Oh my word..."

Nicole scanned the parking lot. She was only able to find the van when it pulled out of its parking spot and turned onto the street. The van drove down Main Street, followed the first bend in the road, and disappeared from view.

Abby Rosmarin

Chapter Fourteen

Andrew was back home from college for a weekend visit. Like they had a thousand times before, he hopped into the driver's side of his mother's car with Nicole riding shotgun, and took off down one of the back roads.

The sun had long set and the roads were unlit, but Andrew effortlessly drove through every winding curve. The windows were down, the music up full volume. Nicole got to choose the music: a mix CD filled with all the pop songs that she never got to listen to when her mom was behind the wheel.

Nicole danced in her seat and sang along to the music. She sang along in a way that she couldn't when her mother was around. She sang along in a way that she couldn't even when she was by herself. She stuck her head out the window and sang into the wind and the darkness with the biggest, widest smile on her face. She didn't worry about how she sounded because she couldn't even hear her own voice. All she heard was the music blaring from inside the car and the wind whipping around her outside the car. She closed her eyes and belted out the higher notes with extra relish.

On previous nights, Nicole would pretend she was a pop star on stage, singing out her latest hit. That night, as she crooned out every note, Nicole felt no envy towards the pop stars. They might be touring around the globe with their band and their fans, but they weren't driving around with their big brother, breathing in the night sky and feeling freer than they ever had before.

The last song on the CD finished up, the car now silent as the album came to an end. Nicole pushed herself back into the car, her wild smile still splashed across her face. She looked over and saw Andrew smiling back just as wildly, as if he had been the one singing the entire time.

Chapter Fifteen

IT ALL GOES SOUTH FROM HERE

There was no sleep for Nicole that night. No sleep as the night slowly morphed into early morning. Nothing but fitful tossing and turning, sporadically interrupted by Nicole opening her eyes, always as she rolled to her right, always looking over at the empty bed next to her.

Counting sheep didn't help. Watching tacky infomercials on the outdated motel TV didn't help. She tried to clear her mind, but her mind refused to clear. She tried to let her mind wander, but every time she started thinking about the wedding or her family or what had happened that night, she jolted from whatever reverie she was in.

Around four in the morning, Nicole got the closest thing to sleep. For forty-five minutes, Nicole dozed, her mind finally and blissfully slipping away into a very light sleep. The dream was a short one: in it, Nicole was in Miami again, desperately trying to hail a taxi. Everyone was ignoring her, speeding up as they went past. Finally, one slowed down, pulling over to the side of the road and rolling down its window. Nicole approached the window, only to realize that the driver was Ella. Ella slammed the button on the meter, leaned over to Nicole, and said, "You know everything is ruined, right?"

Nicole bolted up in her bed, unable to catch her

breath. She pressed a hand into her chest and closed her eyes until her breathing normalized. After a few moments, she let out a heavy sigh, tossed the blankets away from her, slid out of bed, and tiptoed barefoot outside.

Nicole almost backtracked as she came to the railing on the second floor walkway. By the poolside sat a familiar-looking blonde, her legs gently kicking through the water. With pressed lips, Nicole forced herself down the stairs and around the gate to the pool area.

"Can't sleep either, huh?" Ella looked over as Nicole opened the gate.

"One of those nights, I guess," Nicole said with a half-hearted shrug.

Nicole sat down by the adjacent edge of the pool. She submerged her legs into the water and the water lapped against her knees.

"We've been here for three days and not once have we gone swimming," Ella remarked.

"I guess we really haven't had the time," Nicole replied.

"We'll have to rectify that tonight, then, after the wedding," said Ella. "We fly out first thing tomorrow morning."

"Yeah, we do too," said Nicole.

Ella swayed her legs from side to side, creating small waves that broke over the edge, soaking Nicole's PJ shorts.

"Laura's really gone, huh," said Ella.

Nicole looked down at her knees.

"Unless Kevin's a liar," she said.

"Still can't believe he just volunteered like that." Ella shook her head. "Actually, no I can. It got him out of attending the rehearsal dinner. I would've taxied *anyone* if it meant not having to watch the tossing of a ribbon bouquet."

Nicole smiled weakly, her upper lip slowly curling inward.

"Listen, about last night..." Ella began.

Nicole winced and put a palm up.

"I don't want to talk about it."

"But I do," Ella pressed. "You had absolutely no backup, no one on your side, and that was on me. That was really shitty of me to do. I spent this entire trip talking about how much of a joke this whole wedding was, how much of a mistake it was... and when you actually said something about it, I kept silent. And that wasn't okay."

Nicole leaned back and pressed her hands against the wet cement behind her.

"It's in the past. Nothing we can do about it now," Nicole sighed. "I'm just so embarrassed. I wish I hadn't said anything."

"Can I ask what happened?" asked Ella.

"What do you mean?"

"Well, something had to have happened for you to get that upset, right? The straw that broke the camel's back, so to speak?"

Nicole shook her head.

"I want to say it's because I found out Andrew's dropping out of Northwestern..."

"Andrew's dropping out of Northwestern?" Ella repeated, her eyes wide.

"Leaving Northwestern, leaving Chicago, moving here," said Nicole. "Maybe finishing up grad work in Miami, but probably not. Probably will become some community college professor and that will be that."

"Sheesh. No wonder you went nuts."

Nicole bit her tongue and shook her head.

"But, see: I wish it was as simple as that," said Nicole. "I really, really do. That makes me look less crazy. But it was like... I can't even put it into words." Nicole paused and rubbed her palms over her eyes. "And maybe that's my problem. This whole thing has been so messed up and I couldn't say exactly how or why. And I spent so long trying to act like, if it couldn't be said, then it wasn't worth feeling. But it all kind of... boiled over, I guess." Nicole shook her head again. "I don't know if any of that makes sense."

"No, no. It makes perfect sense," said Ella. "And I think I need to apologize again."

"What for?"

"For being a really shitty cousin," Ella answered.

"How in the world are you a shitty cousin?" said

Nicole. "You've been, like, the only person I could talk to this entire trip."

"Because I am. Because it's *your* brother who's getting married and I made it all about me," said Ella. She sighed and added: "And because Kevin's right and I hate that he is."

"What do you mean?"

Ella sighed again.

"I've been so angry," she said. "So frustrated that I keep working and working – that Roger keeps working and working – and we're both still struggling. And then I see people like Cora in the world, who get everything handed to them, no struggle, no work. Everything I had to sacrifice, everything I wasn't allowed to have, she gets. I got so wrapped up and... I didn't even think for one second about how this was affecting you. *Actually* affecting you. Not me projecting my own feelings onto your experience."

"You sound like a psychologist there," Nicole interjected with a slight smirk.

"Maybe I do," said Ella. "But maybe I need to play psychologist for a second. This is a complicated situation. And it's obviously had a complicated effect on you. And I was too busy shooting down the wedding that I didn't stop to think about what it was doing to you. I'd made it all about me – I mean, hell, I'm *still* making it all about me. Even in this apology. I've been nothing but self-absorbed and I really am sorry."

"Again, it's in the past," said Nicole. "Besides, I don't think you being more selfless would've magically made everything better."

"It could've made it easier."

"The only thing that could make things easier is if the wedding got called off," Nicole countered. "And this wedding is going to happen, whether we want it to or not."

"We could always burn down the church," Ella offered with a cocked eyebrow.

"I'm not ready to go to jail over this. It'll just give Sue-Anne more arsenal," said Nicole with her own cocked eyebrow.

"Well, think of this way," Ella said, lifting a foot out the water and gently splashing Nicole. "At least there will be free food."

Nicole looked up. Dawn was settling in around them; the sky was already a hypnotic shade of blue.

"At least there's that."

***

Pam and Gretchen were waiting for them outside the entrance of the church. Both ladies sported the clothing from the day before, as well as large, dark circles under their eyes.

"Okay, okay, we have..." Pam started, anxiously flipping through her pages on her clipboard. Gretchen followed suit with her own clipboard. "Mother of the groom, Annette Winger, aunt and uncle, Pete and Barbara Winger... our ushers, sister Nicole Winger and cousins Ella and Kevin Winger..."

Both ladies looked up from their pages and scanned each person from head to toe with their tired eyes.

"Hair, makeup, and dress all adhere to the expectations set forth in the wedding party pamphlet," Pam continued. "Alright. Annette, you are to follow me to the Mothers of the Bride and Groom suite. Pete and Barbara, you are welcomed to go where you may until 2 p.m. sharp, at which point I must insist you get escorted to your seats. Nicole, Ella, and Kevin, you can follow Gretchen into the main lobby where she will give further instruction."

Nicole locked eyes with Gretchen and Gretchen responded with a weary smile.

"Well, this way, then," Gretchen said, making her way up the stairs.

Nicole, Ella, and Kevin followed Gretchen up to the main entrance. Gretchen held open one of the doors and the rest silently walked in.

Nicole nearly tripped over the doorframe as she went into the narthex. What was originally a simple church lobby had transformed into a botanical wonderland. Flowers decorated every nook and cranny, punctuated by large, fake flowers that had pictures of Andrew and Cora in their centers.

The main area of the church looked more like the inside of a castle on coronation day than an actual, modern-day congregation. Nicole didn't think it was possible, but it was even more decorated than it had been the day before. White satin with blue sashes covered every pew. White and blue rose pedals lined the aisles. A silver strip of ribbon cordoned off the center aisle, looping down from the inner edges of the last row and tied in the center with an intricate knot. A single gardenia had been slipped in between the loops of the center bow. Along the perimeter of the church, people in black suits and gray dresses hurried about, carrying boxes and bags.

"This is very simple, okay?" said Gretchen, reaching under a table draped with a golden tablecloth. "Address every person who comes in with, 'Good afternoon, y'all.' Hand them one wedding program each and then direct them to one of the professional ushers. The ushers will be waiting just inside this center door. The side doors will be closed before the guests arrive, but, in case anyone tries, *do not* let anyone go through either of the side doors. Got it? Redirect them back to the center entrance and the professional ushers can take it from there."

Gretchen slid out a box from under the table, opened the lid, and pulled out an armload of what appeared to be square-shaped novellas. She turned to Nicole, Ella, and Kevin and handed each of them a four-inch stack.

"When y'all run out, one of y'all may get additional ones," Gretchen continued. "But *only* one of y'all can restock at a time. And this *must* be done when there is a lull in guests and *only* done by the person facing *farthest* from the entranceway. We can*not* have the flow of guests disrupted because of this. Do I make myself clear?"

"Yes ma'am," Ella responded with a grotesquely fake southern accent.

Gretchen sighed and eyed Ella up and down.

"I'm needed with the bridesmaids now. If you need anything, you can talk to one of the ushers and hopefully they'll be able to help you."

"Sounds like a plan," said Kevin in his normal,

alarmingly casual voice.

Gretchen said nothing and instead buried her face in her clipboard, spun on her heels, and zoomed away, leaving the three to stand there, the only still people in a sea of moving bodies.

"Well, now…" Ella started.

"I'm pretty sure there are drill sergeants who are more lenient," said Nicole.

"And I'm pretty sure I've had textbooks that were thinner," said Ella, flipping through one of the programs.

"She's just doing her job." Kevin shrugged. "I'm sure she was given that list of requirements from somebody above her."

"Like Sue-Anne or her little minion Rachel?" Ella replied.

Kevin shrugged again.

"Like somebody," said Kevin.

Ella said nothing. She closed the novella-program she was flipping through and walked towards the main area of the church, stopping at the doorframe and sending a sigh down the center aisle.

"So… it's actually happening," Ella said, resting her stack of novella-programs on her hip.

"I guess so," Nicole replied, leaning against the doorframe, hugging her stack of programs to her chest.

"I cannot believe Andrew's *actually* going to go through with it," Ella continued.

"Now, I might be totally crazy here, but this conversation might not be the best to have – y'know, right before the wedding, and where the wedding is *actually* going to take place," Kevin warned.

Ella gave out a loud sigh. She eyed the center aisle one last time and joined Nicole by the door, her hand resting on Nicole's shoulder. She gave Nicole's shoulder a gentle squeeze before using both hands to hold her stack of programs.

Nicole just stood there for a while, taking in the overall chaos. The harpist was tuning her harp in one corner while the string quartet tested their instruments in the mezzanine. A group of girls that Nicole surmised to be the cheerleaders were spending their time testing out the bubble makers and giggling over something that Nicole couldn't pick up on. The men who appeared to be the professional ushers tidied and then re-tidied their suits as they moved around the church, pausing to scan the rows of pews, mouthing out names, numbers, and letters.

As the minutes dragged on, the florists, seamstresses, and a whole bevy of other people whom Nicole could never place a profession towards slowly left the building. The two entrances on either side of the main doors were eventually closed. The cheerleaders took their places along the outside edges of the congregation, their bubble wands ready.

Before long, Aunt Barbara and Uncle Pete came out to the front.

"We'll gladly be your first guests," Aunt Barbara said to Ella. "May I have a wedding program, please?"

"Of course!" Ella said with sardonic gusto, handing over one of the novella-programs. "Some light reading to pass the time. And – since I am required to say it – might I add, 'Good afternoon, *y'all*.'"

"They don't *really* have you saying that," Aunt Barbara cocked her head to one side, flipping through the program as she did so.

"They *really* do," Ella replied, mimicking her mom's head movements. "And don't forget to let the *professional ushers* help you find your seat." Ella gave a broad smile before handing her father a program as well.

"Well, we'll see you inside," Uncle Pete said, waving the hand that was holding his program before leading his wife through the archway, where they were immediately greeted by one of the ushers.

When Aunt Barbara and Uncle Pete were far enough from the entranceway, Nicole whispered to Ella, "Do they know?"

Ella leaned in to Nicole.

"Know what?"

"Do they know about last night?" Nicole whispered, her hands tightening around her programs.

"They knew you stormed out of the restaurant. Sue-Anne told them what she told everyone else: that you'd had too much to drink and needed some fresh air," Ella whispered back. "They asked me where Laura was and I told them the truth: that you two got into a fight and she left."

"Great," Nicole replied flatly. "Sue-Anne wins out and my own aunt and uncle think I'm a drunk."

"Well, I don't think so," Ella countered. "I think they assumed that what really happened is that you and Laura got into an argument and Sue-Anne made up the drunk part as a cover-up."

"Well, thank God for small blessings," Nicole muttered.

Just then, an elderly couple gingerly made their way over to Nicole and the rest, *ooh*ing and *aah*ing over the decorations in the narthex.

"Good afternoon, y'all," Nicole said to them with a forced smile and no hint of a southern accent.

For the next hour, guests streamed into the church. Kevin systematically slipped off to the side to get more programs, filling up Ella and Nicole's stacks as well as his own. Nicole greeted and smiled and directed everyone to the professional ushers, not recognizing a single face in the crowd.

It quickly dawned on her that, of all the people invited, essentially everyone was a resident of East Braedonton. Aside from Jacob and Evan – who were in the wedding party – and Andrew's immediate family – their mom, Aunt Barbara, Uncle Pete, Ella and Kevin – there was no one from Andrew's life at the wedding. No childhood friends, no fellow football players, no fellow Northwestern grad students. No neighbors or mentors. Just a steady stream of people with exaggerated accents.

"My, my. You are *so* kind – for a yank!" one old lady said as she took a program from Ella. Ella's smile quickly devolved into a grimace.

"Thanks. I do my best."

The guests came in at a steady pace, the stream of people unrelenting, the professional ushers bringing everyone to their assigned seats with superhuman efficiency. Every once in a while, one of the cheerleader's bubbles would stray, floating out of the main congregation and into the narthex. Nicole would watch them as they gently drifted across the room – the one calm entity in the midst of all the chaos – before they bounced against the edge of something and popped.

About fifteen minutes before the ceremony was scheduled to start, the inflow of guests slowed to a trickle. Ten minutes before the ceremony, it slowed further to the occasional guest or two. Five minutes before the ceremony, Sue-Anne came out, draped in a shiny blue dress that dramatically flared out at the hips, her hair in a large bouffant, a huge smile plastered on her face.

"Oh, how wonderful," Sue-Anne beamed. "Everythin' is goin' off without a hitch! Kevin, Ella, if y'all would like to see y'allselves inside, one of the ushers will be able to sit y'all next to y'all's parents."

Kevin gathered up the remaining programs and returned them to the box under the table. Ella gave Nicole a look that Nicole couldn't quite decipher.

"See you inside," Ella said.

Nicole could only nod, her eyes following her cousins as they left. Each pew was filled to the brim, guests sitting shoulder to shoulder from one side to the next. The idle murmur from everyone almost drowned out the harp.

"Now, as for you, I need you to help me here," said Sue-Anne. She brought one hand close to her face and started rubbing the pads of her fingers against her thumb.

"Um, okay. Sure," Nicole responded.

"We can't have any stragglin' guests interruptin' things like, say, the procession," said Sue-Anne. "Or anyone, for that matter, tryin' to come through any of these big doors. Do you follow me?"

"Um, yes?"

"So I need you to stay right here – but not *here*, of course, by these here center doors. That's where the procession will be." Sue-Anne swiveled to her left, her dress billowing out as she turned. "No, no. I need you *there*."

Sue-Anne pointed to a small door towards the end of the narthex.

"You can keep an eye out for any guests that our *professional* security staff might miss during the procession. You'll be able to direct them – as well as anyone comin' in *after* the procession – to that door, right there." Sue-Anne placed a cold hand on Nicole's shoulder. "And do make sure you open the door quietly for them. We can't have any disruptions during the ceremony itself."

Nicole felt like shrinking inside of herself, as far away from Sue-Anne's touch as possible.

"Um, yeah."

"I figure, given all the recent events and – uh – *revelations*, you wouldn't mind missin' some of the weddin'," Sue-Anne continued. "I'm sure you'll know when a good time'll be to come on in. There'll be a chair just on the other side of that-there door, saved just for you for when you're ready to join the rest of the guests."

Nicole could barely think, blink, or breathe. How she was able to stay standing – and how she was able to nod to Sue-Anne – was a complete and total mystery to her.

"Oh, bless your heart." Sue-Anne flashed a large smile, exposing the gums of her upper teeth. "I knew you'd do it. Now, if you'll excuse me, I need to join up with your *wonderful* mother and get ready for the ceremony."

Sue-Anne leaned past Nicole and got the attention one of the ushers on the other side of the doorframe. The usher turned around to see Sue-Anne pantomiming a tap on the invisible watch on her wrist.

"Right away, ma'am," the usher whispered. He caught the eye of the usher across from him, who followed him out into the narthex.

"If you'd excuse us, miss," the second one said to Nicole as they walked past her.

Nicole numbly stepped back. With a polite smile, the ushers walked to the outside doors and, after a quiet countdown from three, slowly closed the doors behind them. They marched in unison back into the main area, where, after another quiet countdown from three, pulled the central doors' handles, slowly closing themselves and the rest of the church off from Nicole.

Sue-Anne let out one long, satisfied sigh, looked Nicole over one last time, and left. Nicole stared at the main doors, gave out her own, defeated sigh, and walked over to the small door in the leftmost corner.

She pressed her back against the wall by the door and closed her eyes. She took in tiny, shallow breaths. She let her head hang forward and her shoulders hunch over.

Before she could fully process what had just happened, Pam came darting up into the narthex from the stairwell on the opposite side, her hand pressed onto the earpiece of her headset.

"Yes, yes, we're ready to go. Groom and priest are coming up now."

Pam spun around and stared down the stairwell that she had just emerged out of. Moments later, Andrew walked into the narthex with a middle-aged man in clergy robes to his right. Andrew's tux was sleek, with a rose boutonniere pinned to his lapel. His hands were clasped in front of him, his knuckles white.

"Okay, you and you, right in front of the main door," Pam spoke in a hurried whisper. "The music will change and they will open the door. Just like in rehearsals, wait two beats and then walk. Is that understood?"

"Understood," Andrew said.

Nicole wanted to step forward and say something. She stared at Andrew, hoping he would catch her looking at him. In her mind, they would exchange glances, and Nicole could somehow communicate to her brother just how much she cared for him, even with everything going on. She'd be able to give him a look of pure love and understanding, something that would make up for everything that had happened. But Andrew's eyes were locked on the center doors in front of him.

The music changed – organ music now playing alongside the harp, practically drowning out the harp entirely – and the doors opened. Pam pushed the microphone portion of her headset close to her mouth and mumbled something into it. Andrew and the minister started walking forward in sync with each other and to the beat of the music. Moments later, Nicole's and Cora's mothers walked up the stairs and stopped a few feet in front of the center doorway. They paused for a few beats before walking in as well. Neither her mom nor Sue-Anne looked over her way, and part of her was incredibly relieved for that.

Nicole pressed herself against the wall, making herself as small and as invisible as possible when the wedding party came up. She felt a wave of embarrassment and humiliation wash over her. She closed her eyes and prayed that she wouldn't faint or throw up – or, worse, be seen by anyone in the wedding party.

She didn't want Jacob to see the girl he'd known since she was in middle school sitting outside the wedding like a forgotten club bouncer. She didn't want Meredith or Ashley to see her like this, in what was clearly payback for how she had behaved the night before – perhaps for how she had behaved since she had touched down in Florida. Only Rachel glanced over, briefly eyeing Nicole up and down before suppressing a smirk and walking down the aisle. Everyone else focused on Pam's hushed directions before disappearing through the double doors.

Eventually, the music stopped, and the doors to the narthex closed. For a moment, everything became incredibly quiet. Pam looked over at Nicole for the first time. She paused to give Nicole a pitying look before cupping her hand over her mouthpiece and turning to the doors that lead outside.

The music started up again, and the doors connecting the main area of the church to the narthex reopened. Two professional ushers marched in sync directly across the narthex, towards the outside doors. Both stopped at the door handles, facing each other with stoic expressions. As the music began to crescendo, the two ushers opened the front doors.

Nicole could hear the entire congregation standing up from their pews, the ruffling and shuffling almost drowning out the music. Cora and her father walked up the front steps and into the narthex, pausing a few feet from the entrance into the congregation.

Cora was decked out in a large, white gown, one that hugged her slim torso before billowing out in all directions. Cora glanced over at Nicole and gave her a look. Before Nicole could respond or even decipher what the look meant, Cora looked over at her father, smiled, and disappeared through the archway. The ten-foot trail of Cora's dress was the only thing Nicole was left with – until it, too, disappeared. As the music ended and the wedding guests cheered, the two ushers closed the front doors, walked through the archway, and closed the second set of doors behind them.

Nicole scanned the narthex and realized that, at some point, Pam had left as well. She must've disappeared down the staircase when Cora was looking at Nicole.

What did Cora mean when she did that? Did she feel like she had finally won? Was it pity? Was she thinking anything at all? What was going on in her mind in those brief seconds?

Did it matter? At the end of the day, Nicole was alone in the narthex, deliberately excluded from her own brother's wedding. She had absolutely nothing, save for a quiet entrance through a side door and a chair by the wall to witness the event.

Nicole collapsed against the wall and slid down to the floor. She tucked her knees into her chest and placed her head in her hands. She could hear the muffled ceremony going on behind her. She knew she could probably sneak in now and experience the ceremony from her designated spot in the back. But that was the problem: she would have to sneak, so as to not disturb anyone, and wait in the shadows.

That was what she had been reduced to.

So she sat there, tears silently running down her face, her head clouded with a thousand different thoughts. She was tempted to leave the church, walk all the way past the East Braedonton border, catch a cab, and fly home to Chicago. But what was waiting for her there? A temp gig, set to end as soon as the project she was on finished? An angry girlfriend, potentially ex-girlfriend? Nicole clasped the back of her neck, tears streaming down harder.

She wasn't sure how much time had passed. At some point, the entire congregation *aww*-ed and applauded, and it was enough to disrupt her crying. Nicole wiped the tears from her cheeks and got up. With a slow, steady breath, Nicole opened the side door and snuck in.

To her left was a metal folding chair, tucked behind one of the large canvas photos on an iron stand. If Nicole had sat down, she would have had the view of the back of the canvas and nothing else. Nicole couldn't help but chuckle – really, at that point, all she could do was laugh – and stood beside the photo instead.

The congregation started applauding again. Up at the front of the church, inside the gazebo-pergola, stood Andrew and Cora, holding hands and staring into each other's eyes. Even from where she was standing, she could see Andrew was smiling from ear to ear.

"The demonstration of love goes beyond the giving of rings," said the minister with a melodic southern accent. "May your holy union provide a lifetime of demonstration for love and giving. By the power invested in me, I now pronounce you husband and wife. You may kiss the bride."

Nicole's heart sank as Andrew and Cora leaned in for their kiss, the entire congregation going wild. She immediately blamed the kiss, the pronouncement of marriage, for how she felt. But as Andrew and Cora turned to the crowd and as the minister proclaimed, "Ladies and gentleman: the new Mr. and Mrs. Andrew and Cora Winger!" and as the congregation applauded even louder, Nicole knew the real reason.

There was her brother, walking down the aisle with his new wife, and Nicole had missed the entire wedding. At that moment, she didn't care about the events leading up to it, or the mystery surrounding Cora, or the fact that Nicole had been intentionally left outside during the procession. It didn't matter that she could easily blame everyone else for her situation. All that mattered right then and there was that Nicole had missed watching her brother get married and it filled her with a sadness that transcended words.

She stood there by the canvas photo as Andrew and Cora walked down the aisle, bubbles and rice and harp music filling every square inch of space. She stood there as the rest of the wedding party went down the aisle, followed by her mom and Cora's parents, followed by the minister. She stood there as the rest of the congregation left, vacating pew after pew after pew. She stood there as the room emptied out and the bubble blowing cheerleaders exited, followed by the professional ushers.

She stood there as the musicians up in the mezzanine got up and left. She stood there as the harpist stood up and stretched, the church suddenly silent as she exited out a side door.

Nicole stood there a moment longer, just her and the empty church. With a heavy sigh, she went through the side door she had just come in before sneaking out a side exit in the narthex. She wove her way through the parking lot and stood by the rented minivan and waited for the rest of her family.

"There you are!" Uncle Pete exclaimed, the sole family member walking to the van after what felt like an eternity by herself. "We were looking for you! I told them that she would probably wait by the minivan if she couldn't find us. And – lo and behold – I was right!"

"Yup," said Nicole, her arms tightly wound across her chest. "You found me."

"Oh man, wasn't that something?" Uncle Pete remarked, his fists resting on his hips, sweat stains forming around the folds of his shirt. "I mean, I don't think I've ever been to a wedding like that before!"

"Tell me about it," Nicole said flatly.

"I mean, kudos to Sue-Anne and her family for putting this all together," Uncle Pete went on. "Seriously: wasn't that something?"

"It sure was."

***

The reception took place on the connected rooftops along one side of the main street. The rooftop area had been completely transformed, with slick hardwood floors resting on top of the asphalt. Stringed lights floated delicately from post to post over the dining area and dance floor. There were rows upon rows of long tables covered with white silk. Silver table runners went the entire distance of each row, pinned down by an overwhelming assortment of candles and flowers and miniature ice sculpture replicas. White flower bouquets hung from the wooden posts holding up the lights.

Guests entered through the restaurant that Nicole and

her family had had brunch at during their first morning in town. The restaurant interior had been transformed: its wooden tables and metal chairs removed and replaced with more long tables covered in white silk. A round table holding an ice swan accented the center of the restaurant, with hors d'oeuvres arranged around the sculpture. The atmosphere was chic and ethereal, turning the diner into a type of upscale cocktail lounge. In one corner, the formerly-on-standby string quartet were now playing what Nicole could only assume were classical covers of country songs.

The beginning of the reception was reminiscent of the beginning of the Chicago engagement party, only with Pam and Gretchen running around instead of Rachel and Sue-Anne. Everyone milled about before being ushered towards their assigned seats. In lieu of place cards, each guest's name had been embroidered into the silk tablecloth, the thread of the embroidery the same shade of silver as the table runners. Nicole sat down by her name, acutely aware of the empty seat next to her, of Laura's name intricately stitched in the cloth.

The lights dimmed before two projector screens descended from either side of the DJ booth. The screens lit up with a view of the sidewalk area just outside of the restaurant. Through the video feed, the guests watched as an antique limousine pulled up. One of the professional ushers opened the back passenger door and Rachel and Fred stepped out. The guests erupted into applause as Rachel and Fred walked into the restaurant, up the stairs, and onto the dance floor. They did a lap around the dance floor before stopping to the left of the DJ booth.

Another antique limousine pulled up; this time Susanna, the solo maid of honor, came out. She made her way up to the dance floor with a smile on her face and her head held high. Nicole watched as the pattern continued: an antique limousine would pull up and let out one or two members of the wedding party, and those people would slowly make their way up to the dance floor. She watched Sarah round out the adult wedding party with Evan, her left hand strategically by her face, showing off her fake ring. The last limousine to arrive had the flower girl and ring bearer, which caused the guests to give out a collective *aww*.

After a pause and an actual drumroll (supplied by the DJ's stereo speakers), Cora and Andrew's horse-drawn carriage arrived. A red carpet rolled out to meet them. The East Braedonton cheerleaders quickly assembled on either side of the red carpet, blowing bubbles as Cora and Andrew stepped out of the stagecoach.

The new couple walked up the stairs and into the reception. The entire rooftop erupted in cheers as Andrew and Cora made their way onto the dance floor. The DJ announced their first dance as husband and wife, and Andrew gently placed an arm around Cora's waist.

The first dance was jarringly normal. No acrobats or flashing lights. No platforms rising up from the dance floor. No intricate choreography or solo dance numbers. Just Andrew and Cora, swaying from side to side to a slow country melody. When the song ended, the couple bowed to the audience and walked over to the sweetheart wedding table, which had been adorned with a cascade of white roses.

Nicole spent the majority of the reception in her seat, eating her food with a morose slowness. When the second and third courses arrived, she simply pushed her other plates to the side, reassuring the constantly curious waiters that she was planning on finishing her food.

Nicole sat alongside her aunt, her uncle, and her cousins. Her mom was stationed next to Sue-Anne at the wedding party table, which housed the same type of waterfall flower arrangement as Cora and Andrew's table. Her mom checked in on the family once during dinner before returning to the wedding party table and getting lost in conversation with Sue-Anne. Andrew and Cora remained seated at their table, looking up at anyone who walked over to them with huge smiles plastered on their faces.

Not much was said during the dinner portion: a few pleasantries, a few innocuous comments, idle chit chat with whoever was close by. Nicole kept to herself, sporadically looking down at her embroidered name on the tablecloth. It was oddly consoling, in a way. Finally, she had a place where she belonged, a place that she couldn't lose at the last minute, even if it was technically just a seating arrangement.

But the feeling wouldn't last. Eventually she'd look over at Laura's name and lose any type of consolation.

Nicole snapped to attention as the DJ announced the impending cake-cutting ceremony. A waiter silently cleared away Nicole's spot, removing her half-eaten plates before Nicole could protest. Out rolled an ornate, seven-tier cake, sitting on a silk tablecloth and a bed of white rose petals. On top of the cake sat a bride and groom made out of sparking crystal. Andrew and Cora took turns delicately placing tiny bits of cake in each other's mouth, much to the delight of the guests.

Nicole felt some reprieve when the dance floor opened up and a good portion of people left the tables. A few went out to dance, but most simply walked to other tables to chat. Uncle Pete dragged a reluctant Aunt Barbara to the dance floor, where he dramatically spun and dipped her. Aunt Barbara smiled, shook her head, and kissed her husband tenderly.

For a while, it was just Nicole, Ella, and Kevin, sitting alone at their stretch of table. After a few songs, Kevin got up, accepting the dance request of a very persistent flower girl (Alexandra was her name, right? Nicole couldn't keep track anymore). Somewhere in a far corner of the rooftop reception, Andrew was politely chatting with an elderly woman.

"Well, wedding of the century, huh?" Ella sighed and pushed herself away from the table.

"Wouldn't even know," Nicole replied.

"What do you mean by that?"

"I mean I didn't even get to see any of the ceremony."

"Wait, what?" Ella sat up in her seat. "I mean, I know Sue-Anne kept you behind at first but... did she kick you out or something?"

"More or less." Nicole rubbed the back of her neck. "I really don't want to talk about it, to be perfectly honest."

"Understandable," said Ella. "If it's anything, you didn't miss much."

"I don't buy that for a second," said Nicole, her eyes

back on her embroidered name, then Laura's.

"Okay, yeah, there was a whole lot of spectacle going on, I'll give you that," said Ella. "But, I don't know... There was something very formal and scripted about it."

"Scripted? A wedding that micromanaged how people walked down the aisle?" Nicole smirked. "Never."

"Oh, ha, ha." Ella rolled her eyes. "But seriously. It lacked any personal touch. Everything felt unnatural and forced. Kind of like this reception."

Ella paused and motioned towards the center of the rooftop. There was a smattering of people on the dance floor, but most of the guests had simply reorganized to sit and chat by the tables. Cora stood by the end of one row, talking with a group of people.

"I mean, look at her: she's acting more like a hostess at a fundraising event than a newlywed," Ella pointed out. "I mean, we're only a yard or so away from the dance floor, and the energy over here is dead."

Nicole scanned the area around them.

"You have a point."

"I don't know, maybe it's impossible to have a personal wedding when you have this many guests," said Ella. She sighed, shifted her weight, and crossed her arms. "Y'know, some people would consider this the perfect fairytale wedding. It's got everything: a harpist and a string quartet, a horse-drawn carriage, a huge guest list, an exotic venue..."

"You consider East Braedonton exotic?" said Nicole.

"We might as well be in a strange, foreign land," said Ella with a grin. "But, still, though. This has all the trappings of a perfect wedding, to the T. And maybe I'm just trying to make myself feel better, but, seeing all this, I'm suddenly very grateful for the wedding I had." Ella paused and sighed. "I mean, yeah, I didn't have any of this. But – the people who were there for my wedding? They were nearly as ecstatic as me. There was heart, which is what this gigantic event is missing. Missing in spades."

Nicole could only nod along. She watched Andrew's college friend Evan bring maid of honor Rachel out onto the dance floor, holding her begrudging hands and smiling wickedly as he shimmied from side to side. Rachel rolled her eyes and let a small smirk come out. Across the rooftop stood Sarah, talking to a small group with exaggerated expressions. She twirled the fake engagement ring around her finger and occasionally tossed a poisoned glance over at Cora. At one of the tables sat Karen, her eyes glued to her phone's screen, a content grin on her face as she typed away. At another table sat Susanna, holding a bouncing baby as she talked to the man next to her. Both the man and Susanna had their eyes on the child, their smiles wide and joyous.

"I don't know. I hope it works out for Andrew and Cora," Ella continued. "I don't know anything about them or what their relationship is like, but, y'know, at the end of the day, I hope he's happy. The wedding was ridiculous, but if he's happy, that's all that matters. Right?"

"Sure," said Nicole, and the ache in her chest returned.

"C'mon, let's at least get our boogie on," said Ella, getting up from her seat.

Nicole sighed, smiled, and followed her cousin onto the dance floor. The music had been consistently country music – something Nicole never really fancied – but the beat of the up-tempo songs was enough to keep her moving. Nicole kept looking over at Andrew, who had not entered the dance floor since his first dance with Cora. When a slow song came on and couples paired up on the dance floor, Nicole leaned in towards Ella.

"I'll be back," she said.

"Where are you going?" Ella asked.

"To the DJ booth," Nicole replied. "There's a song they have to play."

"Have at it," said Ella. "I'm getting off the dance floor before any creepy dudes ask me to dance."

Nicole shot two thumbs up as her reply. Ella shook her head and laughed before disappearing from sight. Nicole turned and made her way over to the DJ booth.

There was one song Nicole knew would make Andrew smile. It was an old pop song that Andrew would sing alongside Nicole back when she was a teenager. It was the one song that could send Andrew's toes tapping as Nicole pranced around the house, the radio blaring way louder than their mother appreciated. She wanted that song to be her olive branch. She wanted to steal her brother away from the idle chatter and polite pleasantries. She wanted to bring him onto the dance floor and maybe help him remember where he came from.

"I'd like to request a song," Nicole said as she approached the table.

"No requests, ma'am. Sorry," the DJ responded.

"What do you mean 'no requests'?" Nicole asked.

"Ma'am, I cannot take requests. I'm sorry," said the DJ.

"But I'm the sister of the groom," said Nicole, her eyebrows furrowed. "That has to count for something."

"I have a very specific playlist to play, ma'am," the DJ replied, his fake southern accent getting a little thicker with each sentence. "I was told that, under no circumstances, can I deviate from it. Rules are rules, ma'am. I can't take requests. I'm sorry."

"...But I'm the sister of the groom," Nicole meekly repeated.

"Ma'am. I'm sorry."

Nicole bit her lower lip, nodded slowly, and turned away from the DJ booth. As she turned, she caught a glimpse of Andrew and Cora talking to a group of people at one table end. Andrew was speaking in a lively manner, his smile still from ear to ear, as Cora stood by his side.

As if knowing someone was watching her, Cora looked over at Nicole.

Nicole didn't know what to make of this exchange, either. Unlike at the church, Cora continued to look at her. Cora stared with big, round eyes, not smiling like a blushing bride or smirking like a woman who got her way – both things that Nicole would have expected. Instead, there was something else. Something Nicole couldn't put a finger on. Before Nicole could make sense of it, one of the ladies at the table touched Cora's arm, and Cora immediately returned to the conversation. Nicole walked away from the DJ booth and the dance floor, found the stairwell, and made her way down to the first floor.

***

Nicole spent the rest of the reception in the downstairs restaurant area, listening to the string quartet and smiling politely to anyone who passed her by.

After a while, she went over to the ice sculpture swan and pressed a hand into it. She retracted her hand only when the cold started to burn her skin. She returned her hand to that same spot on the swan, holding it there for as long as she could stand it. She kept repeating this until the swan's left wing had a discernable handprint-shaped dent in it.

"There are better ways to wash your hands," said a familiar voice.

Nicole snapped around to see Cora's father picking at the remaining hors d'oeuvres on the table.

"So, how are you enjoying the wedding so far?" Dan Bachman asked, his voice deep and slow. It was at that moment that Nicole realized he didn't have any trace of a southern accent. That, or Nicole was hearing him drop it for the first time.

"Oh, it's great. It's beautiful and Cora's beautiful and..." Nicole started gibbering.

"Oh, don't lie." Dan popped a decorative cheese ball in his mouth. "You've been unhappy since you got here and you spent most of that wedding in the lobby."

Nicole's hands gripped around her cocktail plate.

"How do you know that?" she asked quietly.

Dan shrugged.

"Ah, I have my ways."

All Nicole could do was nod in response.

"That little stunt my wife pulled? That wasn't okay. But that's my little Sue-A for you. She means well. And Cora's her youngest. She's going to be protective," said Dan. "What can you do, ya know?"

Nicole swore she could hear the slightest hint of a New Jersey accent begin to creep out.

"I don't blame you, though," Dan went on. "About everything. I get it. I do. We're very similar, you and I."

"Oh?" was all Nicole could say.

"I didn't like East Braedonton when I first got here either. But it's a good town, with good people. Loyal people. Great place to hide away, or hide a body."

Dan paused and winked at Nicole. Nicole just stared at Dan, her mouth slightly open.

"Oh, I'm just messing with you," said Dan with a knowing grin. "But really, this town grows on you. It has its – shall we say – quirks, but the heart is in the right place. Much like its people. Give it time, and you'll realize they're not so bad."

"I really have been having a good time. I swear."

"Oh, sweetheart. You're a terrible liar," Dan remarked. "And I'm notorious for figuring out liars."

Nicole bit her lower lip, her eyes involuntarily widening.

"You don't have to pretend with me. I told you, I get it. I just wanted to reach out to you, make you understand that. You're family now, so I want you to be comfortable."

"I am comfortable," Nicole found herself saying.

"Ah, hon. You got a good heart. You really do," Dan said, gently patting Nicole on the shoulder. Nicole stood perfectly still. "I should get back upstairs. I'm sure I'm scheduled to be somewhere right now. You take care of yourself, okay?"

"Okay."

Dan patted Nicole's shoulder one more time.

"You're a good kid. Call me if you need anything. Anything at all," he said with another wink before disappearing upstairs.

Nicole looked back at the ice swan, at the part she had melted with her hand. It looked like someone had tried to clip the swan's wing, but ended up breaking it instead. She filled up her plate with room-temperature hors d'oeuvres and found a nook to sequester herself in.

There, she was even more invisible than before. She was even more of an observer, an outsider looking in. She stared out the diner's windows. She listened to the music and muffled chatter and compared it to the eerie stillness of the main street – empty, save for the streetlamps glowing orange. She listened to the gentle hum of the air conditioning as it came through the vents. She took in the transformed diner and the deformed swan and the feeling of the wall against her back. She closed her eyes and, for a minute, imagined a completely different wedding, in a completely different town, with completely different people, and with a completely different outcome.

"Alright, alright, y'all!" the DJ called out. "It's comin' up on that time of the night. The time when we save the best for last and the bride n' groom have their last dance. But first, I must direct y'all's attention upward, as the East Braedonton fire department will be setting off only the most beautiful fireworks y'all've ever seen!"

Nicole put down her cocktail plate and made her way back upstairs. She returned to her assigned seat with her embroidered name, where she found her mom talking with Ella, Aunt Barbara, and Uncle Pete.

"Oh, you're just in time!" said Uncle Pete to Nicole. "Did you hear they're about to do fireworks?"

"I did," Nicole replied.

Ella smirked knowingly and gently shook her head.

"This really has been a special evening," remarked Aunt Barbara to Mrs. Winger. "You must be so proud."

Nicole's mom blushed.

"I'm so happy for my little boy," she said.

"That was seriously an incredible wedding," said Aunt Barbara.

"Well, you know what they say – after the wedding day, it's all downhill from here," Uncle Pete remarked, chuckling to himself. "Or, should I say, it's all goes *south* from here." When no one responded, Uncle Pete repeated: "I said – it all goes *south* from here…"

"We heard you the first time, darling," Aunt Barbara said in a warm, yet sarcastic voice.

Kevin walked up to the family and rested his hand on his father's shoulder.

"Did you hear, Kevin?" Uncle Pete turned to his son. "They're about to do fireworks!"

"I heard, Dad. I heard," Kevin replied, looking over at Nicole with somber eyes.

"All this – *and* fireworks? Can you believe it?"

"I really can't," said Nicole before the night sky lit up with the first firework.

Abby Rosmarin

Chapter Sixteen

THE REAL WORLD

"Y'know, we've been in Florida for nearly a week and not once have we gone swimming," Uncle Pete said during the drive back to the hotel.

"I was just thinking that, earlier today," said Aunt Barbara.

"Well, if everyone isn't already too tired, I say we make use of that hotel's pool before we fly back up north," said Uncle Pete.

"I think that's a great idea," said Mrs. Winger.

Uncle Pete tilted his head towards the back of the van.

"What say you, rugrats? Feel like going swimming at night?"

"I could definitely use a swim," said Kevin.

"Sounds good to me," said Ella.

"Sure," replied Nicole.

Aunt Barbara pulled into the motel parking lot. The family entered their rooms in their wedding attire and reemerged in their bathing suits. Nicole was the last to get ready, walking out of her room as everyone else was getting into the pool.

"Cannonball!" Uncle Pete yelled out before jumping in with his knees to his chest.

"Really, Pete?" Aunt Barbara lowered her head with a smirk at her husband. "Remind me again how old you are?"

"Oh, age is nothing but a number!" Uncle Pete threw his arms back, splashing everyone in the process.

"And a broken hip is nothing but an insurance deductible," Kevin added.

"Hey now! Your old man isn't that old yet!" Uncle Pete turned and splashed Kevin.

"Come on in, sweetie. Glad you could join us," Nicole's mom called out to her as Nicole slowly walked through the gate entrance to the pool area.

With a half-hearted smile, Nicole placed her towel on one of the chairs and cautiously dipped her toes into the water.

"Water's surprisingly warm, isn't it?" said her mom.

"I blame Uncle Pete for that," Kevin quipped.

"Hey now, I'm not old enough to break a hip and I am certainly not old enough to be incontinent," Uncle Pete bantered back.

"Did you have a good time at the wedding, dear?" Mrs. Winger asked, slowly walking through the water towards Nicole. "I'm sorry I didn't get much time to talk with you at the reception."

"It's okay, Mom," Nicole replied, sitting down by the edge of the pool. "It was a big day. I understand."

"I know things haven't really been the easiest for you, and I want to say I'm proud of how you've been holding up," her mom added. "I know it was hard, especially after everything with Laura."

"Mom, really, it's okay," Nicole repeated. "Can we just... focus on something else, instead?"

"Of course we can, sweetie," she said. "But if you do want to talk about it, I'm here. Okay?"

"Okay, Mom," said Nicole. She felt a tightness forming in her chest. She scanned the pool and locked eyes with Ella, who nodded knowingly in response.

"So, what I want to know is: can I use visiting Andrew as an excuse to fly down to Miami?" Ella asked, her voice loud enough that everyone, including Nicole's mom, turned to her. "Like, do you think I'll be able to get a discount with the airlines if they think it's purely for visiting family? I mean, I obviously promise to see

Andrew at least once while I'm down here..."

"The area certainly is beautiful," said Mrs. Winger. "I'm glad he chose such a beautiful location to move to. It's not Illinois, but it's a close second."

Nicole's jaw went slack.

"When did you find out he was leaving Illinois?" Nicole asked slowly.

Mrs. Winger turned back to Nicole.

"At the end of this past semester. Said he was transferring out of Northwestern and going for his PhD in Florida."

"He already told you he was dropping out of Northwestern?" said Nicole, her breathing short and shallow.

"Of course he did, hun," her mom added. "Didn't he tell you?"

Nicole looked up at her family and bit the insides of her cheeks.

"Yeah, yeah. Of course he did. I mean, why wouldn't he?"

***

The Winger family stayed in the pool until long after midnight. Around one in the morning, Mrs. Winger retired for the night, followed closely behind by Aunt Barbara and Uncle Pete. After an additional ten or so minutes, Ella got out of the pool as well.

"I should get some sleep before our flight tomorrow," she said as she wrapped the towel around her. "Can't assume you'll get a nap on the plane." Ella shimmied on her sandals and wrung out her hair one more time. "I'll see everyone in the morning?"

"See you then," said Nicole.

Nicole was in one corner of the pool, her elbows propping herself up, her legs dangling weightlessly in the water below her. Kevin was in the opposite corner, propping himself up in similar fashion.

Nicole watched Ella as she made her way up the stairs and into her room. Nicole stared at the motel door as it shut behind Ella before she turned to Kevin.

"Don't you need to get some sleep, too?" she said.

Kevin tilted his head to one side and shrugged.

"It's not that important," he replied. "I try to stay where I'm needed."

"I'm not following," said Nicole.

Kevin took in a slow breath.

"*Did* Andrew tell you he was leaving Chicago?" Kevin asked.

Nicole looked down at the water.

"Of course. He's my brother. Why wouldn't he tell me?"

"Because your relationship with your brother has been strained ever since Cora came into the picture?"

Nicole shot a frantic look at her cousin before nonchalantly rolling her eyes.

"Nothing is wrong between me and Andrew," Nicole stated.

"Nicky, there are a lot of things you are very, very good at. Lying is not one of them."

Nicole hung her head back and closed her eyes.

"Whatever. It doesn't matter anymore."

"I'm going to ask my question again, but this time slightly differently: *if* Andrew told you he was leaving Chicago, *when* did he tell you?"

Nicole stayed silent and focused on the subtle sounds around her. She became aware of the breeze rolling through the trees, the water as it gently lapped against the edges. She opened her eyes and gazed at the stars above her.

"At the rehearsal dinner," she admitted after a spell. "And he probably wouldn't have told me then, either, had I not said something about Chicago."

"That explains a lot, then," said Kevin.

Nicole rolled her eyes.

"I'm *so* not here to get psychoanalyzed," Nicole said. She tried to smile, only to feel her upper lip quiver.

"I mean it," Kevin pressed. "There's a lot you've been holding in, and that was probably the tipping point. Everything that happened last night makes sense."

"Because otherwise I would've just been a raving lunatic."

"No. You would've been a very upset sister who felt like she was losing her brother."

Nicole lifted her elbows from the pool edges and let her body submerge completely underwater. She let her head bob just below the surface for a moment before coming back up and pushing the water from her face.

"Can we not talk about this?" Nicole asked.

"I think we kind of have to," Kevin replied. "Last night is what happens when you *don't* talk about it."

Nicole sighed and looked down at the water.

"Are you going for your master's in psychology or something?"

"I'm just trying to help out one of my favorite cousins," said Kevin.

"I'm, like, one of your only cousins," Nicole retorted.

"Hey, I have a few on my mom's side, thank you very much," said Kevin. "But, regardless, I love you guys, and I don't like seeing someone I love feeling so down."

Nicole shrugged.

"It is what it is."

"Y'know, it's okay to let it out," said Kevin. "It's okay to admit that this whole situation sucks – to admit that dropping out of Northwestern is probably a bad idea. To admit that, wherever 'okay' is on the map, you're on the opposite end of it."

Nicole couldn't help but snort out of a laugh.

"That's one way of putting it," she said.

"I'm just saying..." Kevin trailed off, and the sounds of the breeze and the water filled the space around them again.

"I just wish he had never met Cora," Nicole said into the silence. "Is that so terrible to want?"

"Not in the least," said Kevin. "Everything has changed, and him meeting Cora was the catalyst."

"I mean, why did it have to be *her*? Why'd it have to be someone who's ruined everything?"

"I know it feels like that."

"That's because it *is* like that. Everything was fine before she came into the picture. And then suddenly he starts shutting me out. And it's only been getting worse."

"He did shut you out. There's no way around it," said

Kevin. "But that's Andrew's personality. He cares so much for you that the last thing he would ever want is for you to be unhappy with him. So if there were ever anything that you might not approve of, he didn't talk about it."

"So, suddenly my big brother can't tell me when he actually likes someone?" Nicole snapped.

"Knowing him?" said Kevin. "Yes. Because he was afraid you wouldn't approve."

"And why *would* I approve?" Nicole shot back. "She's practically half his age, definitely half his maturity... I mean, did you see the town she grew up in?"

"Love is funny like that," Kevin replied. He looked to the water, pursed his lips, and then added: "I'm going to tell you something that you cannot repeat to Andrew. Or to anyone. No one can know that you know this."

"Okay... what, then?"

"Do you remember his sophomore year, when Andrew decided to spend his winter break in New York?"

"Yeah?" Nicole replied.

"There's a reason why he didn't invite you or your mom out with him," said Kevin. "And that's because he was thinking of dropping out of school and moving to New York."

"Wait – what? Why?"

Kevin sighed.

"There was a lot going on," Kevin explained. "I guess he met someone and she really broke his heart and he hated his classes and hated his professors and... I guess he thought living in New York City would be what he needed."

"He never told me any of this," said Nicole. "And he has never shied away from talking about his dates. I mean, until Cora, that is."

"Even when you were 14?" Kevin countered. "Remember he was a sophomore when this happened."

"I... I guess not."

"Andrew's MO is to protect the people he loves, at all costs. It's an admirable trait, but it's flawed. He hid all that from you and your mom because he was afraid of how you guys would react," Kevin continued.

"But he obviously had no issues telling Mom he's leaving Northwestern."

"I can't answer for Andrew. I can't tell you why he does everything he does. All I can do is try to give my view on things," said Kevin. "He told your mom only a few months ago, even though he probably made the decision way before that. Maybe he felt like your mom could handle the news at that point – and he didn't tell you because he knew it would still be hard for you to take."

"That's ridiculous."

"But that's Andrew," said Kevin. "You're his baby sister. He'll be protective of you in ways that he might not be for anyone else, including your mom."

"So that means he can shut me out and get snippy with me?"

"No, but it does show just how much he equates 'love' with 'protection'," Kevin explained. "And, because he loves Cora, he's going to be protective of her, too."

"It's not a good excuse," said Nicole, turning to face the edge of the pool. "It doesn't give him the right to act like this."

"It doesn't," said Kevin. "He didn't handle the situation properly. But no one did."

Nicole scoffed and rolled her eyes.

"See? Still the bad guy here."

"No, you're not the bad guy," said Kevin. "No one is. Not even Cora."

"Not even the girl who is dragging him away from Chicago?"

"Who said he was getting dragged away?"

Nicole crossed her forearms on the pool's edge and rested her chin on them.

"He should've known better," Nicole mumbled.

"You hold your brother to an impossibly high standard," said Kevin. "Which is understandable. He's been as much like a father to you as he's been a brother. But he's still human. He's going to do things that aren't perfect."

"Like marry Cora?" Nicole jeered, turning back to Kevin.

Kevin gave Nicole a look that made her bite her tongue and cast her eyes down. Nicole sank into the water until the water danced over her shoulders.

"I thought, when Andrew got married, I would gain a sister," Nicole let out. "Instead, I feel like I'm losing a brother."

"Does he know that?" Kevin asked. "Or does he just think you don't agree with the choices he's making?"

"Why do I have to spell it out for him? Can't he tell that I'm upset? If you could figure it out, then why can't he?"

"We can't go through life assuming the people around us understand what's going on in our minds," said Kevin. "We have to have those open and honest discussions. We have to communicate."

"I just..." Nicole shook her head and looked around her. The hotel courtyard was deserted. There were no lights coming out of any of the rooms. The pool reflected the full moon in dancing ripples. "I just don't understand how he could fall for someone like that."

"She got into Northwestern. She studied law. She's a smart girl, regardless of how she presents herself," said Kevin. "And she had the initiative to go to a difficult school halfway across the country. Maybe there's a side she doesn't really show the outside world. A side only Andrew knows."

"But life would be so much easier..." Nicole started.

"And we know that for a fact, how?" Kevin interjected. "I don't know what goes on in their personal lives. Honestly, it's not my business. And it really isn't yours, either. All that matters is that he's happy."

"How do we even know he's happy?"

"This might not mean much, but I never saw someone light up the way he did when he saw Cora walk down the aisle," said Kevin. "I can't say that they'll have a happily ever after, but I also can't say that about anyone, or anything. Life is life. There's no predictability."

"But he's going to throw away his PhD," she said. "He's making a huge mistake."

"He might be, but that's his mistake to make," said Kevin. "All you can do is be there for him. Standing around, telling him he's making a mistake – or, worse, not communicating with him at all – won't help. You stand by the people you love. You have faith that they know what they're doing. And you get ready to support them in the event they make a mistake."

Nicole stayed silent. She pushed herself away from the edge of the pool and treaded water in the middle of the deep end. She watched the waves she'd created travel away from her, hit the sides, and then ripple back. For a moment, she felt weightless as she kicked the water underneath her.

"Everything is so messed up," she said at last.

"Life is messed up," said Kevin. "Things don't go according to plan. Things change when we don't want them to change. But you find a way to deal and move on."

Nicole went silent again, looking down at the water, watching her legs kick and make circles.

"I really messed up with Laura," Nicole added, her head still tilted down, making it look like she was saying it to the water.

"You did. There's no other way around it," said Kevin. "But that's in the past now. All you can do now is learn from it and move on."

"But what if I can never fix things with Laura?"

"Then things don't get fixed."

"I thought you were here to dispense advice."

"*I'm* here to get a little more pool time in before our flight tomorrow," Kevin replied with a smirk. "But – and it pains me to admit this – I don't have the answers to everything. No one does. And turning to anyone – your mom, Andrew, Laura, me, whoever – to solve your problems in life will only result in disappointment. I'd like to think I'm a cut above the rest, but, still, all I can really do is tell you what I think needs to be said."

Nicole continued to look down, focusing on how it felt to move her hands through the water.

"Listen," said Kevin. "Relationships are tough. All types of relationships. We're all flawed. We're complex and distractible and shortsighted. There are certain aspects of ourselves that will always be part of us. Certain things that will affect our relationships. We can try to minimize it, but it'll always be there. Andrew will always be overprotective. And you will always, to some degree, close yourself off instead of communicating. The same way every person, to some degree, will think others are being malicious when they might just be acting careless. It's human nature to have an irrational side to us. And sometimes relationships fall apart because of it. The question isn't in changing or hoping other people can change, but in learning how to adjust and deal."

"Still doesn't excuse how I treated Laura," Nicole said wearily.

"It doesn't. And it's going to be up to Laura to decide if she wants to continue being with you – if she thinks it's worth it for both of you to figure out ways to handle each other's shortcomings," said Kevin. "And only time will tell with that."

Nicole started to swim backwards until she reached the pool ladder.

"Can I just constantly keep you around for your words of wisdom?" Nicole jested, floating on her back while one hand held onto the ladder. "I'll probably need it even more if Laura decides we're actually done."

"I could follow you around, constantly dispensing advice, but it won't solve what needs to be solved," said Kevin. "Sometimes all we can do is set out on our own, recognizing that we're the only ones who can solve our problems. And, even then, some things are just out of our control."

"I feel like we should've had this powwow at the beginning of this trip," said Nicole. "Maybe even before ever meeting Cora."

"It probably wouldn't have done much, back then," said Kevin. "Advice is only as good as the level it can be taken in. I think only now are you in the right mindset to start rethinking things."

Nicole grabbed the ladder with both hands, dunked her head under the water one more time, and pulled herself out of the pool.

"Had enough for one night?" Kevin asked.

"Oh I've had enough for an entire lifetime," said Nicole.

Kevin pushed himself out of the pool, swung his legs onto the cement walkway, and stood up.

"I know I just talked your ear off about solving your own problems, but, if you need me, I'm just a phone call away. Ella is, too. Whenever you need us."

Nicole wrapped her towel around her back and shimmied her shoulders dry. She brought the towel up to her hair and shook it across her scalp.

"I guess it makes me a hypocrite, all this talk about losing a brother and I haven't been properly keeping in contact with my only set of cousins," said Nicole, wrapping the towel around her.

"No, it doesn't make you a hypocrite," Kevin replied. "It makes you human. I can repeat that whole spiel again if you want me to. And you know I could. Verbatim."

Nicole laughed and picked up her room key.

"I think I've received enough advice for one night," she said with a tender smile. She went over to the pool's gate and opened it for Kevin.

She looked back at the pool. Part of her really wished that they had taken advantage of it more, that she had taken Laura up on her offer to go swimming. She felt a strange sense of loss as they made their way to their respective rooms.

"Well, I'll see you bright and early tomorrow, then," said Kevin when he reached his door.

"Back to the real world," Nicole stated with a wry grin.

"The real world isn't actually a thing. Didn't anyone tell you that?" Kevin remarked.

"You're this close to quoting song lyrics, by the way," Nicole warned.

"Eh, I'm too tired to come up with an original reply. So sue me," he said, opening his door. "See you in the morning."

Nicole smiled one more time.

"See you then."

Nicole walked into her room, silently changed into her pajamas and, with her hair still wet and smelling of chlorine, crawled onto what was once Laura's bed and instantly fell asleep.

Abby Rosmarin

Chapter Seventeen

SO...WHAT NOW?

There was very little waiting for Nicole when she returned to Chicago. She had been relegated to menial tasks at her temp job; and, when the project she was on finished, Cassandra Evans approached her, thanked her for her time, and informed her that they would not be needing her for any additional projects.

She attempted to call Laura twice. Both times, her call went to voicemail. Both times, she hung up before she could leave a message.

The season shifted from the blazing heat of summer to the tame winds of fall. After a string of failed interviews and unanswered queries, Nicole picked up a job at a local coffee shop. At some point during all this, Andrew had officially moved out of Chicago – something Nicole only knew because her mom brought it up in conversation during one of their lunches together.

Much like Laura, Andrew had not spoken to Nicole since the wedding. And, just like with Laura, their last conversation had been the one that had happened at the rehearsal dinner.

She had never talked to him about what had happened that night – or what others may have believed had happened – or why Laura had suddenly disappeared. She wondered which version of the story would upset

Andrew more: Nicole being drunk and belligerent, or Nicole lashing out after bottling everything up for so long.

She spent the first months after the wedding in a fugue state. She felt like she had taken on someone else's life and there was nothing for her to do but go through the motions until she was finally back to herself. In some ways, it was a blessing: it made it easier for her to take on multiple shifts at the coffee shop as she attempted to pay the bills on tips and minimum wage.

Nicole was sweeping the area behind the pastry counter one afternoon, so lost in the hypnotic pattern of it that the person on the opposite side of the counter had to tap on the counter's surface in order to catch Nicole's attention.

Nicole looked up from the floor and froze.

"Um, uh... hey, there," Laura said cautiously.

"Hey," was all Nicole could say. She didn't realize how hard she was pressing the broom into the ground until the spindles curled up and poked the outside of her ankle.

"Um, yeah, hey... I know this is awkward but... is it possible for us to talk on your break?" Laura asked.

Nicole leaned the broom against the wall and wiped her hands on her apron.

"Um, yeah. Yes. Of course." Nicole cleared her throat. "I'm sure I can go on break now if I ask. Do you mind waiting for a second?"

"No, not at all. Not at all. I'll find a place to sit." Laura darted her eyes over towards the tables before staring back at Nicole.

Nicole forced down a dry swallow.

"Alright, I'll see you then," said Nicole, nodding at nothing in particular as she started walking towards her shift supervisor. Moments later, Nicole was removing her work apron and walking over to Laura, who was sitting at a table by the window.

"Hey," Nicole said as she stood a foot away from Laura's table.

"Hey, as well," Laura replied. "Um... have a seat?"

"Yeah, that'd be great," said Nicole. "Thanks."

Nicole pulled out a seat and gingerly sat down, her

back rigid and her legs crossed tightly together. She interlaced her fingers underneath the table and looked out the window.

"So, I see your working at the Café Jungle now," said Laura.

"Uh, yeah." Nicole laughed nervously. She unlocked her hands to swipe a sweaty palm against the back of her neck. "The temp gig kind of… ran out. I'm doing this until I can find something else." Nicole looked up at Laura. "How did you know?"

Laura blushed.

"Purely by accident," she said with an embarrassed smile. "I walked in here one day, saw you working, and, well, walked right back out."

Nicole closed her eyes and nodded.

"I stayed away after that," Laura continued. "I didn't want to come back until I was ready to talk to you. There's a lot of stuff we need to talk about."

"Agreed," Nicole replied, sliding her hands over her hair until her fingers touched her ponytail. "Can I at least start by saying I'm sorry?"

"You can," said Laura. "And I can say I'm sorry, too."

"Sorry for what?" Nicole asked.

"For reacting so dramatically."

"The only dramatic person was me," said Nicole. "I was out of line."

Laura laughed and shrugged her shoulders.

"Well, you were. There's no other way around that one," said Laura. "But I also get that a lot of stuff was going on, and you were just reacting to it."

"I'm still sorry."

"I know."

Laura took in a deep breath and smoothed out the table space in front of her.

"You're lucky your cousin is so smart," she said after a moment.

Nicole didn't say anything. She simply looked at Laura and bit at the inside of her cheek.

"If anyone else had driven me back, we probably wouldn't be talking," Laura admitted. "I would've decided that the relationship was over and I was obviously better off with someone else – someone who'd actually appreciate me."

Nicole forced down another dry swallow.

"But – Kevin – he's a smart guy. He understands how people tick pretty well," Laura continued. "He pointed something out that really resonated with me."

"What did he say?" Nicole asked quietly.

Laura placed her hands on her lap.

"He told me what I already knew," said Laura. "That you were being difficult. And that there was nothing I could say to make you see things from my perspective, at least not while it was happening.

"And you *were* going through a lot. I really do get that. And I probably made a bad situation worse by trying so hard to keep the peace. Me never calling you out when things started to go sour meant that nothing got nipped in the bud. But I also couldn't just stand around while you mistreated me."

"I see," Nicole said quietly.

"So your cousin pointed out that, at the end of the day, there are just certain behaviors we all fall into, even if we don't mean to. And the question isn't whether or not someone is bad because of it, but if two people's behavior patterns can coexist in a relationship," said Laura. "I can't just assume that, because you hurt me – and you did, you really, really did – our relationship is beyond repair. But I also can't assume that, if we got back together, things would change. You are who you are and I am who I am. We can both try to better ourselves, but we'll inevitably fall back into old habits at least once in a while."

"This sounds an awful lot like a break-up speech," Nicole said with a tired grin.

"That's not what I'm trying to get at," Laura replied. She looked away, took in a deep breath, and sighed it out. "I spent the last two months trying to figure out if this was worth working on. If we actually have what it takes to have a healthy relationship, or if we would just fall apart every single time we hit an obstacle. And, I mean, neither of us ever really had serious relationships before this. We don't know what's right and what's wrong, what's healthy and what's dysfunctional. We have nothing to compare it to. And we never really had our relationship tested before – although we certainly failed *this* test."

"I can't tell you how sorry I am," Nicole found herself pleading. "I really, really am."

"This isn't about 'sorry' or 'not sorry'. This is about us, and what it takes to make it work in the long run," said Laura. "All I know is that I love you, and I *do* want this to work out. I don't want this to stop, but at the same time I can't pretend that everything will be fine because we love each other and that's all that matters." Laura sighed and gave Nicole one of her biggest, most endearing smiles. "But I really, really, really want this to work."

"I want this to work, too," Nicole replied, blinking away tears.

Laura covered her face before rubbing her temples with her fingertips.

"I don't know where I'm going with this," she said. "I mean, there are always going to be things that need adjusting, but if we have to fundamentally change who we are in order to keep the relationship going, then it's not worth continuing."

"So, what? What do we do?"

"I don't know." Laura closed her eyes. "The day-by-day ruler can't be too wrong. We can see where life takes us and hope it keeps us on the same path."

"Well, this is depressing," Nicole nervously laughed out. "Just as an FYI: if we ever get married, you are *so* not allowed to write your own vows. 'Til death do us part,' would turn into, '50% of all marriages fail'."

"Just an FYI: what you just said is the *opposite* of 'day-by-day'."

Nicole burst out in hysterical laughter. Laura soon joined in, her eyes brimming with tears. They laughed in a way that made the rest of the coffee house glance over at them before quickly returning back to their own lives.

When the laughter died down, Nicole looked at Laura and reached her arms across the table, her palms facing up.

"We're going to be okay, right?"

"I sure hope so," said Laura, her hands sliding over Nicole's. "I sure hope so."

***

"So, how's the job search going?" Nicole's mom asked during one of their lunches together.

Nicole shrugged, pushing her salad around her plate.

"It's going. Haven't heard back from anyone," she said. "There's not a lot out there. Not right now, at least."

"I know, sweetie. I know," said her mom. "But I have faith something will turn up."

"Hopefully," said Nicole, stabbing at a piece of romaine. "How's life at the firm?"

"Oh, you know. Still as chaotic as ever. But I wouldn't trade it for the world."

"That's always good to hear," Nicole said with a smile. "And, um, how's Andrew?"

"He's good, but – haven't you been talking to him as well?" her mom asked, her brows furrowing with worry.

"Well, not really." Nicole tilted her head to one side and looked away. "We haven't really spoken since the wedding."

Mrs. Winger's face dropped.

"Nicky... that was three months ago."

"I'm well aware of time, Mom."

"But, you two were always so close," said Mrs. Winger. "Have you tried calling him?"

"No, but, then again, neither has he." Nicole paused and let out a sigh. "A lot changed after he met Cora. And neither of us handled it well. I mean, you saw how I acted in Florida." Nicole pushed the remainder of her salad to the edge of its plate. "The last time we talked, I was yelling at him for leaving Northwestern, and telling him that his marriage was a mistake. I haven't really gathered the courage to get in touch with him since."

"I'm sure he misses his baby sister," said her mom. "A lot. Anger or no anger."

"I guess," said Nicole. "I don't know."

Nicole sighed at her plate.

"You spend your whole life seeing someone as almost a demigod, only to realize they're just as human as you," she added.

"I think that's one of the hardest lessons anyone has to

learn while growing up," said her mom. "That even our heroes need a bit of understanding." She paused, looking at her daughter with tired eyes and a warm smile, before adding: "But how are things with you and Laura?"

"They're getting better," said Nicole. "We're still trying to figure everything out but – I don't know – I have faith we will."

"I hope so," said her mom. "You two have always been such a cute couple."

"I've been saving up a little bit. Hopefully I'll soon have enough to take her on a mini-vacation."

"Well, that's a great idea. To where?"

"New York City," said Nicole. "I figured it would be fun to go spend time in New York, see Uncle Pete and Aunt Barbara, Ella and Roger, Kevin..."

"And maybe Kevin's girlfriend, if he has one yet?" her mom added.

"Sure, maybe Kevin's hypothetical girlfriend, too," Nicole said with an exasperated laugh. "I don't know. It just seems like a step in the right direction. The vacation, I mean."

"You could always call up Andrew and Cora," her mom offered. "I don't know if Cora has seen the Big Apple, but I'm sure that's something they'd love to do."

Nicole sucked in her breath. She sat there in silence for a moment before letting her breath out.

"That's not a bad idea," Nicole said warily. "But I think I need to patch things up with Andrew first."

"First things first, as they say."

"Yeah. First things first."

***

By the time December rolled in, life had fallen into a weirdly comforting routine for Nicole. Her time at the coffee shop was starting to feel normal. At the very least, it felt like something she could handle until she found that next job, whenever that would happen. Being with Laura was part of that comforting routine, and it was a comfort that Nicole swore she'd never take for granted again.

At least once or twice a day, Nicole would feel the

urge to call Andrew. But even when the urge was strong, she wouldn't pick up her phone. She couldn't find the courage. She didn't know what she would say, or how she would say it. And she feared what Andrew would say in response.

Every time she left work and found a voicemail notification on her phone, Nicole's heart would skip a beat, hoping that maybe it was Andrew attempting to reach out first. When it would turn out to be her mom, or Laura, or Ella, she couldn't help but be disappointed – and, if she was being honest, a little angry as well.

Angry at who, she couldn't really tell. Sometimes she'd be upset at Andrew for not reaching out, not trying to get in touch with his baby sister. Sometimes she'd blame Cora for why Andrew hadn't phoned. Sometimes she'd even be upset at whoever had called her, for getting her hopes up. And, every time, she'd get upset at herself for feeling the way she did.

But she knew that there was no point repeating those old patterns. There was nothing to be gained. No hurt would be relieved. And she knew that there was no way she could move forward with anything if she allowed herself to hold onto such resentment.

Granted, understanding what she needed to do and actually doing it were two separate things. And she had already learned the hard way that denying how she felt would only make a bad situation worse. In some weird twist, once Nicole accepted that she was going to have those negative feelings, it became a lot easier to handle them.

Yes, she still felt like life would be a lot easier if the wedding had never happened, if Andrew had never met Cora. And maybe it would. But maybe it wouldn't. Life happens, and it never happens in the way you want it to. Maybe it'll unfold for the better. Maybe for the worse. Or maybe it will just be different. While Andrew's path in life had gone in a completely different direction than Nicole could ever have anticipated, it was still Andrew's life. And nothing would change how much she loved her big brother, the man who served as mentor and best friend and father figure. Those titles might've made Nicole expect more from Andrew than could ever have been reasonable, but they also served as reminders that their bond was more important than whatever stalemate they were currently in.

It was an unseasonably warm day in December when Nicole left her shift at the coffee shop. She punched out, grabbed her things, and instinctively checked her phone. She checked her voicemail, where two messages awaited her. The first was from Laura, letting Nicole know that she had just picked up takeout for dinner that night.

Nicole couldn't help but smile at Laura's message. It was those little quirks – like picking up takeout and immediately informing Nicole of it, or the fact that Laura always did things like leave voicemail messages for mundane things – that reminded Nicole just how much she loved Laura, and just how willing she was to make things work. She knew nothing was guaranteed, and she knew good intentions couldn't ever replace what's lacking in a relationship, but she was willing to keep going, regardless as to where it was destined to go.

Nicole saved Laura's message and listened to the second one.

"Hi there. This is Katy Sinclaire calling from Stephenson Publishing," said the voice in the message. "We've received your résumé and feel you would be a great fit for the team. We would love for you to come in to interview with the design manager. If you could call us back at 312..."

Nicole took in a sharp breath, filling her lungs to the point that she thought they would explode. She repeated the message over and over again until she had every word, every number memorized. With her mind still racing, Nicole called the publishing company and, to her surprise, was able to talk to the design manager and personally schedule an interview with him. The manager wished her a good night and Nicole squealed to herself after she hung up.

Nicole could no longer feel the ground below her. With her phone still in her hand, she dialed Andrew's number and brought her phone back to her ear.

What it was about this bit of news that finally got her

to make the call, Nicole couldn't say. Perhaps it was the elation erasing all doubt, fear, and worry. Perhaps the news served as a perfect excuse to call up her brother. Or perhaps it was simply time to finally take that step forward; that this was the exact moment to say something after months of silence.

A million thoughts ran through her head as she waited for the call to connect. She thought about how her brother would sound, or what he might say. She thought about what had been happening in his life over these past few months and she thought about whether or not Cora would be there.

As the phone started to ring, she also thought about how little she knew about Cora. The majority of her opinions on Cora were based on one meeting and Andrew's behavior surrounding her. It can be far too easy to judge someone based on a pair of leather pants and a fur coat – the same way it can be far too easy to judge someone based on an emotional outburst just outside of a restaurant.

Maybe Cora wasn't exactly her cup of tea. Maybe Nicole's personality and Cora's personality would never fully mesh. Maybe she'd always find it peculiar that Andrew dropped everything to be with her. Maybe Nicole would always feel that, in a way, Andrew dropped her as a sister to be with Cora. But these little resentments were not enough to justify shutting out one of the most important people in her life.

Who knows: maybe she could even try calling up Cora directly. She *was* family now, technically. Maybe the conversation would falter. But maybe it wouldn't. She couldn't see them becoming best friends, but maybe a little more time around Cora would help her understand what made Cora tick. Maybe it would make everything else seem a little more reasonable and understandable.

And if Andrew really was making a mistake? Then Nicole would be there for him, no questions asked. She knew the statistics. She knew how common it was for marriages to fail. Even if she and Cora had become like sisters from day one, even if Andrew stayed in Chicago and got his PhD at Northwestern, Andrew and Cora would still have the cards stacked against them. And all she could do – whether it involved attending their 50ᵗʰ anniversary party or giving him a hug at the divorce proceedings – was be there for him. Because that's what family does.

The phone rang seven, eight, nine times before cutting to her brother's voicemail.

"Hey, we're not here right now, but leave a message and I'll try to get back to you." The message was intercepted quickly by a beep. Nicole took in a shaky breath.

"Hey, uh," Nicole began. "How are ya? I, uh, I wanted to call because I... well, I got an interview, for a job. It's my first in a while, and it seems like a really cool company. I don't want to jinx anything, but I have a good feeling about this one." Nicole paused and bit her lip. "I hope everything's going well. I'd love to know how your honeymoon went. I know, I know, it's been ages. But I miss you. You're my big brother, and, I love you, and, I'm always here for you. And there's nothing that can change that. So – yeah – call me back sometime. We have a lot to catch up on, I feel." Nicole sighed and looked up to the sky. "Well, I'll talk to you soon, okay?"

She placed her phone in her purse and made her way to the Ohio Street Beach. She slipped off her shoes and walked directly towards the shoreline, her feet sinking in the cold sand. She dipped her toes in the frigid water, just enough so she could gingerly kick the water around. With the downtown area to the left of her, the park behind her, and all of Lake Michigan in front of her, Nicole felt like she was in the center of everything that nourished her. Off in the distance, someone in a wetsuit was swimming just a stone's throw from the Lakefront Trail. Her eyes went past the swimmer and followed the water out until it disappeared into the horizon. The sun was setting to the left of her, turning the sky a vibrant red directly above her.

"Red sky at night. Sailor's delight," Nicole murmured to herself with a warm smile. With one last kick, Nicole walked away from the water and back onto concrete. She wiped the sand off her feet before slipping her shoes back on and making her way back to the trains. By the time she had gone through the turnstiles and was walking up to the platform, Nicole's phone went off.

"What time are you coming over tonight?" Laura had messaged.

Nicole grinned and typed back:

"I'll be there before you know it."

ABOUT THE AUTHOR

Abby Rosmarin is a writer, model, and yoga instructor. She is the author of *Chick Lit & Other Formulas for Life*, *I'm Just Here for the Free Scrutiny*, and *No One Reads Poetry: A Collection of Poems*. She's been featured on the Huffington Post, Bustle, Thought Catalog, and others. While always a Bostonian at heart, Abby currently lives in the mountains of New Hampshire with her husband and their array of animals.